ABOVE AN ANG_

2ND EDITION

ABOVE AN ANGRY SEA

MEN AND MISSIONS OF THE UNITED STATES NAVY'S PB4Y-1 LIBERATOR AND PB4Y-2 PRIVATEER SQUADRONS

Pacific Theater: October 1944–September 1945

Schiffer Publishing Ltd

4880 Lower Valley Road • Atglen, PA 19310

ALAN C. CAREY

Acknowledgments

Many veterans, family, and history buffs spent considerable time and effort providing me with information and images to update this book originally published in 2001; their dedication to preserving United States Naval history is appreciated. Therefore, I would like to thank the following people and organizations for making the story of Navy Liberator and Privateer operations in the Pacific War possible: Bob Baird, Roy Balke, Peter P. Bresciano, Billy Buckley, John Dienst, Richard M. Douglass, Eddie Harding, Steve Hawley, Sterling Hays, Val M. Higgins, Richard Jeffreys Jr., Eugene L. Kern, Bob Kirk, Chris Longcrier, Al Marks, Davis McAlister, T. W. McCarthy, James McKay, Mahlon K. Miller, Kamada Minoru, Dave Mullen, Hal Olsen, Frank Nevins, F. T. Pierce, Ted Rowcliffe, Kenneth Sanford, James C. Sawruk, Norman B. Sellman, David Smith, Paul Stevens, Louise Thoman, H. J. Thompson, Bill Thys, Dick Webb, and George Winters (image credits appear in the captions).

Emil Bueler Library, National Museum of Naval Aviation
WFI Research Group
Navy Historical Center
National Archive and Records Administration at College Park, Maryland (NARA)
San Diego Aerospace Museum

Copyright © 2017 by Alan C. Carey

Library of Congress Control Number: 2017933335

Type set in Chaparral Pro/Times New Roman

ISBN: 978-0-7643-5368-0
Printed in China

Published by Schiffer Publishing, Ltd.
4880 Lower Valley Road
Atglen, PA 19310
Phone: (610) 593-1777; Fax: (610) 593-2002
E-mail: Info@schifferbooks.com
Web: www.schifferbooks.com

For our complete selection of fine books on this and related subjects, please visit our website at www.schifferbooks.com. You may also write for a free catalog.

Schiffer Publishing's titles are available at special discounts for bulk purchases for sales promotions or premiums. Special editions, including personalized covers, corporate imprints, and excerpts, can be created in large quantities for special needs. For more information, contact the publisher.

We are always looking for people to write books on new and related subjects. If you have an idea for a book, please contact us at proposals@schifferbooks.com.

Contents

Glossary

Enlisted United States Navy Ranks
AMM: Aviation Machinist's Mate
AMMC: Aviation Machinist's Mate CAviation Carburetor Mechanic
AMMF: Aviation Machinist's Mate Aviation Flight Engineer
PhoM: Photographer's Mate
AOM: Aviation Ordnanceman
AOMB: Aviation Ordnanceman-Bombsight Mechanic
AOMT: Aviation Ordnanceman-Aviation Turret Mechanic
ARM: Aviation Radioman
S1c: Seaman First Class

Numbers following each rating:
1c: First Class
2c: Second Class
3c: Third Class

Japanese Aircraft Engaged by PB4Y Aircraft
The Americans gave code-names given to each model of Japanese aircraft.

Name   Model/Type
Zeke: Mitsubishi A6M/single-engine fighter
Hamp: Variant of the A6M
Hap: Variant of the A6M
Pete: Mitsubishi F1M2/single engine float-wing fighter
Rufe: Nakajima A6M2-N/single-engine float-fighter
Kate: Nakajima B5NS/single-engine Torpedo-bomber
Irving: Nakajima Gekko J1N1-S/twin-engine night fighter
Betty: Mitsubishi G4M/twin-engine bomber
Mavis: Kawanishi H6K/four-engine reconnaissance flying boat
Nell: Mitsubishi Type 96 G3M/torpedo bomber
Oscar: Nakajima Ki-43/single-engine fighter
Tony: Kawasaki Ki-61/single-engine fighter
Jill: Nakajima B6N/single-engine Torpedo-bomber
Val: Aichi D3A/single-engine dive-bomber
Nick: Kawasaki Ki-45/twin-engine fighter-bomber
Tess: Nakajima-Douglas DC-2/twin-engine transport
Topsy: Mitsubishi Type 100 Ki-57 (L4M)/transport
Tojo: Ki-44/single-engine fighter
George: Kawanishi N1K2/single-engine fighter-bomber
Peggy: Mitsubishi Ki-67/bomber
Frank: Nakajima Ki-84/single-engine fighter-bomber
Frances: Yokosuka P1Y/ twin-engine bomber
Grace: Aichi B7A/single-engine Torpedo bomber
Jack: Mitsubishi J2M/single-engine Fighter
Dinah: Mitsubishi Ki-46/twin-engine patrol bomber
Helen: Nakajima Ki-49/twin-engine bomber
Sally: Mitsubishi Ki-21/bomber
Sonia: Mitsubishi Ki-51/single-engine bomber
Nate: Nakajima Ki-27/single-engine fighter
Tabby: L2D2/5 transport

Introduction
Summary of PB4Y Operations, February 1943–September 1944

The names of those who in their lives fought for life
Who wore at their hearts the fire's centre.
Born of the sun they traveled a short while towards the sun,
And left the vivid air signed with their honour.
–Stephen Spender (From the VPB-124 Squadron book)

In the summer of 1942, the Navy needed long-range aircraft to patrol the vast reaches of the Pacific. Other Navy patrol aircraft, such as the PBY-5 Catalina, PBM, and the PB2Y were too slow and lightly armed; a distinct disadvantage if they were to patrol close to enemy-held islands. In July 1942, the Army agreed to the Navy receiving a quantity of B-24D Liberators, which changed the designation to PB4Y-1 for patrol bomber-four engine. A rumor still exists that the Army gave the Navy B-24s that failed their inspection—not good enough for the Army, but just right for the Navy.

The Navy's use of the Liberator made it possible to cover wider search sectors than before and, more importantly, extensive photographic reconnaissance could be made before a major operation. The squadrons to be established would be designated VB for Navy Bombing until October 1944 when the designation was changed to VPB for Navy Patrol Bomber.

The Navy Liberator had to be modified to suit the needs of long-range patrolling over the Pacific. The first Navy Liberators sent to the Pacific varied little from the Army B-24D, retaining the distinctive Plexiglas nose with free-hand machine guns mounted to protect against frontal attacks. This type of defensive armament would soon prove to be inadequate. Furthermore, a few of the earlier models were not equipped with the Sperry ball turret under the fuselage; instead, they had twin-fifty caliber tunnel guns that were manually fired by a crewmember. This piece of equipment was all but useless, in part because it gave the gunner vertigo bending over the guns while firing. By the summer of 1944, the tunnel guns were gone.

The distinctive Navy version of the Liberator was introduced when most of the conventional B-24s were modified with the Erco bow turret in the nose that extended the length of the aircraft by three feet. The bow turret had twin .50-caliber guns and carried twice the ammunition supply of other turrets—800 versus 400. It also had armor plating in front that gave the pilots additional protection. However, some squadrons, such as VPB-111, received J, L, and M models with the Emerson nose turret. A total of 977 PB4Y-1 Liberators (the majority being D and J models) were received by the Navy before the war's end.

Brown Baggers Retreat. **She was PB4Y-1 Bureau Number 65385 and possibly belonged to VD-1.**

PB4Y-1 Bureau Number 38894. She flew with VD-1. *Courtesy of Steve Hawley*

PB4Y-1 Liberator Specifications

Length	67' 3"
Wingspan	110'
Height	17' 11"
Wing Area	1,048 square feet
Empty Weight	36,950 pounds
Gross Weight	60,000 pounds
Power Plant	R-1830-43/65
Armament	10 × .50-caliber
Bomb Load	8,800 pounds
Maximum Speed	279 mph
Cruising Speed	200 mph
Service Ceiling	31,800 ft
Range	2,960 miles

During the war, PB4Y squadrons were based at such places as Espiritu Santos, Guadalcanal, Munda, Green Island, Morotai, Owi, Los Negros, the Philippines, the Ellice Islands, Midway, Apamama, Tarawa, Eniwetok, Kwajalein, Saipan, Tinian, Guam, and Okinawa. For many of them, these bases were temporary homes that changed as the war progressed. This book covers the period from October 1944 to August 1945, from the time Navy heavy bombing squadrons (VB) were re-designated as Navy patrol and bombing squadrons (VPB) to the last days of the Pacific War. I covered the first two years of Navy PB4Y operations in the Pacific in *We Flew Alone: Men and Missions of the United States Navy's B-24 Liberator Squadrons Pacific Operations: February 1943–September 1944*. Here is a brief summary of what transpired during that period.

A pair of PB4Y-2 Privateers in flight. *Courtesy of F. T. Pierce*

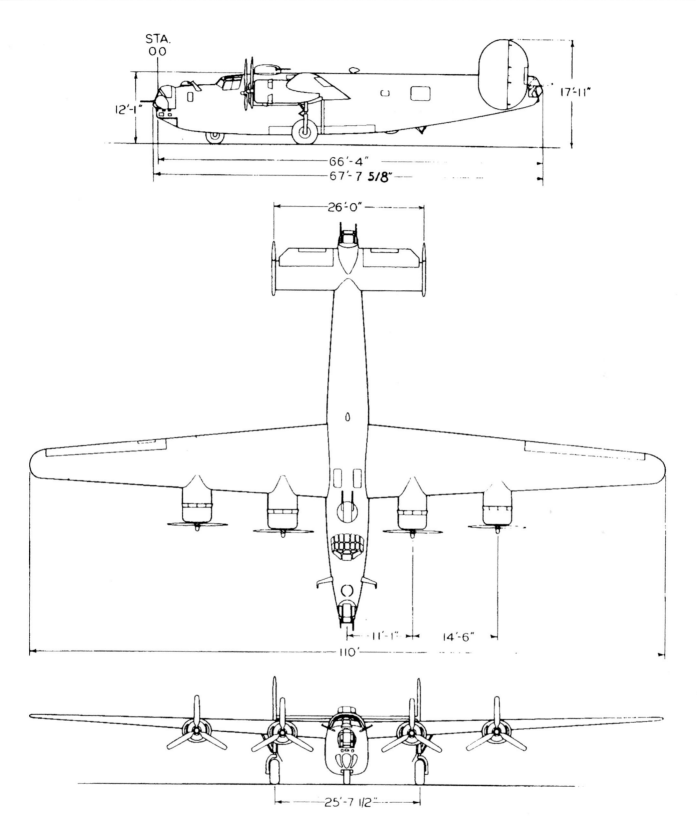

B-24 (PB4Y-1) Liberator dimensions.

PB4Y-2 Privateer with the Erco bow turret. *Courtesy of San Diego Air Museum*

Navy PB4Y operations began in the fall of 1942, when VP-51, under the command of Cdr. William A. Moffitt, Jr., traded their PBY Catalina flying boats for ex-Army B-24D Liberators. After a few months of familiarization with the new aircraft, the squadron moved to the South Pacific and became the first such outfit to fly combat missions. In February 1943, VP-51 was redesignated as VB-101 for Navy Bomber Squadron 101.

The next squadrons in the Pacific were VD-1 and VB-102. The former was the first PB4Y photographic unit, while 101 became the first squadron to fully outfit their aircraft with the Erco bow turret.

A Privateer with the Emerson nose turret. *Courtesy of San Diego Air Museum*

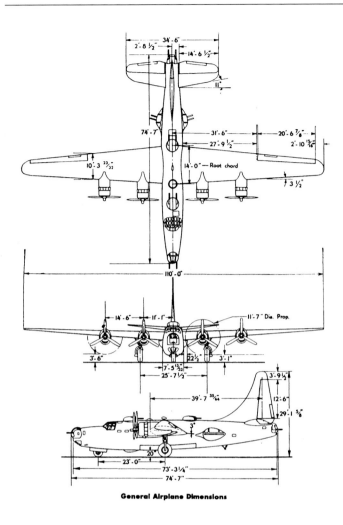

PB4Y-2 Privateer dimensions.

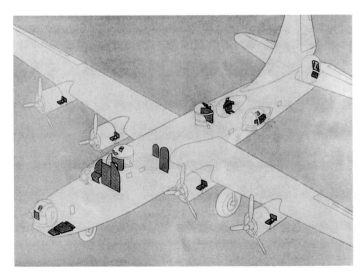

The PB4Y-2 afforded considerable armor plating for the crew.

It was not until the arrival of VB-104 (the Buccaneers) in August 1943 that low-level bombing tactics were successfully used. A year later, PB4Y squadrons were operating across the Atlantic and Pacific with the primary mission of armed reconnaissance.

In the Central Pacific, VB-108, 109, and later 102 and 116, were given the task of neutralizing Japanese forces in the Caroline, Gilbert, Marshall, and Mariana Islands. VB-109 would become the first land-based heavy bombing squadron to attack the Bonin Islands and Iwo Jima.

PB4Y patrol plane commanders used their aircraft in ways that designers at Consolidated Aircraft Company never dreamed of—pushing these big, lumbering bombers down to altitudes of only twenty-five to fifty feet as a tactic to avoid enemy radar, to surprise them, and to hit the targets with accuracy. Attacking targets at masthead height (altitudes of less than 200 feet) or just being a member of a flight crew was hazardous duty, as some 300 men were lost.

By late September 1944, the military might of the United States was poised to strike the Philippines, while in the Central Pacific, PB4Y operations continued with their war against bypassed Japanese-held islands. However, their war was far from over, and they would take part in several major operations, including the invasion of Iwo Jima and Okinawa.

The Liberator served the Navy well from 1943 to 1945. However, the Navy questioned the time and cost of modifying ex-Army B-24s for over-sea patrolling. In 1942, it was reasoned that the Liberator would be more stable with a single fin, and three XPB4Y-2s were built and tested with the single fin and rudder modification. In May 1943, the Navy contracted with Consolidated-Vultee Aircraft Company for the new bomber.

At first, the aircraft was named the Sea Liberator. However, since approximately fifty percent of the bomber's internal components were changed and the belly turret deleted, it was essentially a new model, and was finally called the Privateer. In addition to the single fin, seven feet was added to the length, and two Martin upper turrets and twin Erco waist blisters were installed.

Although the belly turret was deleted, the defensive armament of the Privateer was not diminished with it, having twelve 50-caliber machine guns compared to ten on the Liberator. Therefore, the PB4Y-2 was a heavily armed gun platform and could readily defend itself from fighter attack while unleashing punishing blows on Japanese shipping and shore installations. In April 1945, some Privateers were modified to carry the SWOD Mk-9 "Bat" and were designated as the PB4Y-2B.

In January 1945, the first squadron outfitted with the Privateer arrived in the Pacific. By war's end, the Navy received 739 singletailed PB4Y-2 Privateers. Unlike the PB4Y-1s, which were scrapped at war's end, the PB4Y-2 continued serving with the United States military and other countries well into the 1950s, and even found its way into civilian use as fire bombers. Examples of it can be found in aviation museums and will be seen for generations to come; unfortunately, the same can not be said of the PB4Y-1 Liberator.

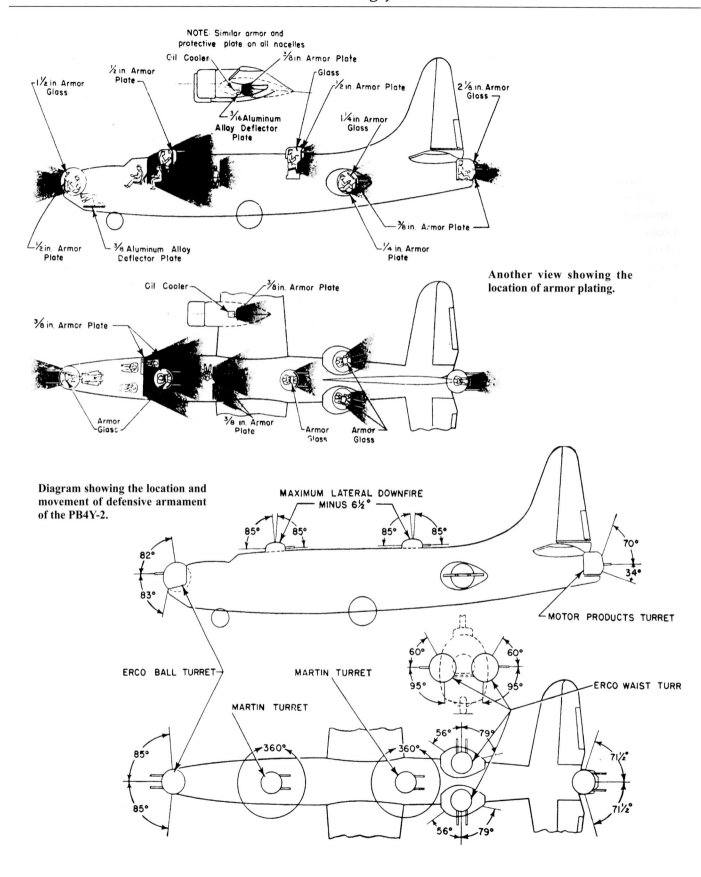

Another view showing the location of armor plating.

Diagram showing the location and movement of defensive armament of the PB4Y-2.

One of the only known examples of this plane lies under the Pacific Ocean off Maui, Hawaii.

The veteran "survivors" of VPB-124 meet for a reunion. This PB4Y-2 squadron suffered severe casualties while deployed on Okinawa between June and July 1945.

PB4Y-2 Privateer Specifications

Length	74' 7"
Wingspan	110'
Height	29' 2"
Wing Area	1,048 square feet
Empty Weight	37,765 pounds
Gross Weight	65,000 pounds
Power Plant	R-1830-94
Armament	12 x .50 caliber
Bomb Load	12,800 pounds
Maximum Speed	250 mph
Cruising Speed	200 mph
Service Ceiling	19,600 ft
Range	2,630 miles

Navy Liberator and Privateer crews often flew alone on searches that extended 800 to 1,000 miles across an empty and unforgiving ocean. When a crew was lost, more often than not, their fellow squadron members never knew what happened to them. The crews simply vanished without a trace, or, every so often, a passing plane would see dye marker spreading across the water where a plane had gone down. A temporary sign soon to disappear that there once was a plane with eleven men on board. They are the forgotten few who often flew alone on patrols that lasted up to twenty hours. This is their story, and the book is dedicated to all those who served with United States Navy B-24 (PB4Y-1) and PB4Y-2 Privateer squadrons in the Pacific.

1

The Philippine Campaign
October–December 1944

Fall 1944 marked the beginning of Gen. MacArthur's return to the Philippines. October brought about a new designation for Navy Liberator squadrons, with Privateer squadrons soon to follow. The Navy changed such multi-engine units to VPB for Navy Patrol Bombing Squadron. On September 30, they were called VB, and the following day, clerks filling out reports had to change it to VPB. This may have been a minor irritation for the yeomen who had to type it, but for the Navy Liberator squadrons operating in the region, it was to be a very heavy operational period.

The two Navy Liberator squadrons operating in the Southwest Pacific at the time were 101 and 115, under the command of the 7th Fleet and operated under Fleet Air Wing 17 (Task Force 73.2.3 and later 73.4.3). Joining them were the 310th Bomb Wing of the 5th Air Force. For the Bulldogs of VPB-115 time was short; they

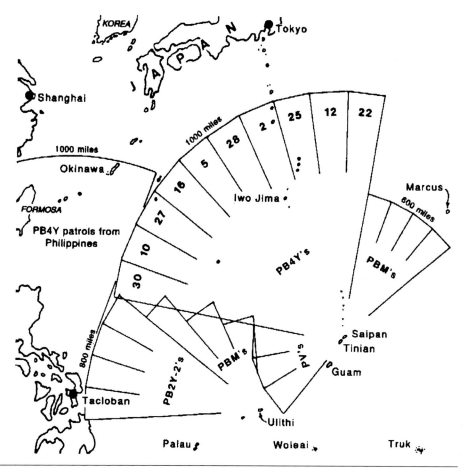

Allied patrol plane search plan.

VB-115's *Baby Shirley* (Bureau Number 32150) was lost in action along with its crew on 5 June 1944. *Courtesy of Art Adair*

VB-106's executive officer originally flew *Bales Baby* before a VPB-115 air crew obtained it and totalled it in October 1944. *Author's Collection*

would go home the following month. In the interim, both squadrons continued with their job of seeking out, and when the opportunity presented itself, attacking the Japanese. For one of them, a squadron commander would be lost, only to return after a two-month journey. Late October 1944 was disastrous for VPB-101, losing five aircraft and some thirty men between the nineteenth and twenty-fifth, beginning with the loss of the squadron commander's crew.

Morotai Operations

Both squadrons, based at Owi Island, coordinated seven daily single-plane searches ranging 750–1,000 miles. During the first weeks of October 115 made successful sweeps against enemy shipping around the Philippines. Most of the shipping was small cargo vessels carrying fuel and troops. However, the impending assault on Leyte required them to move operations to Morotai Island, in the Netherlands East Indies.

Lying ten miles north of Halmahera, Morotai is forty-four miles long and twenty-five miles wide. Except for a small coastal plane on Gila Peninsula, it is a mountainous, jungle-covered island.[1] There were only 500 Japanese troops on the island when the American 31st Infantry Division landed on 15 September 1944. The defenders were rapidly reduced to 200, with the remaining survivors fleeing into the jungle. Engineers began working on an airfield at Wawama which would play an important role in the upcoming invasion, as it was the nearest airfield from which long range patrol aircraft could search north and west of Leyte.[2]

Louis "Louie" Bresciano, a member of VPB-111, wrote a letter to his wife, Irene, in September 1945, reflecting on the living conditions at Morotai after the censoring of mail had stopped.

"Before coming to Leyte we were at Morotai. That was a hell hole. It's a good thing we only stayed there three weeks. Just before we got there they were bombing it every night. That was because

VPB-101's executive officer LtCdr. Smith, attack conducted on 7 November 1944. *Courtesy of the NARA*

A living area on Morotai taken on 18 January 1945. Louis Bresciano of VPB-111 referred to Morotai as a "hell hole." This is from Louie's tent, looking up the road and at the top of the slope toward the wash and shower area. *Courtesy of Peter Bresciano*

An unidentified PB4Y-1 Liberator from VPB-101 leaves a small coastal vessel afire off an island in the Philippines on 19 November 1944. *Courtesy of the NARA*

there was a full moon. We heard after we left they started to bomb it again because the moon was out again. There in Morotai, they bombed the hell out of it. . . Morotai is in the Halmahura group. When I say Morotai was a hell hole, it was. Remember I sent pictures of the tent I was living in? Well, nights there would be rats outside as big as cats. . . They find them any time under your sack. When we went to the head, we would just go right outside and take a gun with us. We were right at the edge of the woods. About a mile in the woods the Japs were fighting all night. You could hear them shooting it out with the Army. The chow was awful. Wouldn't even have bread at times. Boy, was I glad to get out of there. We were a little ways from the Equator. The days were so hot it was awful, and at night it was so damp, when you got up to put your clothes on they were all wet. You'd have to look and make sure there weren't any bugs in them. . . ."

On 19 October, a new search plan was inaugurated consisting of seven search sectors originating from Owi and Morotai. Two Owi-based sectors extended 950 miles along the eastern coast of the Philippine Islands. A week later these searches were abandoned. Sectors from Morotai consisted of one of 840 miles through the Celebes Sea and Makassar Strait and six of 1,000 miles through the Philippines. The new plan coincided with the actual invasion of Leyte on 20 October. For the next month, the military forces of Imperial Japan and the United States battled each other on land, air, and sea.

The invasion would also coincide with the loss of VPB-101's commanding officer. On 19 October, it was 101's turn to fly their search sectors. Lt. D. M. Carroll started in the pre-dawn morning and, on his return leg, seriously damaged a 6,000-ton merchant ship. Next out was Lt. Neal Tyler, who hit moored cargo ships and eight float planes. Coming in at one hundred feet, Tyler made a run down the line of planes and in one pass, his gunners destroyed two and damaged six of them. He then turned around and dropped a string of five 100-pound bombs on the shipping, sinking one vessel.

VPB-101's *Miller's High Life* Goes Missing

In the afternoon, Cdr. Justin Miller made a strike on enemy coastal shipping and seaplanes near Palawan. For some of the crew they would not live to see another day; for the others, it would be the beginning of a two-month journey. The story of their survival was documented by Lt. William Read Jr. and Ensign George H. Martin. Martin was the navigator, while Read was the squadron Gunnery Officer who sometimes joined Miller's crew. This time he would serve as the bow gunner. In the pre-dawn hours, the crew climbed into the Liberator named *Miller's High Life* and headed on a search that would take them out over the lower Philippines and out into the China Sea. Martin remembers approaching Palawan, the long westerly island of the Philippines.

"We were able to get a good look at Puerto Princesa, the capital of Palawan. I do not know who said it, but someone of our crew shouted on the inter-phone, 'Christ, look at that base down there!' And there it was—a sea plane base, airstrip, and dockage for ships. We took a good long look. There was no attempt at interception by Jap planes—we continued on our outward leg of the patrol. That was our primary job on patrol, to go, look, and see. On the way back that would be different, but first we had to complete our patrol—cover the area we had set out to cover. In fact, we went 350 miles beyond the base at Puerto Princesa, far out over the China Sea. The plans were made for the return trip. We would come in at 4,500 feet to clear the mountains, approaching the base from the west, lose altitude as fast as we could, drop our bombs on the ships and seaplanes, and strafe the airstrip."

Sitting in the bow turret, Read had a birds-eye view of the impending attack while watching for targets to engage with his twin .50-caliber machine guns.

"We let down to about 2,000 feet to avoid being picked up by Jap radar and broke out of the front a few miles from the mountains.

Splashes from machine gun fire and possibly general purpose bombs target a pair of Japanese merchant ships off the Philippines on 7 November 1944. *Courtesy of the NARA*

Climbing again, we cleared the peaks by about one hundred feet and went into a steep glide following the contour of the mountain down toward the town. Wooden houses and bamboo huts whisked under us, and in a few seconds we were over the harbor at about fifty feet, heading for the ships, which were around a dock with the airstrip just beyond.

"There was no visible AA, and I held my fire until we were within effective range and singled out the nearest ship through my sight. Watching its apparent motion, I instinctively figured my deflection—I had lots of practice—and fired several good bursts. The tracers arced out and an instant later, incendiary bursts spattered brightly around where I had figured the engine room and fuel tanks might be. Quickly I changed my aim to another ship, then another, then the warehouse near the dock. The air bomber called 'bombs away' over the interphone.

"The warehouse flashed under us, followed by a clump of coconut trees, and we dipped down even lower and started down the mat. The nearest plane was a Topsy. There were several men loading it and the hatch was open near the tail. I was tempted to worry the men, but we were after the planes, and I figured my deflection for inboard of the near engine and fired. The incendiaries hit, and with another burst the engine began to burn. The men who had been loading the plane scattered and were running for the coconut tree on the edge of the strip. I quickly picked up the next plane, then the next, and so on down the line—some of them were so close together I only had time to get off a few shots at them. Tracers from the upper turret were streaking over my head. There were mud puddles scattered along the strip, and I was surprised to see mud splashes on my Plexiglas dome, apparently kicked up by our bullets.

"We climbed slightly near the end of the strip to clear some coconut trees and headed out over the ocean in a climbing turn. The tail gunner reported good bomb hits and that we had started many fires. As we banked around, I could see three or four plumes of black oily smoke rising out of the harbor and eight or nine more coming from the line of planes on the airstrip, with orange flames licking at their roots.

"The skipper ordered pictures taken and the waist hatch 'Rogered,' and we flew a mile or so off shore parallel to the strip at about 500 feet. Then the skipper announced he had spotted some seaplanes in the harbor and we turned and headed down toward them.

"There were five or six Petes moored in a line near a beach and two or three others just offshore. We were just getting within range when someone called over the interphone, 'They're shooting at us.' I strained to see if I could see where the AA was coming from but could not, and turned and opened fire on the line of Petes, aiming just aft of the engines where I had 'flamed' a few before. I could see the belly turret's tracers joining mine, streaking down, and our incendiaries bursting together. Three or four of the Petes flamed and I changed to another Pete offshore, but it was so near that I hardly had time to get off a good burst. We were over the ships again. They were burning now, and I noticed a building burning near the dock. I fired a long burst into a ship that we had neglected on our first pass.

"Our plane wavered a bit as if something was wrong. Then we turned, climbing slightly, and headed out to sea. We had just begun to turn when I heard the upper turret gunner (I recognized his voice) say excitedly, 'Number four engine on fire!'

"In the waist section, Martin was taking photographs of the action with a K-20 camera. Miller banked the plane and came around again for another attack. The enemy now had the Liberator in their sites and anti-aircraft rounds began hitting the bomber.

"I was hit in the right leg by a .30-caliber bullet, and Villa [Peter A. "Pancho" Villa, AMM1c, 1st mechanic, crew chief, and starboard waist gunner] was hit in the right knee. The skipper and McDaniel up front did not know about our wounds until Rummerfield [Harry A. Rummerfield, AOM3c, port waist gunner], who was temporarily manning the port waist gun, called and told them two men were wounded, then Mac looked out and saw number four engine burning. 'Turn off the gas!' shouted the skipper and Mac rushed back to do

The rest of Miller's crew consisted of Lt. William A. Read Jr.; Harry Rummerfield, AOM3c; Francis M. Ford; ARM2c; Curtis Ford, ARM1c; John F. Coshow, AOM2c; J. W. Eckfield, AOMM; D. W. Doering, AOM3c; and P. A. Villa, AMM1c. Only P. A. "Pancho" Villa (back row, second from right) has been identified. *Courtesy of B-24 Club*

Cdr. Justin Miller (center), Ens. George H. Martin (right), and Lt. Hector S. McDaniels (left) standing next to their PB4Y-1 *Miller's High Life* the day the aircraft was heavily damaged by anti-aircraft fire while attacking Japanese aircraft parked at an airstrip at Puerto Princesa, Palwan, on 19 October 1944. *Courtesy of the B-24 Club*

so, but before he could do so the skipper called him back to help keep the plane on a level keel. He was hardly back, maybe half a minute, when the skipper shouted, 'Have to ditch!'

"The fire had burned a hole in the wing and had burned through the aileron control cables. There we were, without either rudder control or aileron control, and it was necessary to get away from that base. The skipper and McDaniel did all they could to keep her level and straight. We were losing speed and losing altitude all the time.

"I was lying on the deck, trying to stop the flow of blood from my leg wound. Villa was there, too, suffering from pain, shock, and loss of blood. I can see him yet, pointing to the severed rudder control cable. I was waiting for Rummerfield to apply tourniquets.

The Ditching

"Read came out of the bow turret, and he and Coshow came aft to tell us we were going to ditch. This all happened in a few minutes, but it seemed like a year. The plane crashed in the water with the right wing down in. I felt myself thrown forward, reached up, and caught the waist hatch as water came pouring through. I pulled myself out.

"The skipper was thrown through the windshield, seat and all. Mac must have gone through the hole that was made by the skipper, otherwise I do not understand how he got out without injury. Fortunately, he had not had time after starting aft to shut off the gas to number four and returned to strap himself into his seat. Curtis Ford [ARM1c and 1st radioman] and Francis Ford [ARM2c, 2nd radioman, and top turret gunner] were forward, Francis on the radio. Curtis Ford reached for the raft release over

the navigator's table—this opens a flap on the hull over the wing and the raft pops out. He did not reach the release because the impact threw him backward between the pilots' seats.

"Seven of us were aft: Doering [Dean Doering, S1c and tail turret gunner], Villa, Rummerfield, Coshow [John F. Coshow, AOM2c and bombardier], Eckfield ["Zeke" Eckfield, CAOM and belly turret gunner], Read, and I, all bracing for the impact. Eckfield was on the command deck above the bomb bay just forward of the belly turret, where the plane broke in two. While I was in the water, I saw the two sections of the plane swaying back and forth, opening and closing. Eckfield came through there. There was an agonized expression on his face. Perhaps he was squeezed in that vice, I do not know. He was in the water after that, but not for long.

"Villa was in the water beside me. He was still alive then, and able at first to hold on to parts of the plane, which remained afloat for a little while. Villa was losing blood and getting weaker, and so was I. We were clinging to the waist hatch section of the fuselage. Villa was weakening rapidly and losing his grip. I yelled at him to help himself all he could. At first he was able to help support himself a little, but as he lost more blood I was supporting his entire weight. He was murmuring to himself. I shouted to Francis Ford, who was near the bow of the plane, and asked if he could help, but he could not. He could hardly hold himself up.

"And then Pancho was gone. There was nothing I could do further to help him. Loss of blood had robbed him of the ability to fight. It had to be, I suppose, but I shall always regret that I was not able to do something more than I did to help him. I shall think of him often, as long as I live.

"Mac had gone to help the skipper out of his seat. I had lost so much blood that I was woozy, but I managed to climb up on the wreckage. Then I came to a bit as the plane started to buckle. It buckled again, and one of the bomb bay tanks finally broke loose. Curtis Ford and Coshow caught it. Mac came to see how the rest of us were faring.

"He spoke to Dean Doering, who had a life jacket on and seemed all right. 'I'm OK,' he said. However, we never saw him again. Curtis Ford had been struggling with Eckfield, who seemed to be in shock. Zeke had on a life jacket, but he had not pulled the straps and it was not inflated. Curtis inflated the life jacket, left Eckfield, and came over to help with the bomb bay tank. We never saw Eckfield again.

"Somewhere about this time Mac did a good job for me when he used one of my shoe strings for a tourniquet. I had been holding my finger over the wound under water and I must have stopped the flow of blood somewhat. The bleeding had been steady and veinous, not spurting as from an artery. The tourniquet stopped it all right.

"There was a small island about three miles away—a small island with a long sand spit trailing off from the end of it. Fortunately, the breeze was on shore. There may have been a tide, too, and if there was, it was favorable. The skipper, with Mac and Curtis Ford, were swimming and pushing the bomb bay tank raft toward land.

"It was about 3:15 when we spun in—it must have been 6:00 p.m. or later when we made it to the island. We reached the sand spit at last, and we all sat in the shallow water to rest for a while. Coshow was on the tank raft only a short while for a rest, then swam and helped to guide the tank to land. At any rate, he was all right when we reached land—he had apparently recovered from his state of shock. The skipper and Rummerfield could only walk with difficulty—both had badly sprained ankles. Read came to where we were almost immediately. He had a gash in his leg, but otherwise hardly a scratch. The skipper, besides his bad ankle, had a cut on the head near his eye, and he had lost a front upper tooth—rather a bloody affair. Mac had suffered only scratches. Rummerfield, besides his bad ankle, had cuts on both legs. Curtis Ford had gashes on both legs and scratches on his hands, face, and head. Francis Ford seemed in the worst shape, although there was no external bleeding. He was hurt, though—probably broken ribs and a broken collarbone.

"We were in shallow water, but it was about 200 yards offshore. Mac, Read, Coshow, and Curtis Ford got the tank as near the island as possible—Francis Ford and I were back on the tank. I had the feeling my leg was dead, but Read examined it, loosened the tourniquet, and said it was all right.

"The water was perhaps a foot to eighteen inches deep here. I lay back in the water and Coshow pulled me ashore. I was not in much condition to notice at the time what happened to Francis Ford, but I believe he got ashore on his own feet with some help.

"Coshow pulled me up on the beach, where I rested flat on my back for five or ten minutes. Meanwhile, Read had found a crude shelter up off the beach. It was just a framework with a thatched roof. In it there was a raised portion, apparently used to lie on. The able members of our party put the skipper and Francis Ford in there and arranged a bed for me outside."

Unwelcome Visitor

They landed on Ramesamey Island, north of Puerto Princesa in Honda Bay. It was uninhabited, except when natives went ashore to gather coconuts. The following day, in the middle of the afternoon, the survivors heard an aircraft approaching. They ran to the beach and were in time to see a PB4Y-1 intercepting a Japanese "Topsy" transport that had just taken off from Palawan. Confusion as to who shot down the Japanese plane continues, as VPB-115 recorded downing a Betty on 20 October 1944, but that occurred forty miles west of Palawan, while a report dated 22 October reports VPB-101 downed a Nakajima Ki-34 "Tess" (DC-2) off Puerto Princesa, or it could have been a Nakajima Ki-49 "Helen" twin-engine bomber/transport. Martin recalls:

"There was a burst from the bow turret of the PB4Y as our plane turned on to the tail of the Jap plane, and the Jap hit the water just off the land. The Jap ricocheted, ploughed up the beach, through the trees, and came out at the sandy beach beyond where our crewmembers had been frantically waving to attract the attention

Splashes from bombs and machine gun fire from VB-101's LtCdr. Smith's Liberator shows the unsuccessful attempt to camouflage this merchant ship attacked on 19 November 1944. *Courtesy of the NARA*

Apparently the same camouflaged vessel targeted by LtCdr. Smith in the previous image shows the aircraft attacking at the typical anti-shipping altitude of 200–300 ft. *Courtesy of the NARA*

Lt. K. H. Dunn of VPB-101 intercepted a Japanese Tess transport off Puerto Princesa, Palawan Island, at 1300 hours on 22 October 1944. It was brought down by Dunn's belly and bow turret gunner. Three figures were seen jumping from the transport before it crashed. This incident occurred well off shore, two days after Cdr. Miller's Liberator ditched off Ramesamey Island, thus it is unlikely the aircraft of George H. Martin. *Courtesy of the NARA*

of our plane. At that instant tragedy and luck struck us a mixed blow. The Jap plane passed over Mac and Curtis Ford but struck Francis Ford, who was buried under the wreckage. His death was so sudden he could not have known what happened.

"We were all stunned by the suddenness of this thing that had happened. Mac and Curtis Ford must have instinctively dropped to the ground as the Jap plane passed over them—beside Mac was the remains of a tree cut off three feet from the ground—but neither Mac nor Curtis Ford was hurt, although Mac was covered with sand and oil.

"The Jap plane did other damage as its parts flew around and it disintegrated. The muscles and nerves of Read's right leg were severed and the leg bone was broken. Coshow had a bad face wound from the inside corner of his eye down to his lip which would obviously require cosmetic surgery to repair. We learned later that Mac was so shocked by the tragedy that he suffered amnesia for a period of twenty-four hours.

"Read, in spite of his horribly damaged right leg, hopped toward the wreck.

"Flames were boiling from the port engine and wing and spreading to the fuselage, with a column of black smoke climbing skyward. Several Japs had been tossed through the front of the plane and lay bloody and groaning on the sand. I limped around the starboard wing—my leg hurt a little when I walked. The plane had broken just aft of the wing, and the tail section lay fifty feet or so down the path the plane had cut through the underbrush. Scattered around lay several more Japs—some dead, some dying—a machine gun with a bent barrel, a torn belt of ammunition, some tools, many jagged pieces of the plane, and a shiny bent Jap officer's sword was sticking upright in the sand.

"As I neared the opening in the fuselage aft of the wing, I was astonished to see a Jap officer walk out of the wrecked plane, apparently unscathed. He had a 'crew' haircut and a long black beard, a khaki shirt with red and gold collar insignia, a wide black belt with bayonet and scabbard attached, and khaki pants and black boots.

"He and I stared at each other for a moment (after what a movie director would have called a 'double-double take'), and he began to jabber and whipped out his bayonet and the scabbard and waved them menacingly, one in each hand. I talked back to him, and pointing to the mess his plane had made insisted that in view of the disgraceful exhibition his plane had just put on he should commit *hara-kiri* immediately. He did not seem to understand, and I felt if he had a knife I should have one, too, so I hobbled over to the lean-to, which had been missed by fifty feet, to look for my knife, yelling to the others, warning them there was a 'live Jap.' No one knew where the knife was and I hobbled back toward the wreck, picking up a green coconut on the way.

"Mac, who had flopped down to avoid being hit by the plane, was now on his hands and knees, covered with oily sand and trying to collect himself. The Jap had walked over and was menacing him with his knife. Mac took a few steps backward, tripped, and fell on his back. I threw the coconut at the Jap to distract his attention from Mac. It was a lucky pitch and would have 'corked' him, but he saw it coming, ducked, and began jabbering profusely at me. In the midst of his jabbering I understood the word 'Americanos' and nodded, repeating 'Americanos,' and by motioning with my hands tried to convince him that the island was full of Americans and we were going to shoot him. The captain appeared, armed with a coconut, the first radioman appeared armed with a stick, and the Jap, seeing them, must have believed I was giving him the word, for he dropped his knife and ran down to the beach and out on the sandbar. Then, spying the

Ens. P. R. Barker of VPB-115 found a 7–9,000 ton tanker anchored in Marudu Bay, Northern Borneo, on 1 November 1944 and proceeded to sink the vessel with a pair of 250 lb. bombs. *Courtesy of the NARA*

bomb-bay gas tank the tide had left on the northeast side of the sandbar, he waded over to it, pushed it free, and was last seen lying on it, paddling with his hands, heading for the mainland. The captain tried to intercept him, but due to his sprained ankle was unable to do so.

"My leg really hurt now, and I hobbled back to the lean-to and lay down. I took off my shoes and blood spilled out of the right one. My gash was pretty deep, almost to the bone, but had almost stopped bleeding. The captain tore off a piece of his underwear for a bandage. An examination of the wreckage of the Jap plane yielded several cans of fish (probably tuna, but it really stank), two parachutes which came in handy for blankets and mosquito netting, and a kit of tools and a pistol. The tools served us in good stead to open up the coconuts that were our only food—except the stinking Jap fish—for many days."

Rescue
Cdr. Miller knew it was only a matter of time before the Japanese decided to pay them a visit. They had to get off the island and find help. On the twenty-first, McDonald made an unsuccessful attempt to swim to Palawan. The crew built a crude raft, and the night of the twenty-seventh Miller and McDonald paddled away. They reached another uninhabited island the next morning and remained there for several days—their physical condition prevented them from going on. On the thirty-first, they set off again and made landfall on another small island closer to their ultimate destination of Palawan. Finally, on 2 November, they made it to Palawan and were soon in the safe hands of Filipino guerrillas. The remaining men on Ramesamey Reef were soon rescued and reunited with Miller. On 2 December, they were picked up by the submarine USS *Gunnell* and taken to Saipan, arriving there on the fifteenth. Four days later commander Miller was back with 101 after being gone for two months.[3]

VPB-101 lost three more Liberators and two dozen crewmen while the survivors of *Miller's High Life* languished on Ramesamey Island. Ensign Harold H. Lewis's Liberator was shot down by enemy fighters on the twenty-third and the crew perished. Lt. Russell E. Brown and three crewmen were killed when Brown was forced to ditch his PB4Y-1 Bureau Number 32299 one hundred yards off Poro Island, in the Camotes Group. The plane broke into four sections; six of the crew survived, made it to shore, and were later rescued with the help of natives. Bowen, Ensign Joseph Downs, crew captain Charles Newland, and radioman George Sloan were killed. The remains of Bowen, Downs, and Newland were repatriated to the United States after the war, but those of Sloan were not found.

Two days later, Ensign Robert Allen and his crew were killed when their bomber crashed on takeoff from Owi. Lt. A. R. Seiber piloted another VPB-101 Liberator lost on the twenty-sixth after sinking a 5,000-ton Japanese tanker off Southern Mindanao, which was sunk after two aggressive bombing runs by the pilot. The ship sent up heavy defensive fire before exploding, setting the Liberator's No. 4 engine on fire and destroying the aircraft's fuel transfer system. Seiber made the decision to ditch before nightfall since the main fuel cells contained only three hundred gallons. The pilot conducted a textbook water landing some seventy-five miles off Mindanao and all eleven members exited the plane, climbed into three life rafts, and awaited rescue, which occurred sixteen hours later the following day via an Army OA-10A Catalina (call sign "Daylight Two One," flown by 1stLt. Denzil L. Kathman from the Second Emergency Rescue Squadron).

The squadron's last fatality during October was Lt. (jg) Neal A. Tyler's navigator, Ensign Joseph W. Shepard, who died from a shoulder

Lt. Dawes Jr. of VPB-115 destroyed a Japanese naval auxiliary vessel along with a freighter and barge carrying fuel drums (seen here) on 4 November 1944, Coron Bay, Northern Palawan, Philippines. *Courtesy of the NARA*

wound sustained from a 12.7 mm machine gun round fired from an enemy freighter while Tyler was making a low level bombing run.

Return of the Buccaneers

While Miller and crew were stranded, 101 and 115 continued with armed reconnaissance missions. With the loss of Cdr. Miller, the commanding officer of 115 assumed the duties of Cdr. Task Force Unit 73.4.3, with LtCdr. Marvin T. Smith taking command of 101.

In early November, the Buccaneers of VPB-104 returned for a second tour of duty, replacing the Bulldog squadron at Morotai. This time around, the Buccaneers were under the command of LtCdr. Whitney Wright, the father of PB4Y low-level bombing tactics.

The Buccaneer Liberators were unique in two aspects that made it unlike any other sister squadrons. First, some of them were missing belly turrets, and in their place were equipped with APS-15 radar; however, this diminished the aircraft's firepower and made the aircraft susceptible to enemy fighter attacks from below. Second, the planes were void of any of the colorful nose art common in all such squadrons. The reason was Cdr. Wright believed that if a crew was shot down they could claim to their captors they were a fresh replacement crew and maybe receive kinder treatment. There is no documentation that this ploy worked for or against 104.[4]

Their arrival, as with 102 and 116 before them, was marred by a training accident in California, when a plane belonging to VB-117 crashed into a supply building, killing three men of the squadron and injuring four more. Operational losses continued while in Hawaii, when just days before the squadron shipped out to the Pacific the landing gear failed on Lt. (jg) J. D. Shea's plane upon landing and was a total loss; fortunately, there were no injuries. On Morotai, the Japanese greeted 104's return by sending a half dozen bombers to bomb the airfield at Morotai, destroying one PB4Y and damaging four others. It would be repeated, as November was a month of intensive Japanese air strikes on Morotai, with the airfield being the target of thirty such attacks.

Squadron search sectors covered the east coast of the Philippines, southwestward along Palawan Passage, and the west coast of Borneo to the town of Miri, the Makassar Straight, the west coast of the Celebes, and Halmahera. The presence of large merchant shipping continued to diminish in numbers and Navy land-based squadrons could only concentrate on the small coastal vessels that hugged enemy-held islands in the Philippines and Indonesia. For VPB-104, the squadron's first score came on the sixth, when LtCdr. Wright sank two such coastal vessels near Kudat, Borneo.

However infrequent contact with enemy surface vessels was, the Japanese air arm still had plenty of fighters left in the region, and Liberator squadrons operating in the area were frequent targets. On the tenth, Lt. John J. Burton was returning from his 1,000-nautical mile search when he tangled with six enemy fighters. In a running battle lasting twenty minutes, Burton dove his Liberator from 3,500 feet down to 200 feet and managed to evade the fighters by flying low between two islands.

The Buccaneers suffered their first combat loss on 11 November. Lt. Maurice "Tex" Hill and Lt. (jg) Gerald Didier were flying a routine two-plane search at 8,500 feet when two Tonys dove and jumped them over the Comdotes Sea. In plain view, the Liberator crews saw a group of F6F Hellcats working over a couple Japanese destroyers with several Japanese Tony fighters trying to stop them. In the melee, the pair of patrol bombers were pulled into the air battle when several of the Japanese fighters broke away and went for them.

The Japanese pilot conducted a fatal move after downing Hill's plane by crossing over in front of Didier's Liberator, enabling the port waist, bow, and top turret gunners to unleash a deadly hail of .50-caliber machine gun fire. A thick trail of black smoke erupted from the fighter's engine as it rolled over and plunged into the sea.

Four F6Fs tried to intercept the Japanese planes but were too late, as one Tony came after Lt. Hill's plane and scored numerous hits. Inside the Liberator the tail turret guns were disabled, making the aircraft indefensible from an attack from the rear (and due to the belly radar vice the twin .50-caliber belly turret). One of the Tony's pilots noticed the lack of gunfire from the rear and proceeded to attack with 20 mm cannon fire. Hill was killed and several others were wounded as the plane headed toward the water.

Lt. "Red" Anderson, at the navigation table, went into the cockpit and helped copilot Ensign Frederick Pratt lift Hill from the pilot's seat. Pratt climbed into the seat, and with Anderson's help tried to regain control of the bomber. However, the Liberator then banked slightly and crashed in the water, killing six of her crew. The remaining four—Anderson Pratt (AOM3c), John L. Nason (AMM1c), Charles D. Vey, and Dow H. Gothard (ARM3c)—climbed into a life raft and waited for their rescue. It was not long before a group of Filipinos in dugout canoes paddled toward them and brought the survivors to shore.

After several days the men were picked up by an American PT boat and taken to Tacloban, Leyte. After two months of being shuffled from one medical facility to another, the men finally arrived in the United States. For the Filipinos who rescued them, Japanese forces descended on the village in retaliation for harboring the Americans, tied several dozen together, and bayoneted them.

The deaths of squadron personnel did not diminish the Buccaneers' taste for anti-shipping sweeps, as exemplified by Paul Stevens on 12 November, when he departed Morotai in the early dawn for a patrol to the northwest, through the Celebes and Sulu Seas. After reaching the western coast of Palawan Island and very near the northern tip, a search was begun of the inlets and bays that dotted the island at an altitude of one hundred feet. The patrol did not produce any targets until a little after noon.

Just after searching a bay, a large convoy was seen on the horizon, fifteen miles away. The ships, sailing in column, consisted of two large transports in the 8,000–10,000-ton range—a tanker, three destroyers, and a destroyer escort. Stevens describes a typical and successful attack on Japanese shipping:

"I made the decision to attack, as it was judged that with this formation the attack could be executed without too much gunfire from the escorting destroyers. The selected target was the leading FTB [freighter transport] since it was obviously the largest ship.

"My course inbound for the attack was about 200 degrees approaching alongside the column. The trailing destroyer and leading destroyer escort had a clear field of fire as the PB4Y-1 approached. The other two DDs [destroyers] increased speed and began heading into the transport column to position themselves for a better field of fire on our patrol plane.

"I was as low to the water as possible, thirty feet or so, and by over-boosting the engines our speed was just over 200 knots. I transmitted in the 'blind' on the VHF voice radio that I was attacking a convoy, but no acknowledgment was received.

"When about five miles from the convoy the ships began firing with heavy anti-aircraft gunfire, but it was inaccurate. At maximum range (one mile) for our .50-caliber machine guns we began firing on the tanker. An estimated 200 rounds were fired and hits were observed. As we closed on the second transport in line fire was shifted and about 800 rounds were fired, with many obvious hits. Smoke began to rise from this ship due to our heavy firing on its superstructure.

"Closing on the target ship—the leading transport—the anti-aircraft fire became much heavier and the airplane was hit in the forward area. The bow turret took a 20 mm or 40 mm hit which disabled the turret and seriously injured Pedigo [Derral Pedigo], the bow gunner. Also Webber [Lee Webber, the bombardier], crouching just below the bow turret, was lacerated by shrapnel.

"Pressing in close upon the target, I was dismayed to see a haze of gray smoke rising from the ship. It appeared the ship had been hit before, was damaged, and the wrong target had been selected. This view was quickly discarded when it became clear that this was smoke rising from so much gunfire emanating from the ship. Conversely, the gunners on the airplane poured in 1,200 rounds of gunfire. There were many hits, as most of the firing on the ship was at very close range.

"In very close, I was looking up at the ship. Soon I started to ease the airplane up for the bomb release. At one hundred feet altitude, six 250-pound bombs were released with fifty feet spacing. As the bombs fell out of the bomb bay the airplane was pulled up sharply to clear the superstructure. Three bombs hit into the hull from the waterline, stair stepping up to the cabin level. The other three bombs overshot the ship.

"As the bombs exploded there was an additional large explosion. Debris was thrown up 500 feet in the air and flames bellowed from amidships. The large transport ship made a slow ninety degree turn to starboard and came to a stop.

"Clearing the ship, I threw the airplane into a skid and got back down, very close to the water. Now the DDs were unrestricted in their field of fire and bracketed the airplane with heavy anti-aircraft fire. It may have been the wild skid or closeness to the water, but whatever it was, this heavy anti-aircraft scored no further hits on the PB4Y. The escape passed close to the leading destroyer and 300 rounds were fired from the top turret and waist guns. The warship went dead in the water, but was later observed to be underway again."[5]

Stevens headed home with two injured men on board. Pedigo's leg was severely injured and would mean a ticket back to the United States. For Webber, his shrapnel wounds were treated back at base and he later returned to duty. The attack netted Stevens and his crew one large prize, possibly the Celebes Maru, a 6,000-

ton cargo ship. Three days later the same crew would follow this success with the sinking of a larger vessel.

The sinking of the Celebes Maru was followed by a series of successful strikes on merchant shipping. Under clear skies on 13 November, Lt. Cdr. Smith of VPB-101 entered Marudu Bay, North Borneo, around noon and sighted two 2,000-ton transports close to the western shore and a gunboat across the bay. Letting down to 1,000 feet, he made a run on the transports from the stern. He released all 250-pound bombs from 200 feet and all missed. However, the aircraft took a 40 mm round hit near the number two engine so it was feathered, and the belly turret was cut loose and dropped to reduce weight and to improve three-engine performance. The search was completed and the plane returned to base. Subsequent reconnaissance saw one of the ships deserted and resting on the bottom.

Lt. Stevens topped everybody when he sighted the 5,863-ton Borneo Maru anchored off Bondoc Peninsula, about seventy-five miles south of Manila on the fifteenth. The ship had been sighted the day before but not attacked, and Stevens was going to change that.

Coming in at minimum altitude, Stevens pointed the Liberator toward the ship, his gunners opening fire when the plane was 2,000 feet from the target. Webber, back at the bombardier's station after recovering from his wounds, dropped a stick of five 250-pound bombs. The bombs were on target and the ship received five direct hits, which tore out its starboard side. Two days later the burned out ship was photographed near a reef; 2,000 Japanese troops she was carrying would never arrive at their destination.

Borneo Targeted

Preventing the Japanese from reaching Leyte with reinforcements and supplies became the major task of American air forces throughout October–November 1944. On the fifteenth, Lt. A. Y. Bellsey attacked the airfield at Puerta Princessa, Palawan, in broad daylight. Initially approaching the island at 4,000 feet, Bellsey dropped down to 200 feet and released five 100-pound bombs on the runways. Swinging back around, he let his gunners chew up several aircraft parked in a dispersal area. The PB4Y-1 then circled and made a run on a nearby seaplane base and machine gun fire damaged one Jake. Passing a house, the Liberator took small caliber fire and the bombardier received a flesh wound just under his eye. Bellsey was not finished, as he made four more runs on the airfield, resulting in the destruction of a Topsy and two fighters. Two days later, two Liberators from 104 struck the Japanese a heavy blow by sinking several ships.

Lt. (jg) Edward M. Hagen became a one-man task force when he and his crew damaged a 1,500-ton freighter transport with 250-pound bombs and machine gun fire. Continuing on his patrol two 300-ton cargo ships were attacked, leaving one burning on the beach after running aground and sinking the other after a direct hit on the vessel's stern by a 250-pound bomb. Trying to outdo

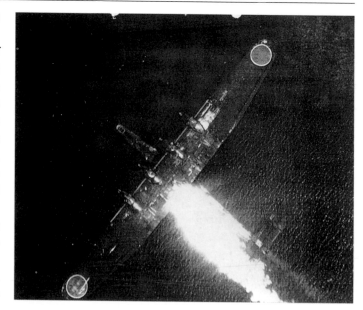

Japanese Mavis seaplane moments before crashing after being set afire by the aerial gunners aboard VPB-101's Lt. Bellsey's Liberator on 22 November 1944. *Courtesy of the NARA*

his counterpart, Lt. William E. Goodman sunk another 300-ton ship and severely damaged another 200-ton vessel.

Patrolling the area around the Philippines and Celebes almost certainly meant interception by enemy aircraft, and that is what happened to Lt. John H. Burton on the eighteenth and Lt. Wood the following day. For Burton, two Oscars tried to chase him down over Marudu Bay, North Borneo. One Oscar managed to damage the Liberator before the pilot could enter some clouds. The damage was slight and Burton and his crew made it home. For Lt. Wood, a formation of eleven Oscars was sighted over Panay Island; fortunately for the Liberator crew only one of the fighters came down to attack. Wood quickly headed for cloud cover and lost the pursuer. The patrol continued, and off Mindoro Island an 800-ton cargo ship and escorting gunboat were attacked, with the merchant ship possibly being sunk and the gunboat severely damaged.

On the nineteenth and twentieth, Liberators from 101 and 104 hit Kudat airfield and shipping in Borneo. Cdr. Smith was the first to strike while nearing the end of his assigned search sector. At 1100 hours he sighted a 2,000-ton cargo ship and a patrol vessel in a bay near Kudat. He went down to one hundred feet and dropped two 500-pound bombs. Both missed the larger vessel, so he decided to use his remaining bomb load on barracks adjoining the airstrip. Smith pickled off three 100-pound incendiaries and two 100-pound general purpose bombs, scoring direct hits that sent up a plume of black smoke that could be seen for fifty miles. The Japanese defenders managed to put up anti-aircraft fire to no avail, as Smith pressed on three more strafing attacks that left two planes damaged on the airfield. The following day 104's Lt. (jg) Hemphill hit Kudat at minimum altitude, destroying two parked Sallys before dropping a string of 250-pound bombs on a barracks.

The seaplane's pilot apparently has control of his aircraft as flames spread along the main fuselage, but seconds later it plunges out of control into the jungle. *Courtesy of the NARA*

A lone VPB-101 Liberator hitting the Japanese-occupied town Kudat, Borneo, on 19 November 1944. Typical missions were conducted by one or two aircraft. *Courtesy of the NARA*

Marvin Smith's VPB-101 and Whitney Wright's VPB-104 squadrons provided invaluable services by impeding the enemy sending reinforcements and supplies to the Philippines, as the Japanese position on the archipelago in late 1944 was unraveling, similar to that faced by American and Filipino forces in early 1942. Japanese land-based fighters flying cover for merchant vessels attempted to bring down a Liberator flown by T. R. Williams of VPB-104 on 20 November as he and his crew targeted 1,000-ton enemy cargo ships at Puerto Princesa. Williams pickled off three 250-pound bombs from an altitude of fifty feet that split the ships in two, sending them to the bottom of the Sulu Sea. Pulling up from the run, Williams spotted seven enemy fighters on a parallel course.

The fighters were soon identified as Oscars, as one came in head on, but was met with the Liberator's bow and top turrets. The Oscar managed to hit the Liberator's number one engine and knocked out the electrical system to the turrets, rendering them inoperative. However, the fighter was hit, burst into flames, rolled over on its back, and then tried to ram the PB4Y-1, but it missed by twenty-five feet before slamming into the water. Another Oscar came in but was quickly driven off, and Williams turned the bomber toward Tacloblan airstrip.

The PB4Y-1 was losing altitude and the crew jettisoned loose gear and prepared for a ditching. Williams managed to keep the big bird in the air and arrived at Tacloban. Touching down, the port tire gave out and the plane skidded off the runway, hitting a gasoline truck that severed the port wing tip. The port strut hit a concrete block, the number two engine burst into flames, and the bomber skidded along on its belly before stopping. The crew climbed out uninjured and watched their plane burn.

Patrol plane crews were covering their search sectors regardless of weather, and many shipping contacts were made and reported. Anti-shipping sweeps were repeated during the next several days, as 104 Liberators flown by Lts. Woodford W. Sutherland, Walter H. Heider, Hagen, Wood, and Burton destroyed ships varying from 200 to 7,000 tons. Lt. Burton even had the honor of dropping bombs on two enemy cruisers. The bombs missed and the Liberator was chased away by an Oscar.

Lt. (jg) Walter Rodgers and four crewmen of VPB-101 were killed when Rodgers was forced to make a night ditching of PB4Y-1 32260 on 25 November, when a bomb released from the aircraft exploded prematurely while conducting a run against a small enemy freighter.

On the twenty-sixth, VPB-101's Lt. A. C. Lubberts came upon a convoy of six merchant ships off the northeastern tip of Marinduque Island. The Liberator went down to 150 feet, crossed over the largest ship from bow to stern, and dropped three 250-pound bombs while his gunners concentrated their fire on the other ships. The bombs missed and Lubberts came around for another run.

On 15 November 1944, while patrolling from Morotai, Lt. Paul Stevens attacked a troop transport off Bondoc Peninsula. Five hits with 250-pound bombs set fire to the ship identified as the *Borneo Maru*. Courtesy of Paul Stevens

The shadow of a Philippine based PB4Y-1 Liberator looking over the remains of a small Japanese freighter destroyed by the bomber's guns and bombs. *Courtesy of the NARA*

This time he was met with heavy machine gun fire that hit the bomber in the tail turret, smashing the ammunition belt and rendering one of the guns inoperative. Lubberts left and went hunting for other game, which was spotted less than thirty minutes later, as three small coastal ships were damaged by strafing twenty-five miles west of Pandan, Pany Island. Lubberts finished his patrol by strafing a dock area at Tanjay Bay, Negros Island.

Close Call at Zamboanga

December arrived with continuing armed reconnaissance missions around the Philippines and attacks on Japanese forces on Borneo. VPB-101's Lt. R. L. Hersherger conducted the first successful mission for the month. Approaching Brunei Bay at 5,000 feet, a 2,000-ton merchant ship was spotted being escorted by two gunboats. Dropping down to fifty feet, the Liberator went in and delivered two attacks with machine gun fire and 100-pound bombs, damaging the larger vessel with a direct hit on her bow. As Hershberger pointed the PB4Y home the merchant ship and both escorts were left burning.

The Buccaneers' score continued to climb with successful attacks on enemy shipping of all sizes. On the third, Cdr. Wright sank or damaged three vessels, including the 834-ton cargo ship Nanshin Maru Number 13. During an attack on his third target a patrol boat sent up heavy anti-aircraft fire that punctured the aircraft numerous times in the bomb bay and wing areas. The damage was so severe the plane was grounded for two weeks. Three days later another Buccaneer crew led by Lt. Hemphill attacked shipping in Zamboanga, Mindanao.

Coming in at one hundred feet, two 500-ton cargo ships were hit by a salvo of five 100-pound bombs. Then it was the Liberator's turn

to be on the receiving end of a deadly hail of anti-aircraft fire. The starboard aileron and flaps were shot away, two of the engines were set on fire, the hydraulic system was shot out, and the vertical stabilizer was perforated. One 40 mm shell entered the nose compartment and exploded, puncturing the fuselage in a hundred places.

Everything that could be ripped from the plane was tossed out as the pilots tried to regain altitude. Leyte was sighted and the landing gear was lowered manually. Hemphill made a perfect landing without an airspeed indicator and flaps. Rolling to a stop, the crew climbed out of an aircraft that would never fly again. The crew was relieved they had escaped death, but war sometimes plays tricks on its participants; the crew walked into the middle of an air raid on the base. Copilot Ensign Joe Wasneski tells what happened next:

"It was just getting dark as we were leaving the plane. The red alert was still going on and the ships were firing at planes out in the dark bay. We were going down the runway in a truck when ack-ack guns at the end of the airstrip started firing. Just then we saw a Jap plane coming right for us, strafing.

"We jumped from the truck and scattered amongst the parked planes. Someone steered me to the right and that's why I'm here today. The Jap plane [a Betty] was hit and crashed into the parked planes. Ensign Madsen [Norman Madsen] was killed instantly when the plane hit him. Don Holton, a mechanic and belly turret gunner, was also killed instantly."[6]

Ensign Wasneski rescued four injured crewmembers, and without thought about his own safety shielded them from the fire and explosions that followed. For his actions he was awarded the Navy Cross.

2

Tacloban Airfield, Leyte, Philippines
December 1944–January 1945

December 1944 in the Southwest Pacific saw the arrival of Cdr. E. O. Rigsbee Jr. and the Blue Raiders of VPB-117 to Tacloban airfield, Leyte, on the first. As will be discussed later, VPB-117 had briefly staged strikes from Tinian, in the Mariana Islands. It was a welcome addition to Fleet Air Wing 10, becoming the first Navy land-based heavy bombing squadron to operate from the Philippines since 1941. The Blue Raiders would also distinguish themselves by producing five aerial aces.

By the ninth, two planes and crews from VPB-104 had joined VPB-117 at Tacloban, and by the end of the month, the Buccaneers would pack their belongings at Morotai and move to Leyte. Back on Morotai, VPB-101 would continue hitting enemy shipping and ground targets until the first of the year.

On the shore of San Pedro Bay, which separates the islands of Leyte and Samar, Tacloban was captured in late October and Army Engineers quickly began work on it; by the squadron's arrival it was operational. Search sectors extended to Camranh Bay, French-Indo China (Vietnam), western Borneo, Hainan Straits to China, and eastward to the Ryukyu Islands, including Okinawa. The job of Navy Liberator squadrons was to support allied forces in the seizure of the Philippines.

VPB-104 and 117 found life difficult at first, because most of their equipment was lost during transit to Leyte. Food was hardly edible, with the crews subsisting on canned goods and native produce. Combined with primitive living conditions was adverse weather, with take-offs and landings taking place in zero visibility. Initially, the runway was loose Marston steel mats laid on sand. Yet the airfield became invaluable during the Second Battle of the Philippine Sea, when battle damaged carrier-based aircraft found a safe haven at Tacloban. In early December, space restrictions at the Tacloban airstrip made it imperative to park airplanes close together, with their noses just off the narrow takeoff/

Tacloban Island, in the Philippines, became home to VPB-117 beginning in December 1944, after the squadron operated in the Central Pacific for two months. *Courtesy of the VPB-117 Association*

Combat Air Crew One of VPB-117. Back Row: Taliafero, Voelzke, and Cox. Middle Row: Jamieson, Ens. Allsopp Skipper, Sqdn.Cdr. E. O. Rigsbee Jr., Lt. Osborn, and Chief Lassey. Front Row: Brewer, Riggs, and Manners. *Courtesy of Dan Kerper*

Lt. Squires, patrol plane commander of Crew Nine, smiles for the camera while behind him another officer lies on his cot inside their quarters. Squires is carrying a standard Navy issue .38-caliber pistol in his shoulder holster. *Courtesy of the VPB-117 Association*

Unidentified members of VPB-117 standing next to PB4Y-1 Liberator Bureau Number 38735, *Pop's Cannon Ball*, that was lost with its crew on 16–17 February 1945. *Courtesy of the VPB-117 Association*

Lt. Brooke was forced to ditch his PB4Y-1 *Pink Lady* (Bureau Number 38773) off Negros Island after being intercepted by a Japanese fighter. Back row: Trotter, Chatman, Nelson, James L. Tedrowe, and Allen. Middle row: Sullivan, Hooper, Taylor, Thompson, and Melvin Long. Front row: Lt. Bradford M. Brooke (far left), Ens. Gregory A. Robertson, and unknown. Not shown is Vergil T. Bolton Jr., ARM2c. Killed in the ditching were Brooke, Robinson, Tedrowe, Long, and Bolton. *Courtesy of Dan Kerper*

This is VPB-117 PB4Y-1 Bureau Number 38761, *Neptune's Virgin*, at an unknown location circa late 1944 or early 1945. *Courtesy of the VPB-117 Association*

landing strip. Little margin for error was provided for the take-off and landing of aircraft. Each take-off was uphill, but on landings this was beneficial, in that very little breaking was required.

On 5 December, one of the first planes to take off was a Marine F4U Corsair. As the fighter was approaching take-off speed the pilot saw another plane taxiing toward him and he veered to the left and crashed into a parked Liberator of VPB-117. A fierce fire instantly erupted and quickly engulfed the fighter and the Liberator. Immediately the crew of 117's Lt. (jg) Sheldon L. Sutton rushed to assist the F4U pilot who, though his legs were pinned in the wrecked plane, was trying, without success, to extricate himself by pulling his body up with his arms and shoulders. Rescue attempts were thwarted as an explosion and fire prevented anyone from assisting the pilot. Within a few seconds the pilot slumped down in the cockpit and fell victim to the fire that consumed his aircraft.[1]

The Blue Raiders lost their first aircraft on 10 December, when two Zeke fighters shot out three engines of Lt. Bradford M. Brooks' *Pink Lady*, Bureau Number 38773. Brooks ditched off Los Negros, but he and four members of the crew were killed, while the remaining seven were picked up by Filipino guerillas and returned to the squadron.

Leaking Fuel and a Navy Cross

For the Buccaneers, on 12 December, Lt. Joseph D. Shea took his Liberator to Brunei Town, Borneo, and proceeded to wreak havoc on enemy installations and shipping. His gunners strafed a convoy of trucks loaded with troops, but the fleeing soldiers managed to take their vehicles into dense foliage and contact was broken off.

Heading over the harbor, he banked the plane and began three bombing and strafing runs, leaving eight ships heavily damaged. Anti-aircraft fire from ships and shore batteries found their range and began bracketing the lone bomber. One hit damaged a fuel line to a main fuel cell and the plane filled with gas fumes. Shea began venting the plane by opening the bomb bay doors as three of the crew headed toward the damaged area.

In the bomb bay, gas was pouring out of several hose connections from the number two and three fuel tanks. One of the crew, nineteen-year-old William E. Abbott (AMM3c), of Peoria, Illinois, began trying to transfer fuel from one tank to the other by holding the hoses together. The fumes overcame plane captain Gordon Martin and he had to get out while Otto Adams and Abbott continued to transfer fuel. In minutes one hundred gallons had been transferred.

The fumes overcame Abbott and he slipped off the catwalk, but crewman Otto Adams grabbed his arm as the helpless sailor dangled out of the open bomb bay; the fumes became too much for Adams as well and he lost his grasp of Abbott, who plunged 1,500 feet to his death. James Harrington rushed over to help Adams but was overwhelmed as well; luckily both men managed to hold on to the catwalk and survived. William E. Abbott was awarded the Navy Cross for his actions to save his crewmates.[2]

The Buccaneers continued pounding away at Japanese shipping, with the squadron damaging or sinking more than 48,000 tons of

Aviation Maintenance Mate Third Class William Edwin Abbott as a nineteen-year-old member of Lt. Joseph D. Shea's crew was awarded the Navy Cross (posthumously) on 12 December 1944. *US Navy*

Two members of VPB-117 standing beside PB4Y-1 Bureau Number 38757 *Dirty Gerty* have the standard tri-color configuration that replaced Army olive drab and gray coloring. *Courtesy of the VPB-117 Association*

shipping while claiming the damage or destruction of thirty Japanese aircraft. Three separate missions are worth noting as examples of the tenacity of 104's Liberator crews to get the enemy by any means necessary.

On the fifteenth, Lt. (jg) Woodford W. Sutherland sighted a large convoy of ships consisting of four transports being escorted by the same number of destroyers and destroyer escorts off the western coast of Luzon, at Scarborough Shoals. Too much for a lone Liberator, Sutherland made contact with submarines *SS-319* and *-366*. He then left. Two days later the squadron received a communique stating that one of the destroyers had been sunk.

Stevens and Sutherland then went out together and attacked the *Shinfuku Maru* in the East China Sea. The merchantman was spotted through a heavy overcast and strong tail wind. Sutherland went in first, his gunners providing suppressing fire, and dropped a 500-pound bomb. The bomb missed by forty feet and Sutherland came back around for a second run. This time he pickled off two bombs, with one exploding near the bridge section that blew off the funnel. The second bomb went through the fantail and exploded ten feet from the stern. Stevens came in and salvoed ten 100-pound bombs, seven of which found the target. The ship began burning fiercely and the crew abandoned the vessel. Stevens and Sutherland met up and headed home with another victory.

Lt. Paul Stevens Spots a Task Force

The day after Christmas, Lt. Stevens went on patrol to Indo-China and found nine Jakes sitting on the water at Carnranh Bay. His orders were to search only and not attack, but Stevens could not pass up the chance—a chance that almost backfired on him later that day. During two strafing runs his guns destroyed one aircraft and damaged two more before he turned back toward home.

At 1600 hours on the return leg he sighted a Japanese task force consisting of the heavy cruiser *Ashigara*, the light cruiser *Oyodo*, and six destroyers approximately 170 miles west of Mindoro Island. It was Vice Admiral Shima's Second Striking Force under Rear Admiral Masanori Kimura, and it was headed for Mindoro to bombard the American beachhead. Flying at 8,000 feet, Stevens approached to within eight miles and was welcomed by a full broadside from the *Ashigara's* main batteries. Stevens made a violent turn toward Mindoro and made a contact report. After landing Stevens reported the ships to Col. Wilson, commander of the bomb wing.[3]

His report signaled a full effort of American air and surface units to engage the enemy. The V Army Air Force sent ninety-two fighters, thirteen B-25 bombers, and some P-61s to meet the striking force. Meanwhile, Adm. Kincaid sent PBY Catalinas and PBM Mariners to assist. Additionally, a task group consisting of the heavy cruisers *Louisville* and *Minneapolis*, with light cruisers *Phoenix* and *Boise* and eight destroyers, was rushed in. For Stevens, his participation was far from over, as the wing commander directed him to refuel and attack the Japanese force. It was a job he did not want, as chances

for a lone Liberator against an entire enemy task force were slim to none, but he went outside and headed for the airstrip.

"While I was gone from the airstrip my crew had begun refueling the airplane with 2,700 gallons of gas from fifty-five-gallon steel drums. This was accomplished by rolling the barrels off a truck and then to the PB4Y-1. Then, using a hand-cranked pump, the AvGas was transferred into the wing tanks. During the final fueling I was guided over to a camp of sorts where a group of soldiers had an open campfire. Here my hosts offered up a less-than-gourmet dinner of cold beans and lukewarm coffee. A condemned man should rate a better last meal than this!

"Walking back to the airstrip, I was surprised to see thirteen B-25s parked near our airplane. Up to this time I had seen no other airplanes or aviation personnel. A red alert was on and Japanese bombers were making intermittent air attacks. Given the current circumstances the airstrip was no place to be. This situation was obviously in the minds of the ordnance gang. They came roaring up in their bomb-handling truck, skidded to a stop, kicked off four 500-pound bombs, threw the tail fins and fuses to the ground, and

The Stinger (Bureau Number 38741) ran out of fuel off Tacloban on 31 December 1944, and flipped over while ditching, killing Lt. (jg) William Benn. *Courtesy of the VPB-117 Association*

Ready to Write a Book?

Our authors are as passionate as we are about providing new and intriguing perspectives on a variety of topics, both niche and general. If you have a fresh idea, we would love to hear from you, as we are continually seeking new authors and their work. Visit our website to view our complete list of titles and our current catalogs. Please visit our Author Resource Center on our website for submission guidelines, and contact us at proposals@schifferbooks.com or write to the address below, to the attention of Acquisitions.

Ⓝ Schiffer Publishing Ltd.

A family-owned, independent publisher since 1974, Schiffer has published thousands of titles on the diverse subjects that fuel our readers' passions. Explore our list of more than 5,000 titles in the following categories:

ART, DESIGN & ANTIQUES

Fine Art | Fashion | Architecture | Interior Design | Landscape | Decorative Arts | Pop Culture | Collectibles | Art History | Graffiti & Street Art | Photography | Pinup | Sculpture | Body Art & Tattoo | Antique Clocks | Watches | Graphic Design | Contemporary Craft | Illustration | Folk Art | Jewelry | Fabric Reference

MILITARY

Aviation | Naval | Ground Forces | American Civil War | Militaria | Modeling & Collectible Figures | Pinup | Transportation | World War I & II | Uniforms & Clothing | Biographies & Memoirs | Unit Histories | Emblems & Patches | Weapons & Artillery

CRAFT

Arts & Crafts | Fiber Arts & Wearables | Woodworking | Quilts | Gourding | Craft Techniques | Leathercraft | Carving | Boat Building | Knife Making | Printmaking | Weaving | How-to Projects | Tools | Calligraphy

TRADE

Lifestyle | Natural Sciences | History | Children's | Regional | Cookbooks | Entertaining | Guide Books | Wildlife | Tourism | Pets | Puzzles & Games | Movies | Business & Legal | Paranormal | UFOs | Cryptozoology | Vampires | Ghosts

MIND BODY SPIRIT

Divination | Meditation | Astrology | Numerology & Palmistry | Psychic Skills | Channeled Material | Metaphysics | Spirituality | Health & Lifestyle | Tarot & Oracles | Crystals | Wicca | Paganism | Self Improvement

MARITIME

Professional Maritime Instruction | Seamanship | Navigation | First Aid/Emergency | Maritime History | The Chesapeake | Antiques & Collectibles | Children's | Crafts | Natural Sciences | Hunting & Fishing | Cooking | Shipping | Sailing | Travel | Navigati

SCHIFFER PUBLISHING, LTD.
4880 Lower Valley Road | Atglen, P
Phone: 610-593-1777
E-mail: Info@schifferboo'
Printed in Chi'

www.schiffe'

roared off. This annoyed me considerably. Since they had no respect for the nature of explosives, the least they could have done was handled the fuses more gently.

"I stood looking at the bombs lying on the ground, knowing that no bomb hoist was available or likely to be found. What to do? I simply said to the three crew members standing there, 'load the bombs.' Lee Webber, bombardier; Garner Culpepper, copilot; and Little, ordnanceman, leaped to the task. They rolled a bomb underneath the aft port bomb bay (the two forward bomb bays had fuel tanks installed).

"With Webber grasping the nose of the bomb and Little on the other end, Culpepper placed himself alongside on his hands and knees. Webber and Little lifted the bomb up about two feet. Culpepper then slid underneath and held it while the other two re-set the grip. Now, with a great combined effort, the three heaved the bomb into the upper bomb bay shackle. My utter amazement continued as our other crewmembers joined in to load the rest of the bombs in a similar manner.

"While the crewmembers were bolting on the tail tins and installing the fuses I walked over to the B-25s, arriving at the same time as their squadron leader. He had just returned from the same colonel and had received the same attack order. As he gave the order for an attack on the enemy task force his pilots and crewmen made a number of 'Oh no's!' They had started an attack on this enemy formation a short time ago, but had broken off because of the very heavy gunfire from the big guns.

"I told the young captain I wanted to join them in the attack and would be ready in just a few more minutes. The squadron leader said they were leaving now and asked if I was ready to join in, but they would not wait for me. As they taxied out and took off I felt as if I was seeing our chance for survival leaving with them.

"Very soon we were ready to go. I called the entire crew together and told them that I needed only a copilot and a bombardier; the rest could stay behind or go with us. It was not stated, but they knew our chances as well as I. To my surprise they all decided to go, and even seemed very eager to make the attack on this major enemy force.

"As we were loading and readying the airplane for take-off, a P38 crash-landed just in front of our parking area. This reduced an already short runway. Dusk was setting in and there was no wind to assist with our take-off. Given the soft runway surface, I seriously questioned whether we would be able to get airborne; thankfully, no more than 2,700 gallons of fuel had been loaded aboard. Any more fuel would have substantially reduced our chances to get off the ground. Had a defueling truck been available I would have off-loaded some gas. However, the Japanese were rapidly approaching and the airstrip would be under fire from their guns very soon.

"There were no flare pots to mark the runway. It was now dark, but a bright full moon had started to rise. We applied full power to the engines and released the brakes. The airplane moved forward and the left wheel sank into the ground. Right brake was applied and the right wheel sank. We staggered left and right, but slowly accelerated. Finally beginning to gain some lift, the airplane steadied and we slowly increased our airspeed.

"I saw the scrub trees at the end of the runway but had no idea of whether we had flying speed or not. I pulled back hard on the elevator controls and we cleared the trees by inches. We were flying, barely, and slowly gaining altitude and airspeed. The landing gear was retracted and the flaps were 'milked' up.

"The moon was beginning to illuminate the area well and visibility was unlimited. Heading to the north along the coast of Mindoro, I could see tracers were flowing in every direction, indicating lots of action. Continuing to climb, I saw the B-25s attacking the task force at masthead level. They were strafing with their forward-firing .50-caliber machine guns. As they made their bombing runs one at a time they were being shot down one at a time. One of the attacking Mitchell twin-engine bombers was hit in the starboard engine and it became a mass of flames. The courageous pilot flew his airplane into a Japanese destroyer. There was a large explosion. This destroyer was later confirmed as having been sunk.

"A number of PT boats began a torpedo attack on the column of enemy ships. The *Ashigara*, in the lead, trained a powerful searchlight at the speedy boats. The other ships in the formation then opened fire. The PT boats appeared to be taking many hits and broke off the attack. Rear Admiral Masatome Kimura, Officer in Tactical Command, was fighting his surface force very well. He was an experienced Imperial Japanese naval officer of considerable reputation in night torpedo actions.

"All of the B-25 attacks had been made down moon and from the Mindoro side of the enemy ships. I decided to make my attack from the other side of the column and up moon. I flew well around the action. Due to being provided instantaneous fuses rather than four to five second delayed fuses, we would make our bombing run from 8,500 feet instead of a masthead run. During positioning there were many other low-level attacks; at the time I believed these to

VPB-117's Bureau Number 38741 *The Lewd Nude* was lost in a ditching off Mindoro on 17 February 1945, but the crew managed to safely exit the sinking aircraft. *Courtesy of the VPB-117 Association*

***Uncle Sam**, also known as *So Solly*, was a J-model Liberator with Bureau Number 38736 and was stricken from the VPB-117 inventory as an operational loss on 14 February 1945. Courtesy of the VPB-117 Association*

be by PBY Catalinas and PBM Mariner Black Cats only [belonging to VPB-20, which flew PBMs, and VP-54, which flew PBY Catalinas].

"I directed Anania, who was operating the radar, and Webber, our bombardier, to pick out the largest ship and set our bombs for sixty-foot drop intervals. In addition, should our bombing run not look good for a hit, Webber was to announce this and I would break off the run and try again. We turned inbound toward the task force from about twenty miles out. I maintained a cruise power setting on the engines. By doing so I could stay in a lean fuel mixture and eliminate any flare from our exhaust.

"Almost immediately Anania called that he had the force on his scope and began giving me small heading changes and distances to the target. Our approach was on the starboard quarter of the *Ashigara*. I was reminded this would be the first Norden bombsight release for Webber since our training back in the States. To this point all of our attacks had been made via very low level masthead bomb releases by visual judgment (seaman's eye). Just after the call 'eight miles' Webber stated very authoritatively, 'I have him, follow the Pilot Director Indicator.' Again, there were a few very small corrections to our heading. We were indicating 140 knots airspeed in stable level flight.

"The anti-aircraft fire was still being directed at low levels. I wondered when the enemy ships would begin firing at us. There was no question we would be shot down. I just hoped we would be able to get our bombs away before we were blasted from the sky. I could see the largest ship in the lead of the column running fast and leaving a long and very bright wake. In close the target disappeared under the nose of our airplane. Webber suddenly called, 'bombs away.'

"I rolled the airplane quickly to the right and just as hard and quickly back to the left. Most of the crew were then rewarded by the sight of one explosion close to the stern and then, very rapidly, two, perhaps three beautiful bomb bursts on the after deck of the *Ashigara*. These bursts were so quick it was difficult to distinguish whether there were two or three. Now the flow of tracers began streaming toward us. I really rolled hard to the right to exit this gunfire and distance us from the task force.

"We had done it! In addition, there had been no hits on our PB4Y-1. Webber was beside himself with joy, having hit a major unit of the Japanese fleet. He repeatedly shouted over the intercom, 'Let's go back and get more bombs.' This, of course, was not possible, given the big shells soon to fall upon the beachhead.

"There was neither a fire nor any other indication of much damage to the *Ashigara* at this time. The ships continued to steam at high speed toward the Mindoro beachhead and airfields. We retired to a safe distance and began to shadow the force. There continued to be occasional attacks by what appeared to be Black Cats.

"Looking up moon as we approached the San Jose area, I could see that all of the allied supply ships, except a burning Liberty ship, had moved out. They were now anchored only several miles away in a protected body of water off the south end of Mindoro Island. I can only assume that Lt. Cdr. Burt Davis, in command of the MTB squadrons and torpedo boat tender [AGP], had gathered and led them out of harm's way.

"At my altitude, I could see both the Japanese task force and the vulnerable logistics ships. I prayed that the enemy would not be able to see them. Should they locate these defenseless ships it would be a massacre. Although the PT boat tender and the supply ship were lightly armed, they would not stand a chance against the Japanese big guns.

"The enemy surface force entered the beachhead area at very high speed and began firing star shells over the area in an attempt to illuminate targets. There was no return fire from the batteries of our forces on the ground. I well understood this to be the best course of action, given that the Japanese vessels heavily 'outgunned' our Army's artillery pieces. To return fire would only have served to generate aiming points for the enemy.

"Finding no targets, the surface force turned away from the beach and started what was to become a square for another run along the beach and anchorage. By this maneuver I concluded the Japanese gunners could not see our supply ships. I was greatly relieved!

"During the second run the Japanese again fired star shells, but still they found no aiming points ashore. However, nearing the end of this run all of the ships of this force fired a volley into the previously damaged Liberty ship. It exploded with a large burst of flame and smoke and disappeared from my view. Completing this square, the task force departed the area on a westerly course. One destroyer was missing from the formation. I could now clearly see that the *Ashigara* was trailing oil and had slowed. Soon it was the last ship in the column. There was no question we had hit the lead ship, and additionally, a PT boat reported a flash in the area at the same time we reported our bomb drop.

"Sporadic attacks by Black Cats continued. These PBY and PBM aircraft were probably attached to Patrol Bombing Squadrons Four, Twenty, and/or Twenty-Five. One PBM contacted us by VHF radio and asked that we report their position on our CW long-range radio. They had been shot down but were afloat on the water. We did so. At 0400, we were getting low on fuel. I knew relief tracking airplanes would soon be coming. Later I learned that, indeed, Cdr. McDonald of VPB-117 picked up the force about this time. We set course for Tacloban."[4]

For Lt. Stevens, it almost resulted in a court martial for attacking the Jakes at Camranh Bay. His role had been to search for the enemy, not attack, hence he had disobeyed orders. How could the Navy court martial a man who had found the Japanese Task Force? They did not. Fortunately, his wing commander interceded and pending charges were dropped.[5]

The raid cost Admiral Kimura the destroyer *Kiyoshimo* and the damage of several more ships. For the Americans twenty-six aircraft were lost, but most of the crews were rescued.[6] PB4Ys continued searching for Japanese merchant and naval forces, and on two different occasions the Blue Raiders found what they were searching for. On 5 January, a 117 search plane spotted twenty-six enemy ships, including eight destroyers, near Swatow, China. Three days later another plane reported fifteen transports and seven warships near Saigon. Within a few days Task Force 38 entered the South China Sea and proceeded to sink thirty-two merchant ships totaling 149,000 tons. This was followed by another attack off Swatow that netted the task force another 62,000 tons of shipping. The Blue Raiders ended the month with a score of twenty-two enemy aircraft shot down and the sinking or damaging of some 25,000 tons of shipping.

Tried and Executed: The Crew of VPB-117's *Queen Bee*

A VPB-117 PB4Y-1 Liberator named *Queen Bee* and its crew commanded by Lt. (jg) Robert E. White was shot down over Tung Kang Harbor, Formosa, during an anti-shipping sweep on 28 January 1945. White, copilot Ensign Harry P. Palritz, ARM3c Frank E. Collins, and AMM3c Albert C. Kalishauskas were killed in the crash, while seven others were captured and taken prisoner. AMM2c Edward W. Sieber succumbed to his injuries soon afterward, while injured navigator Ensign John Bertrang was sent to Japan for medical care and interrogation. The five left behind as prisoners at Taihoku Prison were J. C. Buchanan, AMM2c; Wayne W. Wilson, ARM3c; Delbert H. Carter, AOM3c; Donald K. Hathaway, AMM3c; and John R. Parker, AMM3c.[7]

The five men of the *Queen Bee*, along with nine other army and naval airmen, were interrogated and charged by the Japanese 10th Army District with violating a Formosa military law regarding bombing and strafing on non-military targets. Six trials for each of the men, who were afforded no defense counsel, were held on 21 May 1945, and all were sentenced to death by firing squad on the twenty-ninth. On 19 June 1945, the men were lined up in the prison's courtyard in front of a ditch and executed. The other nine sentenced were 1stLt. Ralph R. Hartley, USAAF; Lt. Harwood S. Sharp, USAAF; petty officer Harry H. Aldo; petty officer James R. Langiotti; Staff Sgt. Bobby L. Lawrence, USAAF; Frederick E. McCreary, ARM1c; Charles E. McVay, AOM2c; and Sgt. Merlin W. Riggs, USAAF.

Their bodies, initially buried in the ditch, were later cremated and placed in an urn. A war crimes trial was held by the US Military Commission at Shanghai 1–25 July 1946 against Chief of Staff of the 10th Army District Lt. General Harukei Isyama and seven others for the murder of the fourteen Americans. Gen. Isayama left instructions with Chief of the 10th Army's Judicial Department Col. Seiichi Furukawa for prosecuting the Americans. Furukawa and Lt.Col. Naritaka Sugiura, the chief interrogator of the airmen, were sentenced to death. Gen. Isayama and Capt. Yoshio Nakano, an interrogator and associate judge, were sentenced to life imprisonment, while Capts. Masaharu Matsui and Tadao Ito, who also participated in the interrogations, were sentenced to forty years and twenty years, respectively.[8]

3

PB4Y Aces

Navy and Marine patrol aircraft claimed at least 377 aerial victories, with a huge majority (317) being claimed by PB4Ys. There is a custom that only fighter pilots qualify as fighter aces. During WWII, eight PB4Y-1 Liberator patrol plane commanders and their crews earned this distinction. The bomber crew of eleven to twelve men, serving together as a team, was like a well-oiled piece of machinery, and together became what few have achieved in war—aces. Lt. Paul Stevens of VPB-104 became one with six kills, as did Lt. Paul J. Bruneau of VB-115 with five, and Lt. Cdr. Neil C. Porter of VD-3. Unequaled by any other patrol squadron was VPB-117. Between October 1944 and August 1945, five Blue Raider aircrews scored five or more aerial kills that propelled them into a distinguished group of military aviators. The aces of 117 were Lts. McGaughey, Hyland, Moore, Sutton, and Carter.

Lt. (jg) Sutton's Crew 18

Lt. Sutton commanded the top scoring Blue Raider crew. Together with the rest of crew 18, he shot down seven enemy aircraft in sixteen combat flights over a two-month period. Their first score came on 12 December, as they skirted along the western Luzon coast after unsuccessfully attacking a convoy of six Japanese ships. Off Mindoro another ship was sighted and Sutton made a run at an altitude of twenty-five feet. Bombardier Pappy Judson released a salvo of bombs toward the ship just as H. T. "Hanger" Jones and Jim Cox, standing at the waist hatches, reported an unidentified aircraft at five o'clock. Sutton applied climbing power and went up to investigate what soon turned out to be a Tony fighter.

The Liberator pilot immediately applied climbing power to his plane in an attempt to catch the enemy. However, as the Liberator climbed the Japanese plane started to slowly descend. The enemy pilot started to follow the coastline in a leisurely fashion, apparently looking for something along the coast. Sutton's plane now had a good height advantage over the Tony and was close enough to dive and overtake it before the Japanese plane could pick up speed. As the larger aircraft closed rapidly on the fighter but was still out of

effective firing range, the crew started to fire their machine guns. The pilot of the Tony must have seen the tracers, as he made a slight turn, then dived for the water. He was too low when he started his dive to attain speed rapidly.

The Liberator continued to gain on the fighter, although less rapidly as seconds passed, and was just within firing range when the pilot of the Tony pulled up in a steep climb. It was a fatal maneuver, because Sutton's plane then closed rapidly and fire from Bill Bolick's and Doug Burdick's machine guns riddled the Tony. The fighter then did a wing over and tried to crash into its adversary, barely missing the American plane's right wing before crashing into the sea.

The following day Sutton was called in to see the admiral. The admiral very nicely told Mr. Sutton that his plane and crew were invaluable to the security of US forces in the entire area. In other words, he was telling Sutton not to take the risks involved in bombing ships or chasing airplanes, as it was too hazardous for the few PB4Ys and their crews. The patrol plane commander acknowledged the

VPB-117's Crew 18 commanded by Lt. (jg) Sutton. Back row (L to R): Judson, Cox, Bolick, Jones, and Boris. Middle row: Davis, Burdick, Major, and Hobert. Front row (L to R): Lt. (jg) Sutton, Ensign Smith, and Ensign Clark. *Courtesy of the VPB-117 Association*

An individual identified as Chief D. T. Ennis, the plane captain and port waist gunner, poses next to B-24 J-model PB4Y-1 *Ready, Willing, and Able* (Bureau Number 38759). The term "Dice Artiste" is in reference to Ennis carrying a pair of drilled dice with the ones to three spots changed to fours and fives so it was impossible to crap out. The chief, a big Texan with large hands, would palm the undrilled dice when playing craps. *Courtesy of the VPB-117 Association*

importance of reconnaissance in the war effort and told his superior officer that he would be more diligent. Sutton would have two additional meetings with the admiral with similar outcomes.

On Christmas Eve, Crew 18 was given the sector skirting the western coast off Mindoro and Luzon and the southern and eastern coast of Formosa. As the plane reached the southern coast of Formosa, a single-engine twin floatplane was sighted. The Japanese plane carried a rear seat gunner as well as the pilot. The rear seat gunner had a 7-millimeter machine gun.

When the US plane reached firing range the Japanese plane began maneuvering, but was no match for the Liberator and was quickly shot out of the air. Sutton and his crew had downed their second plane in twelve days. Soon thereafter another biplane was sighted. After a relatively short chase, which included a few maneuvers only a few feet off the surface of the water, the Japanese plane was destroyed. Two planes shot down in one day.

On 8 January 1945, Crew 18 was given the mission to fly the 1,000 miles to Camranh Bay in search of elusive Japanese warships. Near the Cape of St. Jacques a convoy of Japanese warships was sighted, including a battleship, plus at least three destroyers, four

destroyer escorts, and fifteen transports. Sutton's plane approached the force and the large ship opened fire at the low flying plane. After making a contact report the Liberator's crew spotted a twin-float plane approaching. The ensuing fight was vicious but of short duration. The Liberator was maneuvered to keep at least the top and nose turrets bearing on the Japanese plane. Sutton flew the Liberator like a fighter as the action took both aircraft within 150 feet of the sea. The Japanese plane was destroyed with only a few shots fired. This was the sixth plane destroyed in the air by Sutton's crew in just over a month.

On 20 January, Sutton's crew was given the mission of flying to Okinawa to search for the Japanese fleet. At that time intelligence knew little about Okinawa, except that it had several airfields. The plane took off about midnight for the 2,000–2,100 mile trip to the island, arriving at the northern tip of Okinawa just after sunrise and proceeding down the western side of the island. Just as the plane, flying at about fifty feet, was approaching Ie Shima, the pilot thought he saw some planes taxiing on the island airfield. No verification was possible, as one of the gunners in the starboard waist hatch called out "Plane high and five o'clock." Sutton immediately turned his plane toward the Japanese aircraft, which did not appear to see the US plane.

Black, billowing smoke marks the resting place of a Japanese Jake float plane shot down by Lt. Sutton's s gunners on 24 December 1944. The bow and top gunners started firing 500 feet away, damaging the Jake's engine. Sutton banked his bomber, allowing the port waist gunner to fire, which apparently killed the float plane's rear gunner. The tail gunner then finished it off after the bomber overshot the Jake. *Courtesy of the NARA*

The Liberator, now pulling full combat power, closed on the Japanese plane from the rear and below. When within close proximity the Liberator's gunners (Bill Bolick and Lawrence Holbert) dispatched the Japanese "Kate" dive-bomber in short order. As the plane fell, mortally wounded, a huge column of smoke outlined the plane's track until it crashed into the sea.

As the Japanese plane fell, Sutton's plane quickly descended to an altitude of about fifty feet with the expectation of an attack by Japanese fighters. If there were planes on Ie Shima, they evidently did not become airborne after observing the experience of their brother pilot. No enemy ships or planes were sighted until Crew 18's plane came into the vicinity of Naha, the capital of Okinawa.

When the Liberator was a few miles at sea from Naha several Japanese Zeros were sighted. At first two of the Zeros, flying a parallel course with Sutton's plane, took stations just out of gun range on each of the Liberator's wings. Another Zero was well above and just ahead of the Liberator. Sutton surmised the two planes on the wings were trying to get the Liberator's altitude and keep the plane on a steady course.

To counter the Japanese Sutton turned toward the Zero on the port side and started to chase it. He expected an attack from the other two Zeros, but they kept their distance. The Zero being chased flew toward Naha, and again Sutton made an assumption. He thought the Japanese pilot was trying to lead him over gun emplacements on Okinawa to let the anti-aircraft fire shoot down the Liberator, so he broke off the chase and turned back to sea when the planes approached land. But as the Liberator turned to the sea the Zero followed until the US plane again turned and chased the Zero back over Okinawa.

This cat and mouse play was repeated three times until Sutton's plane, having burned much fuel, proceeded on its primary mission

of searching for Japanese naval vessels. The trip to Okinawa proved to be their last combat mission together as a crew. They had enough points, and they and two other crews were heading home. Together, Crew 18 became the highest scoring PB4Y crew in the Pacific.

Lt. (jg) Nick Carter's Crew 16

Scoring five aerial kills was Lt. "Nick" Carter and crew. Their first kill came on 8 December, minutes after takeoff from Tacloban. Climbing out, an Irving was intercepted while on a reconnaissance mission to the airfield. The Liberator's bow gunner, Eddie Cormier,

VPB-117's Crew 16 commanded by Lt. (jg) Carter. Back row (L to R): Wardlow, Lawrence, Magoon, Burgen, and Plunkett. Middle row (L to R): Shaulis, Eichenberg, Papp, and Cormier. Front row (L to R): Ensign Crawford, Lt. (jg) Cater, and Ensign Pistonich. *Courtesy of the VPB-117 Association*

and top turret gunner, Chuck Blackley, scored damaging hits, causing the Irving to crash on Luzon. Two days later Carter borrowed crew 15 and shot down a Judy off Panay Island. Not long after three Zekes intercepted the Liberator. In an aerial battle that brought bomber and fighters down to fifty feet off the water, the Liberator's gunners appeared to have shot down a Zeke and F4Us that appeared ran off the other two on the scene.

On 28 December, Carter intercepted a Topsy off the southern tip of Formosa. The Topsy was a passenger plane run by the private firm All Nippon Airlines.[1] After a short chase Cormier and Blackley brought the transport down in flames. Crew 16's next kill came on 30 December, as Cormier and Blackley shot down a Jake near the Batan Islands, between Luzon and Formosa. An hour later Carter came up from behind a Val and the two aerial gunners brought down their second plane of the day. Carter and his men continued to seek out the enemy, attacking shipping when it could be found. Their last aerial kill occurred on 11 February 1945, a mission that showed that luck, if there is such a thing, can and will run out.

The crew now owned Sheldon Sutton's plane *Torchy Tess*. While on patrol near Indo-China, Carter found a convoy of merchant vessels with a Jake flying ASW. The Blue Liberator came in, the Jake dropped its depth charges, and the battle was on. The Jake went inland with Carter in hot pursuit. At treetop level Cormier and Blackley opened fire, and within a few seconds the enemy plane was burning on the ground. Then it became the convoy's turn to be on the receiving end of the Liberator's bombs and machine guns.

Carter picked out the largest vessel and went down. With every gun on board providing withering suppressing fire he dropped a string of four 500-pound bombs, scoring one hit. While the pilot was initiating the bombing run the aircraft began taking anti-aircraft hits. The hydraulic lines were shot out and three men were wounded. Ensign Lloyd Bloomquist took a hit to the shoulder and Plane Captain

Another VPB-117 crew to shoot down five enemy aircraft was commanded by Lt. Hyland. Front row (L to R): Holzricter, Fuller, Trottier, McCoy, Jones, and Bryant. Back row (L to R): Brodie, Brosh, Kessels, Lt. Hyland, Ensign Minnock, and Lt. (jg) Campbell. *Courtesy of the VPB-117 Association*

Joe Papp received multiple shrapnel wounds. The attack was broken off and Carter headed back on a 900-mile trip to base. After patching up the hydraulic lines and replacing the fluid with grapefruit juice the Liberator landed and rolled down the runway, ending up at the end of it nose down.

Carter and crew continued with replacements through March and April, searching vainly for an enemy that was rapidly disappearing from their assigned search sectors. Looking around Cam Ranh Bay, Carter's gunners decimated ten Jakes sitting on the water. The remainder of their tour consisted of white cap patrols—patrols that never resulted in an encounter with the enemy. On 4 May, they flew their last mission, minus Carter as patrol plane commander.

4

Armed Reconnaissance
Operations from Tacloban and Morotai
January–May 1945

During the last part of December 1944 and January 1945, special search and reconnaissance missions were flown during the Luzon operations and no bombs were carried during the last three weeks of the month, as directed by ComAir7thFleet. Consequently, there was a sharp decrease in shipping tonnage sunk or damaged. The month started with the temporary loss of a Buccaneer crew and the first successful ditching of a B-24 Liberator without injury to the crew.

Such missions conducted by long-range PB4Y squadrons were extremely long in duration and often boring, as crews scanned the vast ocean and seas below for any sign of enemy shipping. Louis Bresciano spoke for all such aircrews when he wrote a letter to his wife dated 6 September 1945.

"I feel sorry for the boys that fly. They go out every third day and they are gone from fourteen to sixteen hours, and it's not any fun just sitting there. Be different if they had some seats, and the worst thing that everyone hates is the takeoff. Boy do they sweat that take off with all them bombs on. That's how we lost a crew about four months ago. They were swell fellows. When our planes go out, they go out by

themselves. They don't go out like the Army; they send a whole squadron. I don't know why they do that, but the Navy doesn't. . . ."

Sutherland's Ditching

On 2 January, VPB-104's Jock Sutherland and his crew took off at 0700 from Tacloban for a 1,000-mile search that included a stretch of the China coast. On the return leg Sutherland made contact with a barge gunboat. It may have been serving as an anti-aircraft trap set up by the enemy. This vessel was anchored just off the shore where many guns were located, and was tactically positioned to be of considerable value in anticipation of the eventual landing by US forces at the entrance to Lingayen Gulf. The actual landing assault was to take place 9 January 1945.

Sutherland made a low-level strafing run, firing off 800 rounds of ammunition. No damage to the barge was observed, and as he pulled up from this pass shore batteries opened fire with heavy, medium, and light anti-aircraft fire. It was intense and very accurate, with bursts surrounding the PB4Y-1. The airplane was flown violently

Change of command of VPB-117 took place on 31 December 1944, with Lt. Cdr. McDonald taking over from Cdr. Rigsbee. *Courtesy of the VPB-117 Association*

Lt. Cdr. Mulvihill (bottom left) assumed command and became a controversial figure in the squadron's history. *Courtesy of the VPB-117 Association*

Lt. Cdr. McDonald (bottom row far right) commanded VPB-117 for one month before he was transferred and command went to Lt. Cdr. Mulvihill. *Courtesy of the VPB-117 Association*

Attack on shipping in Philippine waters by Cdr. Mulvihill on 7 December 1944. Courtesy of the VPB-117 Association

evade and no hits were noted. Later it was found that the entire communication and radar equipment had been damaged.

Continuing the flight, the pilots and navigator did the best they could under the circumstances to locate the airstrip at Tacloban. Due to heavy weather and failure of the radios it simply could not be done. By 2300 hours, Sutherland accepted the fact they were lost and a night ditching would be required. He recounted his story in the after action report filed after the incident:

"I began to realize the necessity of ditching was rapidly changing from a possibility to an absolute certainty. At 2330, I informed the crew we were going to ditch in about twenty minutes, as we only had enough fuel for a maximum of forty minutes flight. I told the plane captain to jettison all loose gear, such as the waist guns, ammunition, toolboxes, engine covers, spare radio gear, and oxygen bottles.

"Then I told him to have someone knock out the aft bulkhead in the radar compartment. While the boys in the after station were having a big time tearing the ball [belly] turret out of the airplane and throwing out gear I pulled the emergency release wire on the pilot's window and shoved it out. My copilot had difficulty removing his window until he finally knocked it out with a fire extinguisher. Then we buckled on our guns, canteens, and jungle kits, and fastened our shoulder harnesses as tightly as we could get them.

"I told the navigator to open the flight deck escape hatch and the radioman to transmit 'I am ditching.' Then I told both of them to go to the after station, as I wanted no one to remain on the flight deck during the ditching.

"At about 2340 hours, the after station reported that everyone was ready for ditching. I told them I felt confident we could all get down without being hurt and that I was not worried about the outcome in the least. From the comments on the interphone no one else seemed much concerned, either. Not a single member of the crew became panicky.

"After making sure that everybody in the after station was ready for ditching I told them I would ring the warning bell just before we

hit. The radar operator continued to watch the radar and said he was certain there was water to the north, and that all of the land was behind us. As I thought the wind was northerly, I continued to let down on a due north heading until we broke out of the clouds at 2,000 feet. In the moonlight I saw two small islands dead ahead and a large mass of land to port. The water appeared to be calm, with a northerly wind of about eight knots. To ditch a little closer to land I made a wide, 360-degree turn to start my base leg over the large mass of land. Then I switched the radio altimeter to the 400-foot range and told the copilot to put the mixture controls in automatic rich, the props to 2,700 RPM, and to stand by with his hand on the crash bar (master ignition).

"At 400 feet I looked at my watch and saw the time was 2349. Then I switched on the landing lights and fully extended and put down full flaps. At a speed of 105 knots I continued to let down to seventy-five feet on the radio altimeter. From here I was able to

A patrolling VPB-117 Liberator photographed this beached Japanese freighter of some ten thousand tons (codename Sugar Able) on 7 December 1944. *Courtesy of the VPB-117 Association*

judge my altitude visually, but I continued to glance at the artificial horizon to keep the wings level.

"Then, almost on the water, I reduced power, rolled back the elevator tab, and pulled back on the yoke (elevator control) until I felt the tail touch. Then I gradually added power and pulled up the nose still farther until we smashed into the water at about seventy-five knots.

"The initial part of the landing was much like that of a P-boat [PBY flying boat]. There was only a swishing of water while the nose was high. Then, when it became impossible for me to hold the yoke back any longer, the nose dropped and a wall of water crashed up through the cockpit, just as the copilot hit the crash bar. Naturally I had forgotten to ring the warning bell.

"For a few seconds the cockpit filled with water, during which time I released my harness and got out of the window in a hurry. As soon as I was out of the cockpit I yelled and asked if everyone was out. Somebody answered that everyone was out of the after station and the copilot said he was okay, but he was having trouble getting out of his seat because the yoke (control wheel) had jammed down against his legs. I inflated one side of my Mae West and started swimming around to the starboard side. The navigator, who had come up over the airplane from the after station, was there first and helped the copilot twist the yoke around until the open side was down, thus enabling him to withdraw his legs.

"While this was going on one of the men inflated the seven-man raft while another released and inflated the two auxiliary wing rafts, all of which operated perfectly. With an officer in each separate raft, we ended up with three men in the large raft and four men in each of the smaller rafts. Aside from a smashed bow the plane seemed to be in good shape. The top turret had not come down as expected. The props appeared to be unbent and the plane was riding high in the water.

"In questioning the crew on the results of the ditching, I found that no one was even slightly injured. Some of the ditching positions had been peculiar. Two men were in the radar compartment with

Ensign C. J. Sager shown after his rescue. He was a member of Lt. Brooks's crew, which was attacked by enemy fighters, and the bomber was forced to ditch off Los Negros Island on 10 December 1944. *Courtesy of the VPB-117 Association*

VPB-117 living quarters on Mindoro. *Courtesy of the VPB-117 Association*

Strafing and bombing attack on a cargo ship by Ensign Paris of VPB111 on 26 February 1945. *Courtesy of the NARA*

A low-level Liberator from VPB-111 firing at a small, 70–150 ton Japanese cargo ship code-named Sugar Dog. *Courtesy of the NARA*

A pair of camouflaged Sugar Dogs under attack and burning from incendiary tracer rounds by a VPB-117 Liberator flown by Ensign Allen on 18 December 1944. *Courtesy of the NARA*

their backs against the forward bulkhead. The navigator was sitting between one of the men's legs, facing aft. One man was lying on the floorboards beside the belly turret station with feet forward. Three men were also aft lying there with feet braced against the step. One man was in a standing position beside the port waist hatch, holding on to the armor plate brace with one hand and the gun mount with the other. One man was in a similar position on the starboard side. Neither of the men was thrown from his feet during the ditching. This was a first for a B-24 bomber—ditching without injury to the crew.

"As we stood by waiting for 813 [the last three bureau numbers of their airplane] to sink, I noticed we had sufficient survival gear to supply our needs considering we were so close to land. The inventory revealed two bags of emergency rations, two jungle packs, one parachute, ten pistols, and five Very pistols, along with plenty of cartridges and canteens. The Gibson Girl (emergency radio) was lost during the ditching.

"After waiting seven minutes for the plane to sink and noting it did not seem to be settling very rapidly, I told one of the men to remove the gas tank caps. At 1159, exactly nine minutes after ditching, 813 gave her final gurgle and sank nose first to the accompaniment of a rousing cheer from the entire crew.

"We started paddling our rafts toward an island about five miles away. Soon some natives met us and took us to their village. Although it was 5:00 a.m. when we got there, the whole village turned out to greet us. The chief of police took us to his house and we were royally fed fish, rice, and yams. We then distributed all of the things we had brought from the plane. The woman that got the parachute was tickled to death.

"The chief brought up three outrigger canoes and we traveled over to a larger island and settlement. A tremendous welcome was given

and our every wish was anticipated. We were fed chicken, eggs, green coconut milk, bananas, and commotes [sweet potatoes]. The chief sent a runner with a message several miles away, where they had a radio to send a message back to our base. I was given a bed of a wooden board and slept more soundly than ever before in my whole life."[1]

VPB-111 Arrives on Morotai

Lt. Commander James V. Barry arrived on Morotai with his squadron (VPB-111) after a month of duty on Tinian. A considerable number of the men were "old salts," having previously served with VB-111 at Port Lyautey, in North Africa. One of them was twenty-year-old AOM1c Farville K. "Bud" Mills, who enlisted in the Navy at

Aerial gunners aboard a VPB-104 Liberator flown by Lt. Ettinger hitting a trio of Sugar Dogs at an undisclosed location on 26 February 1945. *Courtesy of the NARA*

Ensign Allen of VPB-117 came upon similarly camouflaged Sugar Dogs (seen in a previous photograph) two days later on 20 December 1944. *Courtesy of the NARA*

A Liberator from VPB-117 came upon a solitary Sugar Dog on the high seas on 18 December 1944, and became the victim of concentrated fire, beginning with the bow turret gunner. *Courtesy of the NARA*

seventeen prior to the Pearl Harbor attack. He operated the bow turret as a member of VPB-111's Patrol Plane Commander Lt. Harold H. Ashton's Crew 12, and recalled how squadron operations changed from those conducted from Tinian:

"Our flights and action intensified with strikes against Borneo, the Celebes, and a ship building facility on an island called Tahoe. On one of our patrols to the islands of Clebes we left four ship-building ways with eight ships burning. We struck at Bin Tulu, on the west coast of Borneo, just south of the city of Miri, on the outskirts of the small town Bintulu, where we left an airfield, the hangars, barracks, and storage tanks ablaze after our low level bombing and strafing runs. One of our assignments from Morotai was to drop leaflets on large, sometimes major cities on Borneo, like Balikpapan, Bandjermasin, or Pontianak, after which the Army's "Skull and Cross Bone" B-24 Squadron from the Philippines would follow up with bombings. The leaflets were printed in the local language or dialect, warning the citizens to take cover for the impending bombing. After the leaflet drop we would seek out targets of opportunity, such as river boats, airfields, light houses, or radio towers, which were all considered military targets."[2]

A two-plane section of VPB-111 led by Lt. Cdr. J. V. Barry, with wingman Lt. H. H. Ashton, left Morotai before dawn on 28 January to reconnoiter the western coast of Borneo below Miri. Allied planes had not scouted this area for some months, and it was believed the area might contain worthwhile targets. After a flight across Borneo, the section reached the west coast a few miles below Makah. The section turned to the northeast and searched the coast and adjacent waters.

The first target seen by the flight was a sixty-foot enemy lugger anchored in the mouth of the river below Makah. Lt. Cdr. Barry made one run on the target, strafing it with 200 rounds from his bow

turret and dropping two XM-6 incendiary clusters. The target ship was straddled by the incendiary clusters and by several of the bombs. As the run over the target was begun six crewmembers were seen to dive over the sides and swim away.

Ensign Allen left this camouflaged Sugar Dog burning off the Philippines on 16 December 1944. *Courtesy of the NARA*

Combat Air Crew One of VPB-111 poses next to their PB4Y-1 Liberator Bureau Number 38892 *Lady Luck*. Back row (L to R): Lt.Cdr. J. V. Barry; Lt. (jg) R. P. Tucker; Lt. (jg) C. M. Russ; J. F. Browne, AMM1c; O. B. Proehl, ARM2c. Front row (L to R): C. I. Perry, AMM2c; J. M. Banta, AMMF2c; W. P. Peterson, ARM2c; R. G. Ferreira, AOM2c; K. N. Morrison, AMMFc. *Courtesy of the Tailhook Association via Mahlon Miller*

The second target presented itself as the section approached Bintulu, where an air strip approximately 2,000 feet long with dispersal areas and twenty-two buildings was sighted. At this point the section deployed to attack. Lt. Cdr. Barry took the lead, about one-third of a mile ahead of Lt. Ashton. The first run was made directly over the administration building, where three Japanese flags were seen on flagstaffs. During this run Barry fired 600 rounds from his bow, deck, and waist guns, and dropped two incendiary clusters

that straddled the administration building. Ashton followed over the same building, dropping one incendiary cluster and expending 800 rounds of ammunition into several buildings in his path. During Lt. Ashton's run some twenty to twenty-five enemy soldiers were seen running from the administration building but were gunned down by the Liberator's gunners.

Upon completion of the first run the planes circled and made a second run parallel to the river over a row of buildings. During this run Barry dropped six more incendiary clusters with good dispersion among the buildings, also firing 725 rounds of ammunition from the bow, deck, and waist guns. The starboard waist gunner fired at a small storage tank that burst into flame, sending a column of black smoke 1,200 feet into the air. On his run Lt. Ashton dropped two incendiary clusters among the buildings and fired 1,000 rounds. His bow and tail turrets concentrated on the administration building, and his waist gunners fired at miscellaneous targets among the buildings. At the end of the run ten of twenty-two buildings were destroyed or damaged. Time and gasoline supply did not permit another run over the target or further observation of damage inflicted. During this attack no enemy planes were seen, nor was flak observed. It was the squadron's only major blow to the Japanese before their departure.

Tacloban

VB-104 arrived on Tacloban on 23 December 1944, as part of Navy Search Group, Seventh Fleet, followed by VPB-111 on 6 February 1945, which relieved VPB-117. Routine patrols of twelve to fifteen hours now extended to Okinawa, Indo-China, and the Chinese mainland. A day earlier, Lt. Howard Sires, PPC of Crew 6, went on patrol northward of the China Coast and disappeared. On 8 February, Lt. (jg) Jeff Hemphill went to examine the harbor at Kilirun, Formosa. It was overcast, with a ceiling 300–1,200 feet. Flying underneath the clouds, he spotted a large amount of

A strafing attack on a Japanese lugger (a small wooden cargo vessel) by VPB-117 on 18 December 1944. *Courtesy of the NARA*

Smoke from palm fronds used to camouflage this Sugar Dog set afire by gunners aboard Ensign Allen's VPB-117 Liberator on 16 December 1944. *Courtesy of the NARA*

shipping in and near the one-mile wide bay. Before the Liberator was a 10,000–12,000 ton merchant ship, a hospital ship, eight medium merchantmen, and ten or twelve smaller steel-hulled coastal ships anchored in the bay and up a river. Hemphill decided to go for the largest merchant ship, approaching the target across the bay from west to east. It was not a wise choice. Before reaching the bomb release point the Liberator was met by light medium and heavy anti-aircraft fire from both shorelines. Shrapnel from a 3-inch or 40 mm gun hit the top turret, striking the top turret gunner, Mark A. Hagen (AMM3c), in the head, rendering him unconscious. Due to the intensity of the anti-aircraft fire and the wounding of the gunner the attack was broken off and Hemphill and crew survived to fight another day.

The Liberator's success as a fighter was shown again on 13 February, when Lt. (Jg) Edward Hagen intercepted two Nells off the southwestern coast of Formosa. They were flying in a tight formation, skimming the top of the overcast at 2,500 feet and making about 122 knots. Hagen slowed down to 110 knots using half flaps to drop in behind and join up on the formation. Flaps were brought up when the range closed to 500 yards. The bow turret opened fire on the lead plane while the top turret took on the wingman. The lead plane was quick to dive into the clouds as pieces began to fly off his starboard wing from the Liberator's .50-caliber machine gun fire. The wingman took hits from Hagens's top turret that set the Nell's starboard engine and wing root on fire and the plane went into a vertical dive.

The PB4Y-1 followed through the overcast to see the wing plane burning on the water. Meanwhile, the lead plane had reversed course and was sighted about five miles away. Applying full military power, Hagen soon closed the range and the bow turret started a fire in the port engine and wing root, but it continued on course. All guns on the Liberator were then brought to bear during the ensuing action. The pilot of the Nell finally gave up and tried to ditch, but the high seas stirred up by a forty-knot wind caught him, causing the aircraft to break up and explode as it hit the water.

VPB-104 suffered its first combat losses in many weeks on 18 February, when Lt. (jg) Richard S. Jameson, finding no shipping targets in his sector east of Okinawa, attacked an airfield on Borodina Island. Making a power glide from 1,800 feet, he pulled out at fifty feet over the airfield with his gunners strafing and aiming his bombs at a hangar and adjoining buildings. The Liberator was met with highly accurate and intense anti-aircraft fire and the navigator, Ensign Kenneth R. McHenry, was hit and fatally wounded by a burst of 20 mm fire. The plane was so badly shot up that it had to be surveyed after safely reaching base. Meanwhile, Lt. William E. Goodman and his crew went out on patrol to Formosa; they never returned. Their last report had them seventy miles north of Formosa at 1046 hours, and they were heard by another search plane at 1400. Searches for the missing crew were conducted, but as in most cases, they failed to reveal the circumstances surrounding the disappearance of the twelve men.

Bud Mills Topsy Kill

"Bud" Mills of VPB-111's Crew 12 shot down two Japanese aircraft during his tour of duty as a bow turret gunner, with the first occurring on 12 February 1945, off the coast of Okinawa, when he claimed a Val. Mills recalled the second aerial kill on 21–22 February 1945:

"Takeoff for CAC-12 and its Liberator *Reputation Cloudy* (Bureau Number 38906) was 0440 local time, a time that made for maximum daylight patrolling over the vast expanse of the western Pacific Ocean. Today's routine patrol would take the Liberator out to the Mansei Shoto, "southwestern" chain of islands; otherwise known as the Ryukyus Islands, with Okinawa being the largest in the chain. These islands commanded the sea approaches to the China coast between Foochow and Shanghai, and for Japanese forces, this chain made the East China Sea a Nipponese lake. The bomb load on this day consisted of five (5) one hundred pound general-purpose bombs with an AN-M115 tail fuse, four to five-second delay on impact. A full complement of .50-caliber machine gun ammunition was carried for all gun stations. A little over three thousand gallons of fuel comprised the fuel load for this patrol, and with everything else on board, this would make for another usual heart-pounding takeoff. Negative patrols made for a very long day, but on this day, the homeward leg of the patrol would prove to be anything but uneventful. In the late morning hours, flying at an altitude of 2,000 feet in overcast skies, Lt. Ashton spotted a twin engine Japanese Army Mitsubishi Ki-57 Type 100 Transport, US designate Topsy, and its flight path indicated it was apparently headed for Formosa. The transport was painted an intermingling of brown and green, with red discs on the wings and fuselage. The enemy aircraft was at a position 25 degrees, 43 minutes north latitude and 124 degrees, 10 minutes east longitude, at an altitude of 800 feet. This position put the Topsy just north of Miyako Island, in Nansei-Shoto (southwest group) of the Ryukyu Islands, approximately 224NM from Okinawa and 177NM from Formosa."[3]

A squadron Combat After Action Report recorded the details of the interception. While homeward bound on his search sector among the southern islands of the Nansei Shoto Chain, at an altitude of 2,000 feet in overcast on a course of 180 degrees, Lt. H. H. Ashton sighted an enemy Topsy nine miles away on a course of 270 degrees at an altitude of 800 feet. Lt. Ashton changed course to intercept the Topsy, increasing power to forty-seven inches and 2,700 RPM. He remained in the overcast, ducking in and out of it every few seconds to keep the enemy plane in view and yet remain hidden himself. After a six-minute chase, Lt. Ashton caught up with the Topsy and made a steep dive toward her from about 1,000 feet. The Topsy had meanwhile dropped down to about 400 feet off the water and Lt. Ashton opened fire at a range of 800 feet with his bow and deck turrets. The fire of his bow gunner, F. K. Mills, AOM1/c, was so well aimed that the Topsy's starboard engine and wing root burst into flame after only a few shots had been fired, streaming flames twenty feet behind the trailing edge of the starboard wing. The Topsy started a shallow turn to starboard as the fire broke out, enabling Lt. Ashton's starboard waist gunner to also get in a short burst. As Lt. Ashton passed over the target, the tail gunner fired a short burst just as the Topsy nosed over into a steep dive directly into the water, where it exploded, sending a burst of fire and smoke high into the air. This entire action from sighting to Topsy's "splash" lasted only seven minutes. The identity of the Japanese transport remains a mystery, but it may have been a Nampo Koku transport that went missing on that date.

The Brutality of War

The rules/standards of humanitarian treatment of combatants and non-combatants during armed conflict are contained in four treaties and three protocols established by the Geneva Conventions. There are now Rules of Engagement (ROE) detailing where, when, and how an individual engaged in fighting can and cannot kill his fellow human.

The Pacific War was a brutal conflict in which the Japanese military often committed the most heinous acts against their enemies; furthermore, as the Empire of Japan was not a signatory to the conventions, its military saw no reason to act accordingly to those laws. Their actions in Manchuria and China should have been a clear warning to the United States and Britain that war with Japan would be horrific, and thus allied military forces and non-combatants captured in the Philippines, Indonesia, Hong Kong, and Singapore suffered inhumane treatment from their captors and hundreds of thousands perished.

An untold number of men serving with allied forces adopted actions toward Japanese forces that by definition were nearly if not equally just as brutal as the enemy's. This author has written several accounts of how combat air crews waged war against the Japanese and their actions were brutal. Correspondence from some readers of my works wrote they were aghast that such events occurred and whether such American "perpetrators" would be held liable for prosecution since they allegedly acted contrary to international law. The following account is just one of several acts conducted to prevent the enemy from surviving, and, as some veterans over the years have claimed, including this author's father, it was necessary.

Eugene L. Kern, a member of Blue Raider Crew 10, recalled a special mission on 17 December 1944. Crew 10, led by Lt. Moore, conducted a reconnaissance flight over Cam Ranh Bay, French Indo-China, on 17 December, to locate two Japanese battleships reported in the area. They did not locate the ships, but some twenty Zeke fighters were seen taking off and heading for the lurking Liberator. Thick, low-hanging clouds concealed the American patrol bomber for approximately two hours before breaking into a clear blue sky. A half hour later Gunner Kern spotted two Japanese Tess transports. The Liberator's gunners shot both of the transports down in two minutes: one exploded on impact with the water, while the other dropped its landing gear and ditched. Twenty to thirty of the passengers aboard the second plane managed to exit the plane, but were efficiently and quickly dispatched by Moore's gunners. Two days later one of Moore's gunners, Frank Wharton, was killed when an anti-aircraft round exploded inside his turret, killing him instantly during a bombing run over Lingayen Gulf.

A Betty Goes Down

On 23 February, VPB-111's Lt. (jg) Will Paris and his crew, while reconnoitering Miyako Shima—an island that is part of the Ryuku chain—observed two enemy landing barges full of troops proceeding about four miles away parallel to shore. Paris did not turn to attack at this point because the barges were very close to an anti-aircraft battery on shore, so he continued on his course long enough to allow the barges to clear and turn west around the northeast tip of the island. He then reversed his course, dropping down to an altitude of one hundred feet, and made a straight-in attack over the two barges that were very close together.

He dropped two 250-pound bombs that were very near misses, tipping both barges over so that all of the troops were thrown into the water. During this run Paris's bow and deck turret gunners expended approximately 600 rounds into the barges, with one of them being set afire. Paris circled for a second run and again strafed the barges and the troops in the water. On this run he dropped two 100-pound bombs among the troops, killing many of them. During this run the two barges had run aground and settled on a reef off shore. Three more strafing runs decimated the swimming troops; of the estimated 300 troops in the two barges, less than one hundred were able to reach shore.

The end of February marked a new stage in armed reconnaissance missions for VPB-104, as orders were issued sending them to Clark Field, on the island of Luzon. From their new base, the Buccaneers would continue to harass the Japanese all the way north to within thirty miles of Shanghai, China. For Cdr. Barry's VPB-111, they would continue staging from Tacloban through March until a new base was established on Palawan. For Barry, he would be going home soon and turning the command of 111 over to a new man. Until then, the squadron continued searching for the remains of the once vaunted Japanese military. Occasionally enemy aircraft were engaged, as was a Betty on 3 March.

Lt. K. D. Johnson spotted the enemy bomber off Indo-China, and in a fifteen-minute chase the Liberator caught up to it. Both planes were at 1,000 feet when the Betty's pilot noticed he was being stalked. He immediately dropped down to fifty feet, with Johnson following at 500 feet. The Betty changed course and headed for the coast, but the turn enabled Johnson to gain on him. Now the Liberator's gunners were in direct range and the end for the Betty began. Johnson made four bow runs, with the bow and deck guns firing and securing hits on the starboard engine, as well as on the fuselage.

On one of the runs, the Betty closed within fifty feet with the obvious intent of ramming the PB4Y-1, but Johnson pulled up over the Belly, which apparently had not suffered major damage. Again the Betty attempted to turn on the Liberator's tail, but this unsuccessful maneuver ended in disaster. The Betty lost distance, and after a chase of seven minutes the Liberator closed from astern and opened with the bow turret.

The Blue Raiders of VPB-117's score board. *Dan Kerper*

A fire broke out in the starboard engine and a few seconds later, under the raking fire of the bow and deck guns, in the starboard wing root, as well. The 20 mm cannon in the Betty's tail was firing throughout the encounter, but neither it nor any other guns secured hits on the Liberator. Only a relatively few rounds were fired, indicating inadequately trained gunners or stoppages. All guns were silenced about a minute before the Betty's starboard wing dipped, hit the water, and the plane exploded.

Blue Raiders Mindoro Operations
On 6 February, 117 moved to Mindoro to begin operations under Command Group One, Fleet Air Wing 17. Here they would stay until the end of the war, the only PB4Y squadron on the island. From there, the Blue Raiders would roll up a score unrivaled in the history of PB4Y operations. In the coming weeks patrol plane commanders

like Lts. Sutton and Moore would join the ranks of a select few fighter pilots by shooting down more than five enemy aircraft, becoming top PB4Y aces. Additionally, Lt. Arthur G. Elder would soon establish one of the outstanding individual heavy bomber records of WWII. Within a period of seven weeks beginning on 16 February, he and his crew would sink or damage an estimated 56,000 tons of enemy shipping, shoot down two enemy fighters, and destroy another twelve aircraft on the ground.

Some of his men regarded their leader as a reckless glory seeker bent on winning medals for himself at the risk of his crew. On the

Outbound for a patrol from Tacloban Island, Lt. Stevens of VPB-104 destroys Sugar Charlies. These small wooden-hull vessels of about 200 tons collectively carried a great deal of supplies to Japanese Island bases. *Courtesy of Paul Stevens*

Lt. Sutherland and crew 14 of VPB-104 attacked a convoy of one 5,280-ton and one 3,000 ton cargo ships escorted by one destroyer and a gunboat on 19 December 1944. Hits were scored on the larger cargo ship, the *Panama Maru*, effectively wrecking it. Lt. Stevens came from two search sectors away to hit the ship again. A crewman took this photo just as the PB4Y-1 passed overhead and before the bombs exploded. *Courtesy of Paul Stevens*

* Chapter 4: Armed Reconnaissance *

Lt. Elder and his gunners destroyed five small freighters, damaged another four, destroyed two fuel dumps, damaged a radar station, destroyed a locomotive, damaged a Betty bomber, and shot down a Kate float plane while patrolling over Borneo on 22 March 1945. Here are the Kate's interception and destruction as it explodes. *Courtesy of the NARA*

Machine gun fire from a PB4Y-1 commanded by Lt. Arthur G. Elder of VPB-117 scores hits on a Japanese transport of some seven to eight thousand tons known as a Tare Baker in Saigon, French Indo-China. *Author's Collection*

afternoon of 17 March, his copilot, Ensign Isaac Parker, went in the commanding officer's tent and told him that the crew no longer wanted to fly with him. It was a mutiny of sorts; the crew in their eyes felt the commander was no longer capable of commanding an aircrew. However, in Mulvihill's and the Navy's view, it was a clear case of disobeying a lawful order. The crew won, in a sense, as they never flew with Mulvihill again. Two weeks later, the commanding officer of 117 was relieved of command and was replaced by Lt. Cdr. Roger J. Crowley Jr. The story did not end in the tent on Mindoro; some months after the war Parker stood trial and was convicted of disobeying a direct order.[4]

Before the change of command transpired the squadron continued patrolling. Due to a report of an enemy task force, Lt. Hyland boarded Liberator 38925 on 30 March and headed for the Paracel Islands. Returning down the eastern coast of Hainan, Hyland received a message from a VPB-119 Privateer concerning a large Japanese cruiser and destroyer force. The Liberator headed toward the task force and joined up with the Privateer just as two enemy fighters came up to attack.

The fighters turned their initial attention from the Privateer to Hyland's plane and the Liberator began taking hits that knocked out the number one engine and damaged the fuel cells. The Liberator was in bad shape as the fighters broke off, with one trailing a thin cloud of black smoke caused by Hyland's accurate gunners. The patrol plane commander ordered all unnecessary equipment jettisoned to lighten the plane and to conserve the rapidly draining fuel supply. The Privateer joined up and acted as cover for the stricken PB4Y-1.

There was not enough fuel left to make it back to Mindoro, so Hyland made the choice to head for a small island named Triton 150 miles from the French Indo-China coast. The pilot knew the chances of everybody getting out alive in an open water ditching were next to nil and chanced for a wheel's up landing along the island's sandy beach. Coming in with the numbers one and four engines feathered, Hyland made a near perfect landing. The big bomber skidded along the beach for 200 feet before finally coming to rest. The entire crew exited uninjured. Three hours later, they were picked up by a PBM and went back to Mindoro.

The Blue Raiders' movement was preceded by a change of command on 25 January, as Lt. Cdr. McDonald was detached and was replaced by Lt. Cdr. Thomas P. Mulvihill. McDonald had only been in command for a month before he was promoted and reassigned. Mulvihill was an aggressive patrol plane commander with four aerial kills to his credit. However, he was probably too eager for his crew. His rise to command was soon marred by the only known case among PB4Y squadrons of a commanding officer's crew refusing to fly (see previous).

April and May brought an intense campaign against land targets in Borneo and Indo-China. Now under the leadership of Lt. Cdr. Crowley (whose prior service included a stint as a patrol plane commander with VB-108), targets previously forbidden now became the center of 117's war. Throughout this period oil storage tanks, refineries, airfields, and river shipping in Borneo were hit. However, it was the Tourane-Saigon railway in Indo-China that became the Blue Raiders' favorite hunting ground. French Indo-China was a target rich environment previously somewhat unmolested by the allies. Consequently, the Japanese were able to keep most of their military assets from harm's way.

One of the first crews to venture to Indo-China was led by Lt. Castleton, who hit the railway at a point sixty miles north of Saigon on 9 April. From an altitude of 150 feet Castleton dropped a string of bombs on a locomotive. Six direct hits blew sections of the train into the air, with three freight cars being blasted to bits. Japanese troops fleeing from the wrecked train became victims of the Liberator's gunners.

Four days later, Lt. Arthur Elder went snooping around Camranh Bay and found two small merchant ships. Coming in at full power, Elder told his crew to open fire at the ships. All hell broke loose as the Liberator's guns were met with heavy anti-aircraft fire from shore batteries, killing one crewmember and wounding two others. Elder realized it was a trap and was caught in heavy crossfire so he made a getaway out to sea.

Targets around Tuy Hoa, Phan Thiet, Bink Dinh, and Cape St. Jacques were also the subject of a heavy bombing and strafing campaign during the month. One such mission resulted in the death of one man and the wounding of five others when Lt. Elder was attacked by three enemy fighters off Cape St. Jacques on 25 April. During May, the squadron conducted attacks on coastal shipping and railroads in Indo-China. Additionally, marshalling yards at Bink

Modest Miss **(Bureau Number 38733) of VPB-111 sporting a typical semi-nude woman which adorned many Air Force and Navy bombers.** *Courtesy of Peter Bresciano*

PB4Y-1 *Doc's Delight* **(Bureau Number 38746) was the primary aircraft operated by Combat Air Crew 11 of VPB-111, led by Lt. R. L. Fleming.** *Courtesy of Peter Bresciano*

On 31 December 1944, Lt. Stevens shot down a Nate fighter off Sakishima Gunto. The Japanese pilot was completely surprised and jumped from the burning airplane without a parachute. This was one of six enemy aircraft brought down by Stevens and crew. *Courtesy of Paul Stevens*

Dinh and shipping at Vinh were hit twice during the month, resulting in the destruction of nine small ships. During this period the Blue Raiders added sixty-seven ships either sunk or damaged and four enemy aircraft destroyed to their combat score.

By late May, it was obvious that worthwhile targets were vanishing from regular search sectors. Therefore, the Blue Raiders' searches were extended to extreme range. In June, the squadron suffered the loss of two crews. On 14 June, Lt. (jg) J. P. Dougan and his crew failed to return from patrol. A week later, Lt. Sayre's Liberator crashed into the sea shortly after takeoff, killing all aboard. July began with the loss of another crew. However, this story has a different ending to the often cold and unresolved term missing in action.

5

Missing in Action[1]

Personal accounts from PB4Y combat air crews of being taken prisoner by the Japanese, surviving such an ordeal, or evading capture were rare occurrences, since most missions were conducted at low altitude, making it impossible to safely bail out of a crippled aircraft. The men rode the plane down, hoping the pilot would conduct a somewhat controlled crash landing at sea or on land. Unfortunately, most if not all of a crew perished upon impact. Lacking verifiable evidence of what happened to most combat air crews who disappeared, they were classified "Missing in Action," and remained so until additional information became available.

The story of VPB-101's Commander Miller and his crew in *Miller's High Life* was one of the few instances where some crewmembers of a PB4Y survived a crash. Lt. Commander Marvin T. Smith, Miller's replacement as the squadron's skipper, had a similar occurrence on 13 January 1945, but he and five other crewmen would not survive their ordeal. Six months later three men of a VPB-117 Liberator survived a crash, became prisoners of war, and were repatriated.

Escape from Borneo

Lt. Commander Marvin T. "Smitty" Smith, acting skipper of VPB-101, and his crew aboard PB4Y-1 38840 departed Morotai on 13 January 1945, on what was to be their last mission before returning to the United States. It did become the crew's last mission, but not in the manner in which they would have desired. Smith was a 1931 graduate of Georgia Tech and a naval aviator since 1937. The mission that day had been uneventful, and as part of it they dropped propaganda leaflets over Miri, a coastal city in Sarawak, Malaysia.

Smith headed the plane toward Brunei Bay at an altitude of 7,500 feet when four Japanese fighters, consisting of two pairs of Zekes and Oscars, came out of the clouds and started attacking in pairs at eleven and one o'clock. Within seconds the fighters knocked out two of the bomber's engines and mortally wounded bow gunner Sheridan L. Poston (AOM1c) and wounded copilot Lt. (jg) John R. Graham.

Marvin T. Smith pictured here as a senior at Georgia Tech, where he majored in civil engineering. *1932 Georgia Tech Blueprint Yearbook*

The Liberator went into a sharp glide; emerging from a cloud formation, the plane was down to an altitude of 4,000 feet. Smith leveled the plane, but with two engines it was impossible to gain altitude. He realized that ditching was inevitable, but knew he had to get as far away as possible from the fighters and Japanese-held Brunei and Miri. Suddenly the enemy fighters reappeared, but this time one of the planes was brought down by the Liberator's top turret gunner Reuben L. "Robby" Robbins and waist gunner AOM2c William T. Fischer.

Lt. Graham lowered the flaps using the auxiliary hydraulic gear as Lt. Commander Smith conducted a smooth wheels-up landing along the shore, with the plane skidding for 150 yards before coming to a stop in the waist-deep mud of a rice paddy ten miles east of Brunei. The crew immediately set out destroying classified documents and equipment that may have been useful to the enemy. During the process the crew discovered the extent of Poston's injury—cannon fire from one of the fighters had severed one of the gunner's legs and he was bleeding out.

The rest of the group consisted of plane captain chief aviation machinist mate (CAMM) Talmadge C. Thurmond, AMM2c Melvin J. Roth, ARM2c Kenneth R. Platte, S1c Alvin M. Harms, and AMM2c James R. Shephard. The crew broke out a life raft, placed the gunner inside, and dragged him toward a clump of trees. They took stock

PENDUDOK DI SARAWAK, BRUNEI, LABUAN, AND BRITISH NORTH BORNEO

SUDAH tiga tahun sekarang kamu orang tiada dapat mendengar khabaran2 yang betul, sebab kamu orang sudah kena timpa oleh bebanan Jepun, dan kita tiada sempat mahu membawa khabaran yang betul kepada kamu.

Tetapi sekarang ini bala tentera kita sudah mengumpolkan banyak barang2 peperangan, dan sekarang tentera kita sedang menghalaukan Jepun daripada pulau2 yang di-ambilnya dahulu.

Bagitu juga Jerman di-sabelah Eropah; makin lama makin dia-orang mundor dan kita makin maju dan menjadi lebeh kuat lagi daripada Jerman dan Jepun.

OLEH KERANA ITU KITA SEKARANG BOLEH MEMBOM KEPADA BALA TENTERA JEPUN, DAN LAGI BOLEH MEMBAWA KHABARAN2 SAPERTI INI KEPADA KAMU ORANG SEMUANYA.

Bala tentera kita sudah menghalaukan tentera Jepun daripada pulau Leyte, dekat Manila, dan banyak pulau2, yang ada di-sabelah timor daripada Borneo, sudah di-ambil balek oleh tentera kita. Kapal2 terbang kita sudah menjatohkan bom, dan kapal2 perang kita sudah menghanchurkan banyak benteng2 Jepun di-tanah Belanda yang ada di bawah angin ini. Bagitu juga di negeri China dan di negeri Jepun sendiri. Beribu2 serdadu Jepun sudah mati terlempar di-mana2, dan beratus2 kapalnya sudah tenggelam di laut.

Disebelah Eropah bala tentera Jerman sudah di-pukul mundor balek kepada sempadan negerinya. Negeri Italy sudah taalok. Negeri Franchis sudah lepas dari kesangsaraan-nya, dan bala tentera Jerman sudah dihalaukan keluar daripada negeri Russia.

Bala tentera Jepun tidak boleh menahan tentera kita melanggar, dan lagi dia tidak boleh menahan kapal2 terbang kita membawa khabaran saperti ini kepada kamu semuanya.

OLEH KERANA ITU TUNGGU DENGAN SABAR SAHAJA SEMENTARA ORANG2 JEPUN DIHALAU KELUAR DARIPADA NEGERI KAMU TENTANG KESUSAHAN KAMU AKAN HABIS SEMUANYA, DAN KAMU BOLEH HIDUP DENGAN SELAMAT DAN SEMPURNA LAGI.

A propaganda flyer similar to those dropped over Borneo by Lt.Cdr. Smith's crew on their last mission. *Courtesy of Dan Kerper*

of their equipment, which consisted of five pistols, a Gibson Girl radio, a sail for the life raft, a booklet of Malay terms, a cloth survival map, and two first aid kits containing iodine, gauze, eye location, and adhesive tape. A few hours into the journey the radio became a heavy burden and it was thrown away.

Arriving at the clump of trees, they paused to aid Poston, but he was already dead. As they gathered around the gunner's body a couple natives came out of the bush carrying rice for the crew. They carried blowguns and spears and wore loincloths, and spoke in Malay. The glossary came into use, as the Americans asked them to bury Poston and help them elude the Japanese; however, it quickly became apparent the natives were deathly afraid of the Japanese and would only offer food and bury the bow gunner.

The nine men headed into the jungle, aiming to reach a high range of mountains to the east, but progress became exceedingly slow due to the nearly impenetrable foliage and extreme heat. Insects swarmed around the men, especially mosquitoes and leeches, with the latter penetrating into the men's uniforms. Trudging along several plans were discussed on how to reach safety before finally settling to reach Kudat, on the northern tip of Borneo, as they were briefed back at the base (falsely) that Australian guerrilla forces were

operating from there. The crew figured it would take two months to reach the objective; they needed to find a native guide. The chief of the first village the party came across at first refused, knowing the repercussions if the Japanese found out about helping the Americans. The chief finally agreed to send along a guide to help them to the next village. Thereafter, guides were changed every three to four hours upon reaching each village.

The groups walked twelve hours each day for the next thirteen days, despite swollen feet from infected leech bites. Natives fed them rice and allowed them to sleep on the dirt floors of huts, but they were hastily told to leave each morning. Each day they grew weaker as malaria and dysentery set in. The Tagal village of Long Pa' Sia, on the Matang River in Northern Borneo, was reached after two weeks, but they could go no farther.

The indigenous Tagal, a group belonging to the Murut (hill people) people, live in the interior of Borneo, each of some thirty territorial subgroups, and were known as headhunters, but the practice seemingly began to fade as the Dutch government banned it and many of them converted to Christianity; however, the Allied powers encouraged them and the Dyaks to resume the practice on Japanese occupation forces. Typically the men wore loincloths, sported bowl haircuts, and wore bone or brass earrings, while other tribal men practiced spiritual tattooing of their bodies. The breasts of some women were exposed and their earlobes extended down past the shoulders, caused by piercing and being stretched by brass weights.

The natives were again reluctant to help the men, as Japanese patrols frequently visited the village, yet the chief agreed the group could stay until they were stronger. Smith and his men agreed to split up the group at this point, with Lt. Graham—who began to compile a language dictionary of several local dialects—taking Harms and Robbins to the village of Long Tefadong, six hours up the river. Graham handed Smith his personal .32-caliber pistol while keeping his military-issue .38 revolver before leaving.

Thurmond, Shephard, Fischer, Roth, and Platte stayed behind with Smith. For two weeks the six men ate and rested, but without medication they continued to suffer from malaria and dysentery. On the morning of 12 February, Smith received word from the native chief that a patrol of thirty Japanese soldiers was on its way to Pa' Sia and the Americans needed to leave quickly for the village of Kemabong, on the route to Kudat. Shephard, as the weakest of the group and unable to walk, would be dragged far enough into the jungle to avoid detection and was left in a native lean-to called a *sulap*.

The group headed off to Kemabong, and that afternoon the Japanese patrol arrived at the village and stayed a week while Shepherd remained undetected. He remained in the sulap until the Japanese departed before returning to the village, where a native couple took care of him for another eight days. He stood up for the first time in twenty-five days on 26 February, and immediately requested the natives take him by boat to the house where Graham,

Harms, and Robbins were staying. Harms sat on the river's shore as the boat with Shephard arrived. Neither of the two recognized each other, as more than a month had passed and both were dirty and unshaven, their uniforms filthy, stained, and in tatters.

Harms told Shepherd as they headed towards the house that Lt. Graham had left on 18 February upon hearing news that two Army Air Force men were at the village of Long Nuat; a journey of about four days. The officer handed over a .38-caliber pistol and seventeen rounds of ammunition to Harms and Robbins as they were too weak to make the trip.

Shephard found Harms and Robbins in pretty bad shape. Harms began suffering from dysentery soon after arriving at Pa' Sia, and it continued to worsen to the point that he averaged twenty-two bowel movements a day, and in many instances he could only pass blood. Robbins developed a tropical ulcer—also known as jungle rot—measuring four inches in diameter at the base of his spine. The odor emanating from the ulcer was horrendous and the lesion eroded the skin down to where bone was exposed. The excruciating pain denied him sleep, and on two occasions he deliberately rolled himself into a fire pit, whereupon Sheppard dragged the ill man away, holding him down to prevent him from doing it again. Robbins then became lethargic, stopped eating, and at one point appeared lifeless, so Shephard dug a grave, thinking the man had died. Sheppard checked Robbins and heard a faint heartbeat, but he knew the end was near and explained the situation to the native man taking care of them. The native brought his wife, who started thoroughly chewing a mouthful of rice and then transferred it into Robbins' mouth. Two days of constantly feeding by this method brought back his strength and finally consciousness to the man. Thereafter he could feed himself, and he became strong enough to walk around, although the pain from the ulcer remained constant.

While Shepard's strength increased and Harms and Robbins' condition worsened, Graham had reached Long Nuat, found Staff Sgt. Francis B. Harrington and Cpl. John R. Nelson, and headed back. The two airmen were members of an Army B-24 that was shot down three months earlier. Their plane was hit by anti-aircraft fire over Brunei, with one shell exploding inside the cockpit, killing the pilot and copilot. The remaining seven crewmen bailed out but became separated; Harrington and Nelson found each other and stayed at Long Nuat, hoping the other five crewmen would show up when Graham arrived. The Navy lieutenant collapsed from exhaustion and malaria and had to be nursed back to health by native teacher William Mongan and his wife Maria.[2]

The lieutenant and the airmen left Long Nuat during the second week of March, with hopes of retrieving Harms and Robbins at Long Tefadong and then searching for and hopefully rejoining Smith's group. A day into the journey the native guides became agitated and told Graham that a Japanese patrol was near and they had to return to Long Nuat. The Americans refused and the natives ran off. The officer chose to head toward Long Tefadong while Harrington and Nelson returned to Long Nuat.[3]

Graham arrived at the house at Long Tefadong and found Shephard, Harms, and Robbins too weak to travel, though he wanted to immediately set out to find Commander Smith's group. There he learned that a native arrived on 3 March, and informed Shepherd that Smith and the four men with him were led into an ambush and killed or captured by the Japanese. They had made it halfway to Tenom, in East Malaysian, when their guides turned them over to southern Tagal guides who, unknown to Smith, were pro-Japanese and took them to the village of Tomani to rest in a longhouse. Two days later a pair of Japanese soldiers with Malay and Chinese sympathizers rushed forward, firing into the longhouse. One of the Americans ran out and was killed by a Tagal spear to the back; two others tried to make it into the jungle and one of them was shot dead, while the other made it into the dense foliage. The two remaining navy men surrendered. The unknown airman who escaped managed to hide from the enemy for a week until he was eventually tracked down. The Japanese convinced one of the two men they had captured to convince the individual to surrender and that all three would be treated well. The two returned to the village to find the remaining prisoner being whipped and the dismembered bodies of the two that had been killed earlier burning in a fire. The two Americans became incensed and fought the Japanese in hand-to-hand combat, with one of them picking up one soldier and bashing him to death against a tree. Outnumbered, the navy men were killed.[4]

Graham made the decision to press on back to Long Nuat with Shepherd heading out first, taking turns carrying a cooking pot the natives provided, while the weaker Harms and Robbins would follow carrying bags of rice. Shepherd's health deteriorated rapidly, and by the second day he started swaying, then stumbling, until he finally fell to the ground, unable to continue. Graham could not leave him behind and knew that Shepherd would be forced to move on. The officer thought about a story he once heard about a doctor and a diabetic who went on a trip together and their automobile broke down miles from the nearest town. The diabetic soon needed a shot of insulin, but the doctor had none, and knew the man would go into shock, followed by death; however, he knew that stimulating the adrenal glands could provide a temporary cure. The doctor then confessed to be his wife's lover and that the drive was a plot to murder the diabetic. The cure worked and the man made it to the nearest town safely, but he never forgave the doctor. The lieutenant used the ruse against Shepherd by calling him a yellow coward, a quitter, a son-of-a-bitch, and every derogatory term he could think of. The sailor reacted by rising from the ground intent on murder and he made it to Long Nuat, spurred on by the officer's steady stream of verbal abuse. According to Shepherd he held no resentment, "I would never have got there if Mr. Graham hadn't done what he did. None of us would have got out at all."

Harms and Robbins following behind ran into a heavy rainstorm and both began experiencing malarial chills; they were guided by a young Dayak boy to a hut. The following morning the chills had subsided and they continued on their journey, arriving at Long Naut

A photograph of Joseph Lowder's crew that was shot down over Indo-China on 1 July 1945. Top row (L to R): John Palm, Joe Lowder, Ralph Messick, Robert Hepting, Donald Gross, Charles Playne, and John Klauss. Bottom row (L to R): Charles Fisher, Peter Hourcade, Lester Gottberg, Irving Stark, and William Gore. *Courtesy of the VPB-117 Association*

four days later. The village natives were friendly and the men's diet improved with pineapple, papayas, sweet potatoes, and hog meat. The natives' generosity was due to American missionary Brother John Willfinger, who sacrificed his life two years earlier to protect the natives by surrendering to the Japanese, who in turn executed him.

On 10 March, Graham's group received news of five more members of the Army B-24 staying at a village some four to five days away. Graham, Shepherd, Harrington, and Nelson decided to go meet them, leaving Harms and Robbins, who were once again seriously ill from malaria and dysentery. On the journey they met up with William Makahanap, a Dayak official with the Dutch government, who informed them he had made plans to hide the five airmen at another location and had raised an army of 500 Dayak natives armed with blow guns to harass Japanese troops and keep them out of the area. Native guides took Graham's group to the new hiding place, a house situated at the bottom of a deep, small valley in Punan Silau surrounded by high, precipitous mountains. The men had to crawl down the mountainside, hanging on to roots and bushes along the way. At the house was Mrs. Makahanap, who nursed the men through their recurring bouts of malaria. The five airmen joined them on 24 March: copilot 2nd Lt. Philip R. Corrin, Cpl. Edward J. Haviland, Cpl. James C. Knoch, Cpl. Dan G. Illerich, and Cpl. Thomas Capin, all of which were in far better health than Graham's group.

One of Three: Joseph F. Lowder, ARM2c
Another instance of some crew members surviving capture by Japanese forces occurred when three men survived the crash of a PB4Y-1 flown by Lt. Hepting of VPB-117. The next two months were a time of convalescing, and on 9 April, they received their first communication

from the outside world that a team of Australian guerrillas would attempt to rescue them in six weeks. On 29 April, Maj. Tom Harrisson of the Australian Army, commander of unit SEMUT 1, arrived carrying medical supplies, cigarettes, and news that planning for their evacuation was well under way. Harrisson also showed Graham the flight jacket of Lt.Cdr. Smith that was taken from a Japanese soldier killed by the guerrillas. The nine men left Pa Silau on 12 May, for Long Berang, in which they stayed at a missionary's home until 10 June, by which time the men were nearly back to normal heath due to medical supplies and a healthier diet.

Back at Long Nuat, the health of Harms and Robbins continued to decline with further bouts of malaria, and then Harms developed a serious infection on the bottom of his left foot caused by leeches, swelling it to twice its size. Using sharp bamboo sticks natives pierced his foot in numerous places to let the fluid drain out. His right foot developed an odd purple infection from which purple pus oozed. The infections kept Harms from walking for nearly nine weeks. Australian Army Sgt. Fred Sanderson parachuted in on 9 April, with medical supplies and both Americans began the road to recovery, but Harms remained in no shape to travel. The Australians made the decision to evacuate Robbins at Long Berang, which was closer to where the other seven men were located, while Harms would be carried by litter to Belawit. Seaman Harms was evacuated to Morotai by an RAAF Auster light observation plane on 10 June, while Robbins was evacuated to Labuan Island on 24 June, with Graham and Shepherd leaving four days later. The seven air force men left between 15 and 29 June.[5]

An account of being shot down and taken prisoner was a rare occurrence among PB4Y crews. Two VPB-117 crews were shot down with some surviving, and later dying, while being held by the Japanese. It happened to Lt. Hepting, with only three men surviving the ordeal. One of them was Joseph F. Lowder (ARM2c), who wrote an account of what happened on that fateful day in 1945:

"Especially in combat, no aviator escapes the wonder of what it is like to buy the farm. We see it happening to others and we know

Aviation Radioman Second Class Joseph Frank Lowder was one of four men who initially survived the crash of their PB4Y-1 Liberator off French Indochina on 1 July 1945.

our own chances could turn up any day. 'How would I react?' we ask ourselves, should we realize that this sojourn on earth could have only a few seconds left in it?

"No one can answer this for you. I can, however, relate what I did when it happened to me aboard B-24 Bureau 38907 on 1 July 1945. I was awakened that morning at 03:45, and had set about getting ready for the upcoming mission. It would be our sixth since reporting into the squadron three weeks back as a rotation crew. By daybreak, half of our twelve-man crew was in the back of a six-by en route to the flight line. Takeoff was delayed when we were caught behind several rather large army air strike groups heading for a big push down on Mindanao that had a higher launch priority than ours. It was a bit after 09:10 before we were cleared to go.

"When not on duty and just stretching my legs, I'd sit in the after station and position myself beside one of the open hatches so I could move easily and look around, which was exactly what I was doing while we chowed down. The time was 11:30, and our altitude was 8,000 feet with a ¾-cloud cover of alto-cumulus flat bottom types with tops at 10–12,000 feet, which was great. Then I began to notice a brighter streak along the forward horizon that was smoother and longer than alto-cumulus stuff should be.

"'That's either one of the oddest cloud formations I've seen or it's a coast line,' I thought. My hunch was that I was looking at the Indo-China mainland. Nevertheless, we had been airborne only a tad under two and a half hours—hardly sufficient to have brought us that far. Squinting into the slipstream, I stared at the horizon. Convinced that it was the coast, I got on the intercom and called the flight deck to report my concern. The skipper told me to have Pappy [John Klauss, AOM2c] drop three smoke bombs and he'd have Messick [Lt. (jg) Ralph Messick, pilot and navigator] take a look at them.

"Pappy tossed them out the hatch at two-second intervals. Each one made a tiny puff when it struck the surface. Immediately a thin line of white smoke from each bomb laid down flat against the water and rapidly spread westward! We had been pushed along by a gale-strength tail wind! That was the Indo-China coast.

"'Brother!' I remarked, and shook my head at no one in particular, 'Not a good sign.' Ordinarily we'd have dropped down on the deck while still more than a hundred miles out and made our approach flying either under the Japs' coastal radar or hiding ourselves in their radar's 'grass' at the bottom of their scopes.

"'Battle Stations!' the skipper ordered. The engines were throttled back and the plane banked steeply into a rapidly descending spiral toward the sea below.

"I was already en route forward when we commenced dropping. I had great difficulty maneuvering through the bomb bays from being snagged on the nipples and comers of the bomb racks and the several Gs we were pulling. Visions of newsreels showing bombers falling out of the skies over Europe ran through my head.

'Bad, bad!' I said, talking to myself. Bursting into the nose section that housed the bombardier's equipment, I grabbed the

intercom and reported in. Palm, (John Palm, ARM3c), in the nose on standby, was supposed to switch places with me.

"'For the time being,' the skipper answered, 'let Palm keep the bow.' 'Roger,' I responded. The nose turret was my usual battle station. The plane leveled out, resumed its western heading, and continued losing altitude. I agreed with the skipper's decision, although I felt some frustration at having nothing important to do.

"There were twelve of us, but only eleven battle stations in -24s (we were supposed to be flying PB4Y-2s), so one of us was an odd man. This was the first time for me. How about that—a passenger—'I'll just enjoy the scenery for a change.' I stuck my head into the fisheye window and looked around. The engine nacelles were so close to the water I would swear they were riding on the wave tops. Shortly the coast came into view, this time as a green line. We pulled up, clearing the trees, and turned north.

"Soon the plane angled back toward the sea, then hugging the coastline, continued north. Ahead I saw the mouth of Cam Ranh Bay. Then several ships came into view that were partially sunk or aground on the shallow bottom. I pushed as far into the fisheye window as I could. At mast height, throttles wide open, we weaved across the bay and pointed toward the beach. Just above the tree tops, about two miles ahead, was the superstructure of a large railroad bridge—our target. Two red lights came on, indicating the bomb bay doors had opened.

"We never reached it. I turned to look back. I could not believe what I saw. Number four engine was one big ball of white fire. 'No no no, no!' I kept yelling. There had been no warning. The fire just suddenly appeared. I turned away, not daring to believe it, then looked again. It was very terrifying. I was staring at the end.

"Pappy's attention was on the bombsight. I grabbed his shoulder and yelled 'Number four is on fire!' He looked at me in surprise and seemed disturbed that I had distracted him, but he jumped up to see for himself. I dropped to my hands and knees and headed toward the radar gear in the after station where I had left my chute.

"Opening the door to the bomb bays, I was met by a blast of hurricane force winds whipping through the open bomb bays and tearing at my clothes. From the other end of the catwalk Charlie Playne [Charles Playne, AMM1c], whiter than a sheet and staring wide-eyed right through me, was headed toward the flight deck. I stepped out over the open doors so he would have room to pass. Below the jungle, now a green blur, was rapidly drawing nearer.

"'Pull her up!' I screamed toward the flight deck. 'We haven't room to jump!' Pure fear urged me onward and I plunged into the after station and spun around for my chute. It was not there. I just melted right through my shoes.

"Desperately I reached for the radar dome to brace myself. I had run out of options. There was a tremendous lurch, a screech of metal, and within the space of a dozen seconds a world of things happened. Goot [Lester Gottberg, AOM3C] and Pete [Pete Hourcade, AMM2c] stood transfixed in the glare of the fire streaming by the starboard hatch. I wondered how they could keep their feet while I was weighing tons and being thrown through the bulkhead into the bomb bays. I somehow found the strength to grab the bomb in the top rack and sucked up my legs to keep them from being caught in whatever it was the bomber was skidding over.

"Then there was darkness. Coughing and choking, unable to breathe deeply, I seemed to be looking at myself in pure intellectual detachment. I was sprawled on my back on top of several bombs and noticed off to one side a large tear in the fuselage. Reaching back to help myself sit up I felt wetness. 'Water,' I thought, 'we must have ditched after all.' Trying to see was a problem, and I had to keep brushing my forehead and eyes to keep them clear. In addition, I was getting scared because I still could not breathe deeply.

"'Got to get to that open space, fresh air there.' 'OK,' I answered to myself, 'then, run!' No sooner was I standing when, Kahvoom! A tremendous explosion more felt than heard pushed me out the tear, but on to land. What was the wetness? Gasoline! It was the gasoline from the ruptured fuel tanks that exploded. Bits of shredded vegetation and airplane parts hopped in the concussion. For a few seconds the blast had cleared away the smoke and flames, leaving a terrible heat and no oxygen. Shoreline only forty feet away!

"'Run!' However, I moved in slow motion as I tried to race the flames before they curled back in. Only yards from the surf line I lost and became my own ball of fire. Still holding my breath and with my eyes mashed shut I plunged on until I tripped in the surf, fell in its coolness, and dove toward the sandy bottom. When I 'came to,' I found myself waist deep in shallow surf, facing the open sea.

"My only thought was that my wife was going to receive one of those dreaded telegrams reading 'Missing in Action' and it would make her feel bad. I tried to send her a mental apology for the hurt I would cause. A wave of loneliness engulfed me, and I felt every mile of the 11,000 that separated me from home. I turned toward the beach and saw the wreckage. The scene jarred me back into the present. The destruction was unbelievable. Nothing seemed to be left standing. Yellow-red flames licked the bottom of an enormous column of black smoke that spread back over a swath in the jungle made when the bomber hit at better than 200 miles an hour. I wondered if, indeed, I might be dead.

"'Well, I'll need that survival kit,' I thought, and took several strides toward the beach. Wham! From nowhere a sledgehammer of excruciating pain stabbed so hard it dropped me to my knees, and I pitched face forward into the water and nearly drowned before I could muster my wits. Standing in the slow wash of the surf provided time to focus my attention on me and away from the fact that we had crashed. It was evident that I had to separate my 'head work' from the searing, debilitating pain that my body was experiencing.

"It was some time until I succeeded in 'managing things' by discovering I could keep control to a degree if I could envision myself as two people—twins, intra-related and bound to each other,

where one was 'the thinker' and observer; the other, a body handicapped and enduring incredible pain. Radiating from many places and for different reasons, it was relentless, raw, and resisted any bodily movements with additional stabs of heightened misery. I was aware I had received injuries but blissfully ignorant of their type or severity. At times, in spite of it all, the 'body' succeeded in overriding 'the thinker.'

"Subsequently, I learned the extent of my injuries. A skull fracture, anatomical loss of the right eye, more than half a dozen separate punctures, cuts, tears, bruises, and scratches, a broken ankle, and two bullet wounds (from our own .50-caliber ammo exploding in the fire). I had burns over my face, neck, both hands, strips across my back, right hip, both thighs, and right calf. Added to this, salt water and unburned gasoline in my clothes and the sand, plus the 100 percent heat under a tropical sun at noon, and you gain some appreciation for the plight confronting 'the thinker.'

"I employed this split personality technique in the days to follow, and later into a long dream world. The 'thinker' became 'Stateside Joe' and 'Salty' the one scurrying about the southeastern coastal areas of Indo-China, conniving ways to escape, and also searching for anyone who could provide him with medical help.

"Meanwhile, back at the crash site, I decided I was too close to the wreckage. It would draw the curious, and soldiers, like flies. Laboriously, I angled on to the beach about 200 yards north of the crash. I looked back once, then moved farther away, following the edge of the jungle.

"Attempts to extract myself from the gear were pitiful failures. Zippers, snaps, buttons, all were encrusted with sand. My fingers seemed without tactile knowledge of what to do and tears streamed from my eyes, distorting my sight. The hot flush from the burns aggravated by the sun especially thwarted the task. I had come to an impasse. It was a bad few moments.

"Next thing I noticed—the surprise was so great it ruled my thoughts for a couple seconds—I was standing there stripped of every item of gear and clothing except for my leggings and boonies!

"I have no plausible explanation. I shoved off again. I had not traveled far, as I could still hear the occasional faint cracks of .50-caliber shells going off. Ahead I saw the form of someone approaching. I was hoping to find a native, borrow a boat, and shove out to sea, where our subs were on patrol and I could get picked up.

"Not so, as a man, dressed in Bermuda shorts, neat shirt, and knee socks, walked up to me. For a few moments we just looked at each other. Finally, thinking one of us should speak up, I gestured with my hands like a plane coming in and then blowing up, then pointing at myself said 'American.'

"He responded with a quick nod, saying something that certainly was not English, and waved to someone off on the side. Immediately six or seven soldiers encircled me with rifles and pistols at the ready. The man was a Jap marine and I had just become a POW.

"Our party headed inland and climbed into hills on the outskirts of the city, to a house where I was left standing in a kind of entrance foyer. No one came or went for upwards of an hour. Then I noticed a party of five or six approaching. Stark [Irving Stark, AMM3c] and Goot were with them.

"I was immensely pleased to see them, then just as quickly felt terribly sorry for them. The tales I had heard about war atrocities and the treatment of prisoners made me fear for their well being. In addition, we were aviators. That was supposed to be especially bad. Although I had not been abused thus far, neither had I been shown any consideration for the state of my health.

"If Stark and Goot had made it, why hadn't I noticed them? In addition, could not others have survived? I scarcely had time to wonder when another small group arrived with someone strapped on a door. They were carrying it like a stretcher. It was Pete Hourcade, clad only in his dungaree pants. The soldiers set the door down and cut him loose. He immediately got to his feet and aimlessly started wandering about. The soldiers tried to herd him within a small circle. When he turned toward me I saw he was terribly burned, his head was enormously swollen, and half his face had been sheared off. Blessedly, he was totally out of it. I was mustered into watching him and to keep him put. Once he slipped from the grasp I had on his arm and the meat came off in my hands. He had been literally half barbecued. What power sustained him I could not imagine.

"Then the four of us were put into a garbage pit about six feet square and chest deep. A single sentry could easily watch us. Later we were motioned to move back to the house. Stark and Goot climbed out without too much trouble, but I could not get Pete to climb up and my own strength was not up to bodily lifting him over the edge. The guard observed us a couple minutes and then motioned for me to get out and proceed alone.

"At first I did not think it possible I would make it; I had become so stiff I moved like a jointless statue. Nevertheless, I did, and the new jabs of pain froze me on the spot. The guard gestured angrily for me to get going. I took a few strides and turned back just in time to see the soldier run Pete clean through his chest with his bayonet. It was merciful for Pete. He had never regained his senses and was almost dead anyway. However, it was also a stark reminder to me what to expect if I became incapable of caring for myself. 'The thinker' had increased his resolve.

"Goot and Stark had just nodded to me and I to them when we first met earlier at the back of the house. In the course of our entrenchment in the garbage pit I learned they had seen three of the crew who died—two officers and one enlisted man—but no one else. From some things one of the soldiers, who spoke English remarkably well, had said, all twelve of us were accounted for.

"Stark's and my physical conditions were the exact opposite. I was all but done in, while he had suffered not so much as a single scratch! At some point the tail gunner's turret had been flicked free of the plane and landed in the sea. It skipped along the surface and settled in shallow water. He opened the door and waded a few feet on to the beach. He was mentally in shock, and acted like a zombie. He retained this ploy later when he was mentally 'OK,' but he did not allow any of the Japs to learn he had recovered. There are times when it pays very well to appear ignorant.

"Coot had also been tossed free during the crash, and he too landed in the sea. However, Coot was unprotected and flailed along on the surface head over heels, spraining and dislocating his back and shoulders. He must also have sustained a slight concussion, because whenever he attempted to stand fully erect he would pass out. He had no recollection of anything until he was wading into the beach and saw Stark close by. Soldiers who found them sitting on the outside edge of the fire and wreckage had captured them.

"In Lt. Hepting's crew, only those in the after section survived the crash itself, and the three of us—Coot, Stark, and I—survived prison camp and the war. We were moved from Baie de Cam Ranh on the night of July 2 and transported in an open bed truck to Saigon. We were placed in solitary cells in a former French Foreign Legion barracks.

"After V-J Day we were moved into the main POW camp on Jean Eudel Street, about 200 meters from the Saigon River and about 600 meters from the canal. Japanese warehouses, rail yards, and fuel storage surrounded this camp, so it was a military target area. In this main camp were 1,664 Allied POWs. Of this number, 209 were American. British, Dutch, and Australian army and navy personnel made up the rest. These men had been captured at the outset of the war and had served in working parties on railroads and other construction and maintenance projects, such as the bridges our squadron knocked out. They also helped build the Burma-Siam railroad earlier in the war, which was subsequently made famous following the book and movie *The Bridge on the River Kwai*.

"An interesting fact is that Winston Churchill, wishing to better secure a tenuous British hold on India, sent a general to Saigon the first of September to reestablish the French colonial government in power as a show of strength to India and Burma. The Vietnamese wanted nothing to do with the French and violently rebelled. On September 2, 1945, they began shooting any French they could find and never stopped, and so the Vietnam War was launched. I heard the first shots near the POW camp. The POWs were advised not to stray into the city, because the Vietnamese could not distinguish between the French, whom they shot on sight, and Allied POWs!

"On 6 September, an Army Combat Air Corps squadron out of Burma flew into the Saigon airport in C-47s. They belonged to the first and third squadrons of the First Combat Group. They airlifted the POWs to the 142nd Army General Hospital in Calcutta, India. I stayed about two weeks in Calcutta, then was evacuated by a C-54 hospital plane to NAS Miami, where I was returned to naval jurisdiction. Here I received eye surgery and later convalesced at the Naval Hospital in Bethesda, Maryland. I was medically discharged in February 1946. I'll never forget nor adequately express the relief,

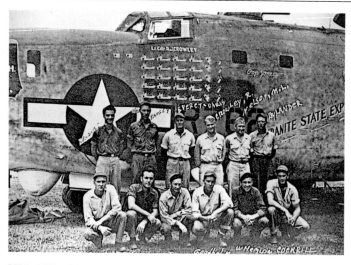

VPB-117's skipper LtCdr. Roger Crowley's crew posing next to a PB4Y-2 Privateer *Granite State Express*, in reference to the state of New Hampshire. *Courtesy of the VPB-117 Association*

joy, and love I felt the first time I came home, stepped off the train, and embraced my wife. It was the day before Thanksgiving, 1945."

Three Came Home

A letter written by Donna Gross, the young wife of twenty-one-year-old copilot Ensign Donald Gross, to Robert Hepting's wife Ruth shows the sorrow they both must have shared. It begins with circumstances surrounding the crew's loss told by Joe Louder's uncle to Mrs. Gross's father during a phone call. Hope of her husband's return quickly vanished when she heard only three of the crew survived:

"It is very difficult for me even now to believe that my Donnie is not among the living. I guess it just won't ever be absolutely final for me. . . . I can only thank God for the very short ten months in which I guess we lived a lifetime. I do know we had a happiness which very few people can achieve in a whole lifetime. I believe this is true for you and Bob also. I do not believe any of the other couples were as completely contented as we four were just being together. It seems while the others rushed to play golf, etc., all our husbands thought of was getting home to us. We must not be afraid to think of these things.

"There is very little left for one to say. This is a pain which only those who have gone through it can realize. We must act as we know Donnie and Bob would wish. They were so brave, how can we be anything else?[6]

Combat operations continued during the closing weeks of the war for the Blue Raiders as Louder, Gottberg, and Stark languished as prisoners of war and as telegrams containing the words "Missing in Action" began reaching the crew's families in the United States. Rail yards in Indo-China continued being the targets of choice. However, the squadron managed to sink or damage an estimated 37,000 tons of shipping in July and August. On 30 July, 117 suffered its last casualty when Frederick Thomas (AMM2c) was killed by anti-aircraft fire during a strafing run on an airfield.

On 11 August, operations were suspended and the squadron was ordered to Tinian. On 6 September, command was transferred to Cdr. Windham, with 117 returning to California in November 1945, where it was decommissioned. Two years later, three of the four former commanding officers accepted the Presidential Unit Citation in an award ceremony in Washington, DC. The squadron lost eighteen officers and fifty-two enlisted men killed, while another six became POWs during nine months of combat operations 11 November 1944–30 July 1945.

Taken from 1942 (left) and 1946 (right) Washburn Wahian, Minnesota, High School yearbooks are images of Donald Gross, Robert Hepting's copilot. *Courtesy of Minneapolis History Collection and Special Collections, Minneapolis Central Library*

6

Operations from Clark Field
March–August 1945

In early March 1945, VPB-104 transferred to Clark Field, reporting for duty under FAW 17, while 111 stayed behind, only to leave the following month for Palawan. From Clark, searches were extended farther north. It was from this airfield that invading Japanese devastated American air power and hastened the fall of the Philippines. Now the base was back in American hands, and would remain so for nearly half a century.

Arriving at the same time was VPB-119, the first PB4Y-2 Privateer squadron to arrive in the area. Commanded by R. C. Bales, he and some of the men were combat veterans from a previous tour of duty with VB-106. Together both squadrons would range across the Pacific, destroying what was left of the Japanese war machine, but many of them would die in the process.

Search sectors ranged from the China coast, to within thirty miles of Shanghai, to Okinawa, Formosa, the Gulf of Tonkin, and Haiphong. These sectors would be extended 1,050 miles during the Okinawa landings (Operation Iceberg). Additionally, night patrols were flown north of Formosa to intercept dawn flights of Japanese aircraft between Formosa and Shanghai.

On 2 March, the first blood drawn by 119 was conducted by the commanding officer and resulted in the destruction of one small freighter and damage to another. Lt. J. W. Holt made the squadron's first big score when he picked up a convoy of three merchant ships being protected by three destroyer escorts.

The Privateer came in at masthead height as the convoy began pouring a steady stream of anti-aircraft fire. Holt pickled off a salvo of bombs that missed one of the transports. However, Holt swung the bomber around and had his gunners sweep the convoy with machine gun fire. A small fire was started on an escort, followed by another fire on *Nichirin Maru*, a 1,000-ton cargo ship. Suddenly, the cargo ship blew up underneath the Privateer and sank stern first. Fortunately the patrol bomber suffered very little damage.

The destruction of the *Nichirin Maru* increased the tempo of anti-aircraft fire and Holt made a hasty retreat. Three days later,

Holt went in alone at Myako Jima Harbor (an island lying between Formosa and Okinawa) and attacked three barges, ignoring heavy anti-aircraft fire coming from shore batteries and four destroyer escorts. Only after his instrument panel was shot away and the hydraulic lines were severed did Holt leave the area.

Back at Clark Field, a new PB4Y-2 for 119 arrived from Owi Island. Sitting at the end of the runway, Lt. J. Reichert waited as a PB4Y-1 from VPB-104 came in for a landing. Reichert had been a patrol plane commander with VB-104 during its first tour. The Liberator came in, landed, and kept on going; its breaks had failed, and it crashed into the Privateer, killing Reichert. A strange twist of fate for a pilot who had survived the Buccaneers' tour in the Solomons in 1943, only to be killed in an accident involving another bomber from VPB-104 less than two years later.

Lt. Stevens, patrolling the west coast of Borneo, conducted a strafing attack on Bintulu Airdrome. Shown is an Oscar under gunfire; although many hits were scored the fighter would not burn.
Courtesy of Paul Stevens

The men of VPB-119 at Clark Field, PI, during May 1945, when the squadron lost twenty-four men in combat, including two entire combat aircrews during the month, building on the previous month's loss of thirty-one men. *Author's Collection*

Lt.Cdr. Bales' Combat Air Crew One of VPB-119 scoring the squadron's first destruction of enemy shipping on 2 March 1945, when two small, 50–70 ton freighters were encountered on the high seas. One of the vessels was sunk after a salvo of five bombs was dropped from 700 feet. Only the fifth 100-lb. bomb scored a direct hit. *Courtesy of the NARA*

Patrolling off Hainan Island, Lt. Stevens sighted a Val divebomber. Hits from the bow and top turrets set fire to the Japanese aircraft. The back seat man jumped from the Val just before it hit the water and burst into a ball of fire. *Courtesy of Paul Stevens*

Both squadrons continued pounding Japanese shipping throughout the month. Most of it was Sugar Dogs (70–150-ton cargo vessels), but several larger merchant ships were successfully attacked. On 5 March, Lt. George Waldeck of 104 sighted a Topsy some 150 miles west of Okinawa; he turned the Liberator around and gave chase for the next twenty minutes. When the PB4Y-1 caught up to the plane the Liberator's gunners poured 200 rounds each into it. Both of the Topsy's engines caught fire, then it made a radical turn to starboard and dived into the water.

Two hours later and fifty miles east of Formosa, the Liberator sighted another Topsy at 1 o'clock high ten miles away; Waldeck climbed and turned to intercept. Robert Golden, in the bow turret, opened fire from 500 feet and blew the cargo plane to pieces with 250 rounds of ammunition, with parts of the plane nearly missing the Liberator. A day later Lt. Adler made a series of attacks on Japanese merchant shipping off the coast of Hong Kong and along the Chinese coast toward Swatow.

The first targets were two 500-ton cargo ships. Six 100-pound bombs were dropped and 1,400 rounds were expended, leaving one ship burning and beached. Thirty minutes later and six miles up the coast, a 100-ton coastal vessel was strafed in passing, leaving it burning. Ten minutes later a 200-ton ship was hit and burned to the water line. He was not done, though, as another coastal was hit, followed by a larger 450-ton cargo ship, and a 250-ton ship was strafed. The Liberator took hits from the ship's anti-aircraft guns and Adler was forced to withdraw.

On 10 March, Lt. Stevens went on a 700-mile search along the Chinese coast. Fifty miles north of Hainan an enemy dive-bomber (Val) was spotted and the Liberator came down for the attack. The doomed Val was hit and plunged into the water. Pulling up from his

Lee Webber, bombardier for Lt. Stevens, cuts away torn metal from the rudder of the PB4Y-1 after a mid-air collision with a Val about to land at Miri Airstrip, Borneo. *Courtesy of Paul Stevens*

attack, Stevens saw a 4,000-ton transport dead ahead in the water. Stevens instructed Webber, the bombardier, to open the bomb bay doors.

As Stevens went in on the bomb run he saw the ship's crew running for their guns, but it was too late. The Liberator went up and Stevens looked back to see the explosions, but there were none. The bombs had hung up in the bomb bay. Stevens came back around and told Webber to drop the bombs manually. Close to the target the bombs fell short, then Stevens realized that his forward guns were jammed and there was no suppressing fire.

Upon completing the outbound leg of a patrol from Morotai Island, Lt. Stevens and crew returned to strafe the seaplane base at Puerto Princesa, Palawan Island. Two Jakes and two Petes were burned to destruction and four other seaplanes were damaged. This action took place on 11 December 1944. *Courtesy of Paul Stevens*

PB4Y-1, Bu.No. 38801, assigned to Crew 11 of VPB-104, Tacloban airstrip, Leyte. *Courtesy of Bill Thys*

A three-quarter view of VPB-104's 38801. *Courtesy of Bill Thys*

PB4Y-2, "Privateer," Clark Field, Luzon, Philippines, between March and July 1945. *Courtesy of Bill Thys*

The ship's crew manned their guns and began firing 12.7 mm machine gun fire. The Liberator was hit in the bomb bay and port aileron, and number three engine was knocked out. Webber's left leg was shattered and they had to give him morphine to ease his pain. After landing back at Clark Field Webber was evacuated to the States. A week later Stevens would go on another mission that would make him a legend among naval aviators.

The VIP Emily

On 17 March, VPB-104 and 119 crews were told to be on the lookout for an Emily flying boat. A top secret (ULTRA) message had been delivered to Gen. Whitehead, commander of the 5th Air Force. The Japanese seaplane was carrying high level Japanese officers and had to be shot down. Stevens' search would take him along the Chinese coast, and in doing so, he would have a chance encounter with a Japanese admiral.

After flying through foggy weather he spotted a 3,000-ton freighter being escorted by a destroyer. He dropped down to one hundred feet and was met by the warship's accurate anti-aircraft fire, but the plane was not hit. At 2,000 yards Stevens' gunners opened fire and began hitting the ship's superstructure. Stevens pickled off ten 100-pound bombs, but many of them fell long or bounced off the vessel. Several more found their mark, causing several explosions that sunk the ship. Three minutes later the copilot spotted two Jakes flying on an opposite course. Stevens applied power and soon joined the formation. The rear seat gunner, sitting behind his 20 mm gun, looked over at the Liberator, then looked again. Too late, as Stevens' gunners fired into the enemy plane and it crashed into the sea.

Thirty minutes later Stevens spotted an Emily flying on an opposite course 1,500 feet above the Liberator. It was the plane he was looking for and he climbed to intercept. His bow and top turrets opened fire and hit the Emily's starboard engines. The gunners then sprayed the entire fuselage with machine gun fire. Stevens recounts:

"As I was running out of airspeed and preferred not to ram the target I pushed hard up on the elevators and we dropped fast. As soon as we gained back enough airspeed maximum ailerons were applied to role left on a course to pursue the enemy; losing 1,000 feet or so below the Emily, we were also now several miles behind. I got right down to the water in hopes they would not see that I was pursuing, and perhaps I would have less head wind that way. Knowing that the big seaplane was faster I wanted every advantage possible. Our engines were howling, but it appeared we were gaining very little or perhaps none at all. The top turret gunner said that one engine on the Emily was throwing smoke, but no other damage was apparent.

"After twenty minutes my copilot asked how far I intended to chase the enemy aircraft. I allegedly replied, 'All the way to Tokyo if necessary!' His question jarred me into the realization that we had run our engines at full power for a considerable period. We were a long way from home, and it came down to breaking off the chase or knowing we faced the distinct possibility of a night ditching. It was with a very heavy heart that I pulled power to maximum range cruise and headed for home."[1]

A report was received that a Sino-American Cooperative Organization (SACO) unit had reported the Emily had gone down. The story was that both pilots were killed during the attack and a non-pilot navigator had taken over the controls and made a crash landing on the China coast. SACO was a US Navy operation with teams located mostly in the coastal areas of China. They functioned as "coast watchers" and weather observers, gathered intelligence, were saboteurs, and cooperated with and provided assistance and support to the Chinese guerrillas.

Lt. Frank Balsley was a member of SACO Camp Eight, which was just sixty miles south of Haimen, where the seaplane made a forced landing. At the time of the forced landing of the Emily Balsley was in the Haimen area. He prepared a report of the incident that was forwarded to the US Naval Unit, Headquarters, 14th Air Force.

The airplane departed Ambon for Surabaya on 14 March 1945. Here they boarded the admiral, his staff, and other passengers. Thirty-three Japanese would make the trip, departing on the fifteenth for Singapore. After remaining overnight, the Emily took off on 16 March for Hong Kong. Due to poor weather there the flight was diverted to Hainan, well short of Hong Kong. After landing they hit a reef and damaged the underside of the hull. During the night repairs were made, and on the fatal day of 17 March 1945, a departure was made for Taipei, on the northern point of Formosa. At the seaplane facilities there the water conditions made a landing questionable. Circling and debating an alternate plan, an air raid warning prompted a departure for Shanghai, although it was acknowledged that fuel for the trip would be close.

One of the Emily's crew recounted what happened as they were flying along the coast of China and a B-24 intercepted. Crewmember Taniguchi operated a 20 mm gun and fired at the enemy aircraft. The gunfire from the B-24 was fierce, with bullets flying through the airplane. The chief engineer, a Navy captain, died instantly from a round that went through his chest. He died with bubbles of blood coming out of his mouth.

The enemy aircraft came so close he could see the pilots' faces. He saw his bullets striking the airplane and was sure that the B-24 crashed. It had dropped from sight very quickly. Fuel was short, and the Emily pilot saw what he believed to be the river at Wenchow. After landing on the water two engines were shut down and they nosed into the bank at a small village. It was dusk, the high tide was running out, and soon the airplane was sitting on the mud.

One of the passengers, a doctor, could speak Chinese, and from a fisherman determined that they were near Lin Hai. Two of the staff and two crewmembers left to find the nearest Japanese troops. As they jumped off the wing about 200 Chinese troops began firing and killed all four. Cdr. Ashiwara then organized a suicide squad to fight the Chinese troops. As they jumped from the wing carrying guns and swords they were shot dead. Taniguchi was firing the 20 mm gun as additional opposition arrived, some approaching from junks. Only five staff officers remained on board.

Hit three times with small caliber bullets in the arm, Taniguchi lost consciousness. He awoke, wrapped his wounds with his scarf, and heard the admiral say, "This is the end, destroy all classified documents and material and then burn the flying boat." He asked Taniguchi to send a radio message. The message was sent to Surabaya, Saigon, Hainan, Shanghai, and Formosa, and it read as follows:

"We engaged in a battle with an enemy plane and made an emergency landing due to fuel shortage. The location is the shore of Huangpu River, near Lin Hai. We will make an attack as a marauding unit. Long live the Emperor! 16:30."

Bu. No. 38809, probably flown by Crew 9, VPB-104. *Courtesy of Bill Thys*

Taniguchi went to the forward fuel room, soaked his scarf with fuel, lit it, and threw it under the fuselage fuel tank. He then went back to see the admiral, sitting with four members of his staff. He heard him say:

"All of you have assisted me well so that I could serve the Emperor and our country. I deeply appreciate your support. You are still very young and have a future. Escape this situation and serve the Emperor. Thank you."

Vice Admiral Seigo Yamagata then drew his sword from a pinkish-brown sheath and without hesitation performed *seppuku* in the classic manner.

The smoke and fire was making it very difficult to breathe. More Chinese were coming—some from more junks—screaming and filing into the airplane. Taniguchi kicked open a hatch and dove into the water, swimming for the opposite shore. Swimming under water, he made his escape as the Chinese fired, nearly hitting him. Crawling up on the muddy bank opposite the Emily, he was soon captured. During one period of interrogation he was shown a photo of twenty bodies lying on the bank beside the destroyed flying boat. He was asked which was the body of the admiral. He answered that none of them were, as he had remained aboard the burning airplane.

Chinese troops rushed to the scene and a melee ensued, resulting in the burning of the plane, the escape of twenty, the massacre of eight, and the burning of three. All were hunted down and killed, except five that were captured and then rushed to Lin Hai.

The following day, a 4,000-ton transport and two Japanese gunboats attempted to recover the plane and passengers. The Chinese mustered 2,000 troops and opposed them. Four Japanese airplanes arrived, but neither the troops, ships, nor planes could find the seaplane, as the Chinese had camouflaged it. In the evening an American airplane came on the scene and the Japanese withdrew. A later report said an American plane sank the transport at 1700 hours.[2]

Patrolling from Clark Field, Lt. Stevens and Crew 2 made contact with a convoy consisting of one destroyer, two destroyer escorts, three gun boats, two large cargo-transports and one medium cargo-transport. The tail end Charlie was hit with four 250-pound bombs resulting in an explosion of its magazine. The small vessel broke in two and quickly sank. *Courtesy of Paul Stevens*

Lt. Virgil Evans and his Crew 15 of VPB-119 found a highly camouflaged Japanese aircraft identified as a Topsy on 19 March and destroyed it with machine gun fire. *Courtesy of the NARA*

Two days after the event, Capt. C. B. Jones told Stevens that he had gotten the admiral. He tried to get further information on the incident but was rebuffed. Neither Jones nor anyone else with the knowledge could tell Stevens. It remained classified for years, and only within the last few years has he been able to find out the full story of the day he shot down Admiral Yamagata.

March Madness

The effectiveness of the PB4Y-2 in destroying enemy fighters was again illustrated by an air battle fought near Formosa. On 18 March, Lt. (jg) William L. Lyle of VPB-119 was flying northwest of Formosa when two Oscars were spotted 2,000 feet above the Privateer. Lyle then used his four-engine patrol plane as a fighter and pulled up behind the Oscars, who were now racing towards the coast and the protection of anti-aircraft batteries.

It was too late, as Lyle's bow, starboard waist, and both top turrets opened fire on an Oscar; it turned over, dove past the PB4Y2, and blew up 400 yards from the port wing. The Privateer's pilot then went after the second fighter using full throttle in a slow dive toward the intended victim. All turrets opened fire and the Oscar went into a dive at full speed, hit the surf near a beach, and exploded. The Privateer headed for home as the shore batteries finally ineffectively opened up at the retreating bomber turned fighter.

Even with the combined gunfire of twelve .50-caliber machine guns, sometimes a Privateer was no match for an aggressive Japanese fighter pilot or a well-trained anti-aircraft crew. On 22 March, 119 had their first combat loss when Lt. Evans was shot down two miles north of Amoy, China. He had been one of the squadron's most aggressive pilots, with seven ships and one fighter to his credit in only three

Lt. Evans ran into enemy anti-aircraft fire near Amoy, China, aboard Bureau Number 59426 on 22 March 1945, causing Evans to crash land his aircraft. Evans and five of his crew survived the crash, along with passenger Mutual Broadcast Company correspondent Don Bell, who had just been released from the Japanese Santo Tomas prison camp in Manila. Front row (L to R): J. R. Pierce, AMMF1c; Ens. F. W. Greene; Lt. (jg) V. J. Evans; Ens. K. W. Lindsley and Flaps; and A. J. Wilson, AMMF2c. Back row (L to R): J. A. Warr, ARM1c; N. J. Meo, AOM3c; C. C. Gibson, S1c; L. R. Jenson, AMMF2c; M. L. Walker, ARM3c; E. F. Reis, S1c; and J. L. Doss, AOMB2c. Greene, Jenson, Wilson, Meo, Doss, and Gibson were killed. *Courtesy of Dave Deatherage*

missions. Evans and six of the crew survived the crash and were rescued by friendly Chinese troops. In the coming weeks 119 would lose several more aircraft and crews, and their would be no survivors to rescue.

March was a productive month for VPB-104, with the squadron claiming 129 ships sunk or damaged, nine enemy aircraft shot down in the air with five probables, and four damaged. During

On 17 March 1945, while flying a special mission, Lt. Stevens sank the AGS-2 Koshu. Within a few minutes, two Jakes were attacked shooting down one. The second Jake ran for the protection of the Japanese destroyer escort protecting the Koshu. Thirty-six minutes later, an Emily aircraft was sighted. A firing pass was made which resulted in the Emily making a forced landing of Vice Admiral Yamagata, all his staff, and flight crew. *Courtesy of Paul Stevens*

119's first month of operations, eighty-nine ships were sunk or damaged for a total of some 72,000 tons. Additionally, eleven aircraft were engaged and destroyed or damaged.

Bloody April

April 1945 turned out to be a bloody month for VPB-119, as it lost two aircraft and crews. The month started with Cdr. Bales and his crew, most of them veterans from VB-106, going on patrol to China—they were never seen again. The aircraft was seen near Hangchow Harbor, but after that sighting nothing was seen nor heard from them. Command of the squadron then went to the executive officer, Lt. Cdr. M. S. Ragan. Ten days later Lt. A. L. Althans failed to return from a routine search of Formosa.

VPB-119 continued anti-shipping strikes against Japanese merchant vessels off the Ryuku Islands and the southern China coast, along with striking land targets in China. Another example of how low the four-engine bombers were being flown occurred on the third, when Lt. (jg) F. D. Murphy attacked two merchant ships off Myako Jima. In his first bombing run one direct hit was obtained with a 250-pound bomb hit, literally blowing the ship into bits. His gunners then strafed the second ship, and as he passed over the tip at 300 feet it exploded with such terrific force that pieces of debris went entirely through the plane.

The squadron's best patrol plane commander conducted another successful mission on the seventh. Lt. J. W. Holt spotted a medium sized merchant ship at anchor in a cove at Myako Jima. After he started a masthead run he discovered the ship was a beached derelict. Intense 12.7 and 20 mm anti-aircraft fire opened up from all sides and he finished his run and withdrew over Myako Jima airfield. Of five Oscars spotted on the field two were destroyed and three were

Cdr. Bales (VPB-119) was the squadron commanding officer, but he and his crew were lost in action on 1 April 1945. Front row (L to R): J. P. McKeon, AOM3c; Lt. (jg) H. W. Evans; Lt.Cdr. R. C. Bales; Lt. (jg) R. L. Fox; and E. F. Fees, ACOM. Back row (L to R): B. D. Guthrie Jr., AMMF2c; E. Atkin Jr., ARM3c; W. R. Gainer, AOM1c; R. N. Thayer; J. O. Ballard, S1c; R. I. Suhl, AMMF1c; and W. J. Wagner, ACRM. S1c. Lt. Evans was apparently replaced by Lt. Roscoe M. Obert, who is not shown. *Courtesy of Dave Deatherage*

Crew 17, led by Aubrey L. Althans, and PB4Y-2 Bureau Number 59514 went missing in action on 11 April 1945, during a routine search in the Formosa Straits. Front row (L to R): J. W. Adams, AMMF1c; H. H. Elfreich, S1c; J. F. Christiano, AMMF2c; C. A. Bagley, AOM3c; C. J. Bogacz, AMMF1c; and B. A. Lawrence, ARM3c. Back row (L to R): W. Harner, AOM2c; Lt. (jg) W. C. Mathews; Ens. D.C. Kirby; Lt. (jg) A. L. Althans; G. H. Stein, ARM1c; and E. A. Jakubiak, AOMB2c. *Courtesy of Dave Deatherage*

Lt. Diddler of VPB-104 attacking small shipping in Suo Harbor, Formosa, on 22 April 1945, with machine gun fire and bombing. *Courtesy of the NARA*

damaged by strafing. During the run Henry Babe (AOM2c) was slightly wounded in the arm and numerous hits were made on the plane, severing the rudder control cables.

The crew, using safety wire and solder, repaired the rudder control cables, keeping the rudder from fluttering. One engine was shot out and the number two fuel cell was hit. Holt had the bomb bay fuel tanks jettisoned and the plane returned safely to base. Holt's tenacity and the crew's ability to perform under such conditions saved them on this trip, but on a future patrol they would not return.

On 15 April, a pair of 119 Privateers ventured to Amoy on an anti-shipping sweep. Lt. W. P. Comstock flew in alone and found a target. Entering the harbor was a medium size cargo ship with a displacement of 1,000–2,300 tons. On his first run he scored a direct hit on the ship's starboard side and the vessel began to burn. Coming back around, he pickled off another 250 pound bomb for another direct hit on the ship's after deck. The vessel blew up, leaving a thick cloud of black smoke drifting in the sky. A few minutes later Lt. (jg) Fette arrived on the scene, and together the two Privateers went after three power barges filled with enemy troops. Strafing by both planes sank the barges and killed many of the passengers.

On the twenty-eighth, Lt. (jg) Walter G. Vogelsang went after shipping and land targets in China; targets he would become an expert in destroying. During the attack strafing near Hong Kong destroyed a lugger and an adjacent barracks area. Near present-day Shaoguan strafing destroyed two riverboats, and four similar vessels were attacked on the Xi Jiang River: three were destroyed and one seriously damaged. Strafing destroyed a locomotive and six cars, with the locomotive blowing up. Vogelsang then hit a railroad dockyard and an unidentified ship mounting a large crane. Going farther into China, a large locomotive and eight passenger cars were blown to bits by three direct bomb hits near Kowloon. The patrol plane commander's final attack of the day was against a Japanese patrol of about fifty men. Coming in at less than 200 feet, the Privateer's gunners decimated them, leaving only a handful of survivors.

The latter part of April through May marked increased strikes on land targets, including blockhouses, barracks, vehicles, and radio stations. Japanese shipping was now reduced to coastal vessels, as the Empire's merchant fleet was all but destroyed, primarily through the actions of American submarines. By this time restrictions against attacking land targets by Navy patrol squadrons (these targets fell under the Army Air Force) had been lifted. Attacking ground

installations resulted in the death of one Buccaneer and the wounding of two others on 27 April, when Cdr. Wright bombed and strafed two blockhouses on Hainan Island. The defenders put up intense 7.7 mm machine gun fire and Robert M. Thornton Jr. (AMM1c) was fatally wounded in the head.

At Clark Field, Quonset huts replaced the tents personnel had been living in for the past six months and recreational activities, including an open-air movie theater and a library, became available. Moreover, the month also brought relief for combat veterans of 104, as six new crews reported for duty when the rotation system kicked in.

The rotation system did not sit too well with many commanding officers that would have to rely on untrained crews. Cdr. Wright wrote:

"It is the opinion of this command that a squadron can do a better job if it has formed together, trained together, and returns as a unit when a six to eight month tour of duty is completed. Individual crews coming and going have thrown a considerable burden on the squadron, the squadron almost taking the aspect of a receiving ship.

"New crews are not trained with the unity that a complete squadron is trained. A process of indoctrination and training is necessary for each new crew, and this process takes valuable time which can not be spared in a combat area. Installation of squadron pride, which means so much to any fighting unit, is greatly hindered by the present rotation system. As far as the squadron itself is concerned, not one single advantage has been observed as the result of the new system, and it is the squadron that has to fight the war."

Lt. Vogelsang's War

VPB-119 started out the month with Lt. Vogelsang having a busy day on Hainan Island. In the coming weeks, he and his crew would make it their job to hunt down enemy troops and destroy all means

Direct bomb hits dropped by Lt. Vogelang's PB4Y-2 of VPB-119 destroy barracks on Hainan Island, off China, while his gunners later targeted a locomotive (left) during a one-plane strike conducted on 1 May 1945. *Courtesy of the NARA*

of transporting the enemy. On this mission he first strafed and blew up a truck loaded with gasoline. A second truck was blown up a few minutes later. Three more trucks carrying troops were then set on fire and many of the troops were killed.[3]

Vogelsang then pickled off three 100-pound bombs in a barracks area, causing numerous small fires. A locomotive and eight flat cars were riddled with .50-caliber fire, resulting in serious damage. Two hits were then scored with 300-pound bombs on a large smelting plant with uncertain results. Small fires were started in a building and barracks area, and flat cars standing on a siding received moderate damage from strafing.

He then attacked Fat Law Airfield. The control tower was strafed, as were administration buildings and barracks areas. Two more locomotives were then strafed, but damage appeared to be slight. The next target was a large railroad center, where strafing destroyed a large locomotive and six empty ore cars. Fifteen runs were made on three more locomotives and they were left in flames. Numerous fires were then started in the barracks area. The final target for the day was a large installation and mine. A thousand rounds of ammunition expended by the aircraft's gunners started fires in some of the buildings near the entrance of the mine.

Vogelsang continued with unrelenting fury against the Japanese. Six days later he repeated the destruction wrought on the first. On 7 May 1945, he attacked land and shipping targets in the Swatow area. A string of five 100-pound bombs were placed lengthwise across a small cargo ship, sending it to the bottom. A large subchaser was then sighted tied to a large barge. Three 250-pound bombs were dropped; two of the bombs hit the subchaser and sank it. The third bomb hit the barge and knocked one corner away. Two smaller subchasers were then strafed with 2,500 rounds; no fires were apparent, but the ships were riddled.

It was now the Privateer's gunners' turn, as they strafed the waterfront area, particularly a power plant and a water tower, causing the power plant to be put out of commission. A matching gun emplacement was the next target; it was strafed with uncertain results, although it ceased firing. The final target was a large artillery encampment, including many field pieces. All through this attack Vogelsang's plane received only minor damage in the bomb bay, tail, port wing, and starboard waist turret.

The same day 119's Lt. T. R. Alkire accounted for several land targets on Hainan Island. Strafing inflicted some damage on a blockhouse, and hits were scored with two of three 100-pound bombs on a locomotive and four ore cars. A second locomotive and five cars were then attacked and bomb hits destroyed the locomotive. The final target was a blockhouse; it was leveled by a direct hit with one 100-pound bomb. The attack resulted in the death of the tail turret gunner, Lloyd Allen Whitten (S1c), who was killed by a 12.7 mm machine gun round.

On 10 May, Lt. Vogelsang inflicted a great deal of damage on the enemy in the Canton area. A bombing and strafing attack left a riverboat burning and beached, a direct bomb hit blew up a locomotive,

Crew Four of VPB-119, commanded by Lt. John W. Holt, was lost on 1 May 1945, when their PB4Y-2 Bureau Number 59559 crashed into a hill approximately a mile from the village of Ling Tou, on Hainan Island. The original crew consisted of front row (L to R): M. F. Smith, ACRM; Ens. M. C. Baker; Lt. J. W. Holt; Ens. F. J. Urban; and J. B. Hutchison, AMMF1c. Back row (L to R): A. H. Busse Jr., AOMB1c; L. G. Benuzzi, S1c; E. M. Loeser Jr., AMMF2c; L. J. Banda, AMMF3c; J. C. Klause, ARM2c; H. B. Babb, AOM2c; and J. L. Middleton, ARM3c. Not shown are John F. Moe (ACMM), Paul D. Wilson (ARM3c), and Fred Kautz (AOM3c), who replaced Hutchison, Loeser, and Krause prior to the last mission. *Courtesy of Dave Deatherage*

Crew Thirteen, led by Lt.(jg) Vogalsang, was one of the most aggressive combat air crews of VPB-119; they were shot down over Hainan Island on 19 May 1945. Front row (L to R): J. E. Rigsby, AOM3c; Ens. A. R. Martin; Lt. (jg) W. G. Vogelsang; Lt. (jg) R. E. Graner; and E. W. Brooks, AMMF1c. Back row (L to R): R. W. Wilson, S1c; C. H. Swift, ARM1c; L. J. Oronoz, AMMF2c; R. Molter, S1c; T. W. Long, AOMB2c; D. C. Hulick, ARM2c; and L. L. Smith, S1c. *Courtesy of Dave Deatherage*

and strafing damaged sixteen railroad cars. Three riverboats were then thoroughly strafed, and two of those were left burning. At this point a 7.7 mm round hit the tail of the Privateer, slightly wounding R. W. Wilson (S1c). This did not stop Vogelsang, as he went after another locomotive and seven cars. A direct hit by a 250-pound bomb knocked the locomotive off the tracks and strafing damaged the cars. The Privateer's pilot then sighted a series of trucks fitted

Lt. Vogalsang hit targets in the Canton, China, area on 10 May 1945, resulting in the destruction of a riverboat (seen here), warehouses, two locomotives, and seventeen trucks. *Courtesy of the NARA*

VPB-119's Crew 12 aboard the PB4Y-2 Bureau Number 59559 crashed at Luichow Peninsula, China on 24 June 1945. Front row (l to r): M. J. McIntosh, ARM3c; W. R. Stuard Jr., AOM1c; P. D. Wilson, ARM3c; H. L. Leonard, S1c; H. C. Everett, ARM3c; and R. J. Henderson, AOMB2c. Back row (l to r): H. H. Fair, S1c; Ens. R. M. Cahow; Lt. F. D. Murphy; Lt. (jg) T. J. Robinson; K. A. Goodwin, AMMF1c; and J. Spatrisano, AMMF2c. *Courtesy of Dave Deatherage*

to operate on railroad tracks and fourteen of them were set on fire. The dock area on the Canton River was then strafed; small fires were started in the warehouse area and the wooden roof of a large cement storage tank was set on fire.

All through these attacks the PB4Y-2 encountered moderate, medium, and accurate enemy fire causing slight damage. As the Privateer departed the area three unidentified planes took off from Whampoa Airfield; being low on ammunition, Vogelsang took cover in the overcast. He and his crew had one additional strike before

they were lost somewhere between Hainan Island and the Gulf of Tonkin on 19 May.

For 119, May was a repeat of the month before, with the squadron losing two more Privateers and crews. On the first, Lt. Holt went on a search to Hainan Island, in the Gulf of Tonkin, and was lost. On the nineteenth, Lt. (jg) Walter Vogelsang went on a similar mission to Hainan Island and did not return. During an attack against Japanese-controlled Sheklock mines on the western side of Hainan Island, the plane was hit by anti-aircraft fire and crashed ten miles west of the mining operation. Less than a week later, a VPB-104 crew commanded by Lt. Richard Jameson was lost while trying to ditch. Search planes arrived at the crash site only to find scattered wreckage floating on the water. There were no survivors.

Summer Operations: June–August 1945

By June 1945, the battle-worn PB4Y-1 Liberators of VPB-104 were being replaced by Privateers; by the end of hostilities, the squadron would be fully outfitted with PB4Y-2s. There was an ample amount of enemy shipping to hunt, and by the end of the month 104 claimed more than 68,000 tons damaged or sunk. It also proved to be a period when 119 lost two more crews.

On 17 June, Lt. Murphy took off on a routine search patrol of Luichow Peninsula and failed to return. The following day special search planes from the squadron sighted the wreckage of the plane on Luichow Peninsula and established there were survivors. All rescue agencies, consisting of FAW-17, VPB-119, COMNAVGROUP China, COMAF, and VPB-28, began rescue attempts. While flying cover for the rescue Lt. Comstock's Privateer crashed and exploded on impact. The burning wreckage was examined by three of Lt. Murphy's crew, and they reported there were no survivors. The rescue attempts were further complicated when a PBY5A attached

Five survivors of Lt. Murphy's crew are shown in this enhanced image waving at a friendly search plane. Seven other crewmen died in the crash. *Courtesy of Dave Deatherage*

Lt. Comstock's Privateer Bureau Number 59553 burning just seconds after crashing near the survivors of Crew 12—there were no survivors among Comstock's crew. *Courtesy of Dave Deatherage*

to COMAF5 was forced to ditch and the crew became stranded. For several days afterward the men waited, and on the twenty-fourth, two officers from AGAS China (Lt. R.C. Scott and 2nd Lt. A. W. C. Naylor-Foote) were parachuted into the area to assist the stranded aviators. Finally, on the twenty-fourth, all were rescued and were returned to Clark Field on 30 June.

July marked a continued decline for tonnage sunk or damaged by 104, with the number falling to 3,000 tons (eighty-one vessels). Therefore land targets, including ground troops, began feeling the brunt of Liberator and Privateer strikes. On 20 July, Lt. (jg) W. G. Bloxham attacked a column of 300–400 Japanese troops with pack horses near Swatow, China.

In the melee that followed (some thirty minutes) countless troops and horses were cut down by strafing and cluster bombing. Bloxham and his crew played havoc again on an enemy troop column of some 1,000 men nine days later west of Macao, China. During five strafing runs the lone patrol bomber wreaked destruction on the enemy. However, this time, the Japanese did not lie down and take the punishment, as they sent up a heavy concentration of small arms fire which wounded navigator Ensign R. E. Smith, who was standing between the pilot and copilot.

On 6 July, Lt. Cdr. H. D. Allen spotted a converted patrol craft anchored close to shore near Hong Kong. The patrol craft commenced firing immediately. On his first run Allen dropped two bombs which did no visible damage. The ship got underway and headed for the open sea. R. G. Friel (AMM3c), the port waist gunner, had his guns jam; determined to get his share of the enemy, he used his .38 revolver on the four runs, expending nine rounds. On the second run three bombs straddled the ship and it stopped dead in the water. Enemy personnel kept up their anti-aircraft fire from guns forward

Lt. Paul Stevens of VPB-104 after receiving news that Japanese Vice Admiral Yamagata was aboard the Emily he intercepted. Stevens would receive the Navy Cross and retired from the Navy as a captain. *Courtesy of Paul Stevens*

and aft on the ship, but did not man the three-inch gun amidships. Two bombs on the third run caused the ship to settle by the bow, but a direct hit by a single bomb dropped on the fourth run blew off the stern and the ship sank stern first.

On 12 July, the first dividends of a new arrangement between ComNavGroup China Coastwatchers and Fleet Air Wing 17 search planes resulted in substantial damage to enemy troops near Amoy. Lt. (jg) A. L. Lindsell was given a target via voice radio by a naval coast watcher in the Amoy area. Led to the target area by means of markers put out by friendly Chinese, he came upon a formation of enemy troops spread along three miles of a mountain trail estimated to be approximately 3,000 troops. Five strafing runs were made, killing many horses and inflicting substantial casualties among enemy personnel.

Retiring for about one-half hour to give the enemy time to reform its ranks, he made another attack from over the top of the mountain, again catching the enemy in formation. This surprise attack also inflicted substantial damage. The following day, the coastwatcher reported to another search plane that among the injured was a Japanese general who was shot in both legs and had his horse killed from under him.

Small, wooden coastal vessel under attack by Lt. (jg) Fletcher's crews during late July–early August 1945 off the Pescadores Islands, Formosa Straight. *Courtesy Emil Buehler Library, NMNA*

A PB4Y-2 Privateer flown by Lt. (jg) George T. Fischer casts its shadow during a strafing attack on a truck in mainland China. He and his crew were late arrivals, serving with VPB-104 beginning in July 1945. *Courtesy Emil Buehler Library, NMNA*

Formosa started getting the attention of VPB-119 as a profitable area for shipping and land targets. On the twenty-seventh, Lt. (jg) H. W. Evans dropped five napalm incendiary clusters on six wooden coastal ships lined up on the beach at Ryukyu Island. Four of the vessels were enveloped in flames, and the fire was spreading to the remaining two when last seen. As this attack was completed a Sally appeared over Takao, headed in the opposite direction. Evans gave chase and was gaining despite the Sally's altitude advantage.

The Sally tried to draw the Privateer over anti-aircraft positions, but the Privateer's pilot elected to avoid them, and by the time he was clear of the anti-aircraft positions the Sally had disappeared. Later in the day two small wooden vessels were sighted a half mile outside Kiirun harbor. Strafing attacks left one of the vessels in flames and the other dead in the water. Fifteen minutes later a large camouflaged 300-ton cargo ship was sighted underway. Having used up all of his bombs Evans made ten strafing runs using 2,700 rounds, setting the ship on fire and destroying it. Shortly thereafter Evans made a strafing run over Suo Harbor, inflicting minor damage on six camouflaged cargo ships and two tugs. The final attack of the day was made on three luggers underway in the Yellow Sea. Three

A PB4Y-2 Privateer from VPB-104 during the last remaining days of the Pacific. The squadron began receiving the Privateer, along with replacement crews, beginning mid-1945. *Courtesy of Bill Woodward*

strafing runs left two of them in flames and the third dead in the water.

By August, even as news of a Japanese surrender filtered down to the men, crews from 104 and 119 continued on patrol. On the fifteenth, Lt. Bloxham, who had decimated enemy ground forces the month before, was on patrol off Formosa when three Tonys and one Oscar attacked him. The fighters made a half-hearted attack with aerial bombs before the attack was broken off. Bloxham then went down to the deck and strafed a small cargo ship. Coming around for a bombing run, a message was received that the war was over. However, squadron aircraft continued to encounter anti-aircraft fire from shore batteries in Hong Kong and Formosa. The last encounter with the Japanese against 104 took place on the twenty-third, when a Privateer flown by Bloxham nearly collided with an enemy cargo plane.

For VPB-119, strikes continued through 14 August, when Lieutenant (jg) S. S. Aichele made the squadron's last kill, a 300-ton cargo vessel. The war had finally come to an end in the Pacific, and thus ends the story of the Clark Field squadrons. Two squadrons flying different aircraft but engaging in the same mission of armed reconnaissance rode the war out together. While 104 and 119 fought the Japanese from Clark Field, three similar squadrons were fighting their war from Palawan.

VPB-119 lost twenty-one officers and fifty-two enlisted men March–June 1945; many of them were veterans of VB-106, including Lt.Cdr. Raymond Bales and most of his crew.

VPB-104's Crew 27 celebrating atop their Privateer upon hearing news of Japan's surrender. *Courtesy of Bill Woodward*

7

The Palawan Squadrons
April–August 1945

In April, another base for Liberator and Privateer operations was established on Palawan. The first squadron to arrive was VPB-111, with VPB-109 coming within two weeks and 106 arriving by the first week of May.

The island is the fifth largest in the Philippine Archipelago, lying between the China and Sulu Seas, and extends 270 miles northeast to southwest, reaching a maximum width of twenty-four miles. Gen. McArthur wanted Palawan as a base to extend air power to the South China Sea and the Dutch East Indies, and on 28 February 1945, the 41st Division's 186th Regimental Combat Team went ashore and secured the island by 22 April. Even before it was wrestled from Japanese hands Navy Liberator operations had begun at Westbrook Field.

Westbrook Field's 5,000-foot runway—part Marston mat, part unrolled coral—was extremely narrow (not more than one hundred feet wide) and did not stand up under the constant traffic of Army B-24s, B25s, and P-38s. The airfield had been built by American POWs. When it was nearly completed, the Japanese herded more than one hundred of the prisoners into an air raid shelter, poured gasoline on them, lit it, and shot down anyone trying to escape the inferno. There were only a handful of survivors.

Now the airfield was in Allied hands. With only one entrance to the taxi lane from the strip, all landings were made downwind to alleviate taxiing back the full length of the strip. The field was closed from sunset to sunrise, and late-returning planes landed only with special permission and after considerable delay. Fully loaded, a Liberator or Privateer could just stagger off the runway.

The living area for PB4Y squadrons was on an abandoned coconut plantation. Tents were the primary habitat, with constant vehicle traffic leaving a fine coat of dust on the dwellings. For the first couple months squadron personnel lived in canvas tents, which invariably leaked during frequent rain showers; by June the tents were replaced by corrugated tin Quonset huts.

Operationally, search sectors from Palawan varied 850–1,000 miles in length, covering the west coast of the Celebes, eastern and western Borneo, the coast of Malay from Singapore to the Gulf of Siam, and south to Indo-China (Vietnam). VPB-111 began operations on 15 April, with seven Liberators fanning out across the South China Sea. Five of the seven search planes made contact with the enemy, with four merchant ships with tonnage ranging 200–7,000 tons being sunk or damaged.

Three days later VPB-111 had its first operational loss when a Liberator flown by Lt. William E. Bartlett Jr. lost an engine on take-off. He came back around for an emergency landing but another engine failed. As the bomber touched down a main tire blew and the plane swerved into a bomb crater, shearing off the landing gear and starboard wing. The fuel tanks ruptured and the plane exploded, killing the entire crew. Two months later a similar fate would take another VPB-111 crew. The loss of the crew coincided with a change of command for the squadron, as Lt. Cdr. Gordon R. Egbert took over from Cdr. Barry. Bud Mills recalled: "On 4 April 1945, VPB-111 found itself with a new 'Skipper,' Lt.Cdr. G. R. Egbert, and on the fifth we were told that we would be moving from Tacloban,

VPB-106's PB4Y-2 Privateer *The Super Chief*, Bureau Number 59400. *Author's Collection*

VPB-111 Crew 14 at West Field, Tinian, Mariana Islands, in December 1944, next to PB4Y-1 Bureau Number 38834. Standing (L to R): (PPC) Lt. W. E. Bartlett; Ens. H. Lee; Ens. F. L. McLean; W. F. Karls, AMM1c; and G. P. Ohligschlager, AMM2c. Kneeling (L to R): J. E. Rinkavage, AOM3c; B. G. Phillips, AMM3c; J. R. Harvester, ARM2c; J. L. Harney, ARM3c; and B. G. Thomas, AMM3c. Lt. Bartlett and this crew were credited with one half of an air-to-air shoot down of a Japanese Betty around noon on 11 December 1944. Lt.Cdr. Bland and Crew 2 were credited with the other half Betty. *Courtesy of Peter Bresciano*

Men of VPB-111 in attendance at the funeral of Lt. William E. Bartlett and Second Radioman ARM3/c James R. Harvester Jr., two of nine crewmembers who died on 19 April 1945, from injuries sustained in the crash. *Courtesy of Peter Bresciano*

Louis "Louie" Bresciano on Palawan Island. Enlisting at age thirty-three, Louie went off to war leaving a wife, two small sons, and a successful cobbler business in Greenfield, Massachusetts. A third son was born six months before he returned from the Pacific. That's what happens when you're stationed so close to home at Quonset Point, Rhode Island, before shipping out for the Pacific. He was a Seaman First Class until the later part of the war, becoming a AMM3/c while at Palawan with VPB-111. Louie was one of a very few squadron members who served with VB-111 and VPB-111 for almost eighteen months continuously. *Courtesy of Peter Bresciano*

Leyte, to the Army Airfield on Palawan Island, Philippines. Our search area became the South China Sea, the west coast of Borneo, Indo-China, Malaya, and Singapore. During 2 February 1945–12 April 1945, our Liberator *Reputation Cloudy* was down for maintenance, needing new engines and her guns replaced. With *Reputation Cloudy* back after extensive maintenance we were back on patrol and were seldom flying over fifteen hundred feet—the cloud base in the South China Sea—and our patrols were back to every third day.[1]

Reputation Cloudy

"With the move to Palawan, we were now on the same airfield with the Army B-24's "Skull and Cross Bones" Squadron, and still supporting them by dropping leaflets as called for. With new engines *Reputation Cloudy* was able to give us a 14.4 hour flight, and as such we were able to sink a ship off the coast of Malaya. Two days later she gave us 13.4 hours, and on a river on the west coast of Borneo we got a bigger boat. We ended the month by bombing a radar station on the east coast of Borneo near Balikpapan, and while we were there we took a look up the river and got two ships, a FTB and a Sugar Baker. On 20 April 1945, our plane [#38906] was on 'stand-by' duty. Another crew, whose aircraft was in for repairs, took our plane *Reputation Cloudy* on patrol, and while on patrol it was severely damaged by anti-aircraft fire and crashed upon landing. Because of the damage our beloved *Reputation Cloudy* was 'stricken for salvage.'

"Our most productive day was 4 May 1945, as we patrolled along the west coast of Borneo near Pontianak. Our single plane patrol was credited with sinking four ships and badly damaging four others, all the while conducting strafing and bombing operations on other installations. By the middle of the month our crew engaged in strikes on Singapore; Grand Natoena Island; Kuching; Borneo; the airfield at Miri, Borneo; the west coast of the Celebes; and Para-Para in the Makassar Straits, and to think, this was only the twentieth of the month. Our last combat patrol of WWII would be five days later, as on 29 May 1945, CAC #12 was relieved from VPB-111 on Palawan Island, Philippines, and ordered to return to the States."[3]

Second Combat Tour of VPB-109

A week after 111's arrival the Raiders of VPB-109 arrived with their PB4Y-2 Privateers. Now under the leadership of Cdr. George L. Hicks (former executive officer of VB109), the squadron was outfitted with a new weapon—the SWOD Mk-9 "Bat." The system was an air-to-ground radar-guided missile, and encased in a plywood shell was a 1,000-pound general-purpose bomb. A Privateer could carry two of them under each wing, and it was hoped it would be a highly effective weapon against enemy shipping. It was not.

On 23 April, Cdr. Hicks and Lt. Kennedy (both veterans of the squadron's first tour of duty) conducted the squadron's first Bat strike. With each plane carrying one of the weapons under its wing, they headed for Japanese shipping anchored in Balikpapan Harbor, on the southeast coast of Borneo, 700 miles from Palawan.

Lt.Cdr. George L. Hicks' Combat Aircrew One of VPB-109. Standing (L to R): Frank S. Graves, AOM1C; Robert O. Blake, ACRM; Ens. Donald F. Hanselman; Lt.Cdr. George L. Hicks; Ens. William R. Wolfram; and Roger W. Clemons, ACMM. Kneeling (L to R): John E. McClean, AMM3c; George R. McKeeby, AMM3c; Albert E. Binch Jr., ARM3c; John W. Davis, AMM2c; John W. Turner, ART1c; and Herbert M. Winter, AOM3c. *Courtesy of Roy Balke*

Fifteen miles from the harbor a large transport, a 4,000-ton freighter, and five smaller merchant vessels in the 300–850-ton range were sighted. From six miles out and at 10,000 feet both pilots launched a Bat. Both weapons traveled erratically and fell short of their intended targets. Due to the weight of the weapon system the Privateers could not carry a conventional bomb load. Not wishing to try strafing attacks on the shipping, the Privateers headed back to Palawan.

For the next two days Japanese radio and radar stations along the Borneo and Malay coasts provided the most popular bombing targets for squadron planes. As Cdr. Hicks and Lt. Kennedy were attacking Balikpapan Harbor, Lt. (jg) Oscar Braddock destroyed radio stations at Tambelan Island and South Natoena Island. On the twenty-fifth, Lt. Thomas Challis damaged a radio and a radio-radar station on Tambelan Island, while Lt. Joseph Jadin damaged a radio station at Cape Paroepoe. Lt. Floyd Hewitt hit a radar station on Baican Island the following day, and Lt. Robert Vadnais destroyed a lookout station at Djemadja Island. On the twenty-seventh, Lt.Cdr. Bundy damaged lookout towers at Mapoeti Island and Lt. John Keeling, ferreting Balikpapan, damaged a radar tower at Kabaladoea.

The Raiders of VPB-109 continued where they left off at the end of their first tour—anti-shipping sweeps. Lt. Jobe, flying 850 miles down the west coast of Borneo at Brunei Bay, planned to attack a 5,000-ton transport beached off Labuan Island, at the mouth of the bay and used by the Japanese as a flak ship. Using cloud cover at 800 feet in his approach, he dived low over a protective peninsula on Labuan Island and made a bombing run on the flak ship.

Coming in at 150 feet across the ship's starboard beam, the plane received light anti-aircraft fire from a 7.7 mm machine gun and took two small bullet holes to an engine cowling. Crossing over the ship,

A PB4Y-2 Privateer carrying two SWOD Mk-9 "Bats." *Courtesy of the NARA*

Jobe dropped one 250-pound bomb and three 100-pound bombs. The flak ship disappeared under a cloud of smoke and flying debris as the bombs exploded close to the ship's hull.

Continuing the search at 1,000 feet, the copilot spotted a radar station consisting of two buildings at Mukah, on the southwestern Borneo coast. The Privateer descended to 200 feet and made one strafing attack on the installations. Both buildings were left smoking after the Privateer's gunners fired 600 rounds into them. Two hours later Jobe sighted a 100-ton freighter off Temadjoe Island. His gunners left it smoking and dead in the water after strafing it with 3,800 rounds of ammunition. Four crewmembers abandoned ship by jumping into the water, only to become the targets of the Privateer's gunners. A short burst from the plane's starboard gun turret quickly killed the men.

Fifty minutes after leaving the damaged freighter, the navigator spotted a small 30-ton cargo boat off Pandjang from the astrodome. The boat was moving slowly as the Privateer circled from 400 feet. Aiming at the boat's water line, Lt. Jobe's gunners sank the vessel within minutes.

Not content with leaving a damaged freighter, Lt. Jobe returned to it and circled eight times as his gunners strafed it with 400 rounds of ammunition. Running short on fuel and ammunition, he finally broke off the engagement without sinking the ship.

On the twenty-eighth, in the early afternoon, Cdr. Hicks and Lt. Donald Chay, each plane carrying two Bats, made another shipping strike at Balikpapan Harbor. Picking out a large transport at anchor in the harbor, a Bat was released nine miles from the target and from an altitude of 10,500 feet. Hick's Bat traveled true, but struck an 800-ton freighter tied up to a dock at the Pandanseki oil refinery a mile short of the transport. He tried to release the second missile, but it malfunctioned electronically and was not released.

Lt. Chay targeted the same transport and released his Bat. The weapon locked on to a small 100-ton picket boat at anchor for a direct hit and the ship was sunk. Releasing his second Bat at the same altitude from seven miles away, it made a forty-five degree turn and followed a larger radar blip of the Pandanseki oil refinery

and scored a direct hit on a large oil storage tank three miles short of its intended target.

Lt. Clifton Davis, while searching the northeastern Malay coast in the early afternoon, was at 1,500 feet when his copilot spotted an eighty foot tug boat three miles away at a speed of eight knots. Lt. Davis reduced his altitude to one hundred feet and circled wide in a power glide. During the first of three strafing runs the tug was set afire before sinking rapidly by the stern, and personnel abandoning ship were strafed in the water, leaving no survivors.

Continuing his patrol along the coast to the north off at seventy feet, the starboard turret gunner sighted a 100-ton picket boat camouflaged with vegetation and its deck loaded with fuel drums. After two strafing runs Lt. Davis initiated a bombing run and dropped three 100-pound bombs along the length of the ship. All bombs missed, but the ship was left afire and moving erratically from the strafing attacks.

After only a week at Palawan, it was obvious that no worthwhile shipping was in the routine search areas to warrant Bat attacks. Having been sunk or driven into areas beyond the range of squadron aircraft, the only possible targets for such attacks were against landlocked ships that presented problems because of the weapon's target selectivity.

Bat tactics were not successful because of the weapon's difficulty detecting the exact target from long range and when there were multiple radar targets at the same range. The device would automatically shift its homing to the best target at the set range. It was also apparent that the only shipping left were small, mostly wooden-hulled coastal vessels (70–100 tons) which hugged the Malay and Borneo coasts. Borneo, which had supplied Japan's military with forty percent of its oil, was rapidly being cut off by Allied air and naval forces, and on 1 May, the invasion of Borneo began with landings by the Australian 7th and 9th Infantry Divisions at Tarakan Island, on the northeastern coast.

In the early afternoon of 1 May, Lt. (jg) George Serbin, covering the eastern Malayan coast from Merchang to Kota Bharu, sighted

Close-up of the plywood constructed SWOD Mk-9 "Bat" guided bomb during testing in the United States. *Courtesy of the NARA*

Lt. Leo E. Kennedy (center, PPC), copilot/navigator Lt. (jg) James D. Marshall, and copilot/navigator Ensign William E. Wassmer of VPB-109 Crew 10 discussing an upcoming mission circa April–May 1945. Kennedy was killed in action on 30 May. *Courtesy of the NARA*

A shipyard in Pontianak, Borneo, became the focus of VPB-109 Privateers 3–5 May 1945. This image taken by a member of Lt. Joe Jobe's crew shows the devastation caused by bombs and machine gun fire. *Courtesy of the NARA*

Serbin pulled up to port, turning inside the Dinah. As the planes met head on Serbin's bow turret gunner opened fire at 150 feet and hit the Dinah's port engine nacelle, drawing smoke. As the planes passed each other the Privateer's number one top turret gunner opened fire with his MK-18 sight set at forty feet, scoring hits on the Dinah's nose and starboard engine nacelle. It began to smoke, and then the Privateer's number two top turret gunner raked the entire length of the Dinah's fuselage. As the Dinah went past his position, the port waist turret gunner concentrated on the Dinah's port engine as the tail turret gunner raked the cockpit. The Dinah's bomb bay doors opened and a 500-pound bomb was jettisoned just as it dove straight into the sea and exploded.

Having completed a 360 degree turn after the destruction of the Dinah, Lt. Serbin turned toward the Jake, which was moving in to look at the remains of the Dinah. The Privateer was at 500 feet and the Jake at 350 feet; as the PB4Y-2 began the chase, the

Lt. (jg) George Serbin's Crew 17 of VPB-109 shot down two Japanese aircraft on 1 May 1945. Standing (L to R): William M. Goreham, ARM2c; Alton N. Druse, AMM3c; Ens. Charles A. Nemish; Lt. (jg) George Serbin; Lt. (jg) Marshall; and Dallas N. Vickers, ARM2c. Kneeling (L to R): Michael J. Scully, AOM3c; Donald S. Ball, AMM3c; James R. Asher, ARM3c; Richard M. Snedeker, AMM2c; and Bernard H. Hornish, AOM3c (Jack D. Tenney, AMM1c, not present). *Courtesy of Roy Balke*

seven freighters at anchor off Redang Island and some other shipping beyond (shortly identified as one destroyer and one escort). Selecting a freighter as a target, at 500 feet Lt. Serbin was about to initiate a bombing run when his port waist gunner sighted a Dinah belonging to the 74th Independent Flying Platoon six miles away at 1,200 feet.[4] Serbin abandoned the bombing run in favor of attacking the Dinah, which had now closed to three miles away and was on a collision course with the Privateer. As he was turning toward the Dinah he sighted a Jake seven miles away over Redang Island.

Lt. George Serbin's gunners aboard a VPB-109 Privateer intercepting a Japanese Jake float plane piloted by Ensign Shigeru Yumura of the 936 Ku on 2 May 1945. *Courtesy of the NARA*

Jake jinked once or twice and then ran, firing out of range with its 7.7 mm machine guns.

The Privateer rapidly overhauled the Jake (belonging to the 936 Ku) and the bow turret gunner fired one burst out of range, then held his fire until the Jake was but 300 feet away. He opened up, hitting the wing roots and both sides of the fuselage. Lt. Serbin chopped the throttles back as he caught and passed over the Jake, which was already afire. As the PB4Y-2 passed the Jake pulled up, and the number one top turret guns raked its port fuselage as the number two top turret guns scored hits along the fuselage and floats, and the starboard waist gunner concentrated on the cockpit and engine fuselage.

Stalling out, the Jake plunged straight into the sea in a vertical dive. As the plane hit the water the parachute of the rear gunner streamed, but was pulled under with the wreckage. Both encounters with Japanese planes had taken less than seven minutes. Short on fuel, Lt. Serbin left the area despite the presence of shipping he had spotted earlier off Redang Island.

Meanwhile, Lt. Chay had searched 900 miles down the Celebes coast before returning up the eastern coast of Borneo to Makassar Harbor. His search was negative until now. In the harbor he found two 100-ton freighters, a 300–800 ton freighter, a 4,000-ton transport, and a destroyer escort camouflaged and tied up to a pier.

Selecting one of the small freighters as a target, Chay made three runs over the ship at one hundred feet. While his gunners laid down suppressing fire on the ship's gun crew during the runs and silenced one 20 mm gun, Chay dropped a pair of 100-pound napalm and general-purpose bombs. The second napalm was a direct hit and the ship was left afire. Upon completion of the second attack, and while withdrawing from the target, the plane took hits from anti-aircraft fire. One 20 millimeter round hit the starboard wing and flap, then exploded inside the wing. Another hit the nose wheel compartment and exploded inside.

The absence of worthwhile targets caused some VPB-109 pilots to extend their search sectors. Lt. Vadnais extended his

search along the west coast of Borneo to investigate Pontianak Harbors, an extension that proved to be a gunners' field day when he found a series of shipyards and newly completed coastal freighters at Pontianak, Borneo.

Following a marked ship channel from Pontianak Bay and leading up the Kapoeas-Kegil River, the pilot sighted two coastals in a stream at anchor a half mile away on his starboard and a mile below the town. He immediately initiated a run on the ships at fifty feet and dropped one AN-47-A2 depth bomb. The bomb missed, but after completing two more runs on the ships one of them burned to the waterline, and his gunner's strafing decimated personnel abandoning the ships. Circling to starboard upon completion of the run and passing over a shipyard and lumberyard on the north bank of the river, he sighted more shipping upstream.

The Privateer headed upstream twenty feet off the water, strafing a two-masted sixty-foot schooner and setting it ablaze. As it passed shipyards were observed along the north bank, with numerous shipping around the intersection of the river and a canal. Two coastals at anchor near the intersection were attacked and left afire from heavy strafing.

Continuing upstream past two shipyards on the north bank and seven coastals anchored farther upstream, Lt. Vadnais made figure eight runs over the area for the next half hour. A shipyard just west of the intersection and containing four ways, each with a coastal, was set afire by bombing and strafing and was destroyed. Six power launches tied up at the yard blazed from strafing, burned to the water line, and sank. Farther upstream one large shipyard upstream from the intersection was heavily and repeatedly strafed during five runs, and an ensuing fire consumed a quarter of the yard and installations before the plane left the area.

The plane returned to the river and canal intersection to attack three coastals anchored in the stream. During five strafing runs his gunners started fires that gutted and sank all three ships. Shortage of fuel and ammunition forced Lt. Vadnais to break off the attack, despite leaving an estimated twenty-five coastals and two more shipyards untouched.

May 5 proved a costly day for VPB-109, when Lt.Cdr. Bundy started for Pontianak, delaying the strike at Jesselton Field along the coast en route. After making a strafing run on an airfield near Papar, Borneo, Bundy followed railroad tracks at 200 feet and flew over a bridge that had AA guns guarding it. The guns opened fire and the plane was hit, critically wounding Bundy. Copilot Ensign Leslie F. Hunt and Lt. Ted Steele, the squadron's intelligence officer, were superficially wounded. Hunt immediately took control and headed for home.

Because the hydraulics had been shot out, plane captain Alvin O'Brien activated the plane's emergency system by rigging a parachute to help stop the plane as it landed back at Palawan. On a separate mission Lt. Turner, preparing to attack shipping at

Aftermath of a VPB-109 raid on a Japanese airbase by Lt. Cdr. Bundy and Lt. Kennedy.

Parepare Bay, in the Celebes, also encountered accurate anti-aircraft fire that killed his plane captain, Joe W. Kasperlik.

VPB-106 Wolverators on Palawan

The following day the squadron was relieved by VPB-106 and ordered to Okinawa. From their new base, the Raiders would venture to the Japanese mainland in search of large shipping. They would find it, and in the process lose an entire crew. For the remaining months of the war on Palawan, 106 and 111 would team up on several occasions for strikes against the Japanese in the Far East, destroying shipping, transportation, and ground installations. Reconnaissance proved to make up the majority of missions due to the upcoming invasion of Borneo scheduled for June and July under code names Oboe 6 and Oboe 2.

As will be discussed later, VPB-106 served in the Central Pacific beginning in February, and had suffered the loss of an entire crew. The squadron had undergone a transformation in name and aircraft flown since its reformation in September 1944. They were no longer nicknamed Hayward's Hellions (in honor of its first commanding officer) and flying the PB4Y-1 Liberator; they were now called the Wolverators and were flying the PB4Y-2 Privateer under the leadership of Commander Sampson.

For some of 106's personnel Palawan would become their last home; they would never see the end of the war. For 111, May brought relief for combat veteran crews, as the rotation system went into full swing. Five veteran crews were relieved by the end of the month, and by June, most of VPB-111's original flight crews would be gone, including Gordon Forbes, a patrol plane commander who would later write a fictional account of the squadron. The squadrons began pairing up for strikes beginning on the thirteenth, and on the sixteenth Wolverator Lt. J. M. Barlow conducted a shipping strike with a Liberator from 111.

The last week of the month saw the Navy squadrons take up snooper missions to Singapore as they played the role of intelligence gatherers. On 23 May, VPB-106's Lt.Cdr. G. C. Goodloe made the first close inspection and photographic reconnaissance of the Singapore area and came back with valuable intelligence on military installations on the island. Several cruisers were sighted, in addition to a harbor full of merchant shipping. The two warships would become the center of attention for Navy patrol squadrons in the weeks to come.

Not wanting to leave the area without a token visit, Goodloe dropped a string of bombs from 9,500 feet. Visits were made four more times during the month by each of the Navy bombing squadrons based in the Philippines. For the first 106 crew to make the initial inspection, they would be lost on a similar mission in July.

Back on Palawan, life continued as it did on many advance airbases. USO shows sometimes found their way to Westbrook Field, there were nightly poker games, there were excursions to the main islands, and several times it was subjected to token enemy air attacks. The bombings did not cause any casualties, but did interfere with sleep. Something had to be done.

Reports on enemy airplane activity at Sandakan Airfield in northern Borneo resulted in a retaliatory strike by the two Navy squadrons. On 28 May, a mission involving two Privateers from 106 (Cdr. Mears and Lt. T. W. Jones), two Liberators from 111 (Lt.Cdr. Albert Ellingson and Lt. William "Chief" Bender), and six PV-1 Venturas from VPB-128 hit the airfield.

Carrying four 1,000-pound bombs each, the two PB4Y squadrons plastered the airfield from 600 feet while the Venturas went in lower, bombing and strafing. There was not much left of the Sandakan airstrip when they were finished. There were no more Japanese air raids on Palawan. Soon baseball fields were built and nightly movies at an outdoor theater became additional sources of relaxation. More importantly, uninterrupted sleep became an escape from the rigors of combat.

Snooping Singapore

On the last day of the month, Lt.Cdr. Goodloe of 106 went on his third mission to Singapore. This time four Oscars and a Zeke intercepted his Privateer, and in the ensuing air battle his gunners managed to damage one fighter without any serious damage to their plane. Unknown to both patrol squadrons, enemy fighters would be waiting the next day for the snooping American planes.

June proved to be a troubling time for both squadrons as reconnaissance missions intensified. The first day of the month brought a special coordinated snooper mission to Singapore involving 106 and 111. A VPB-111 Liberator piloted by Lt. (jg) Fred Heyler carrying an Army photographic specialist and a 106 Wolverator Privateer piloted by Lt. Cdr. "Pappy" Mears took off from Westbrook Field in the pre-dawn hours and headed for Singapore.

In a loose formation, they arrived at the Malay coast after sunrise with Cdr. Mears leading the way. Near Hong Kong they encountered heavy anti-aircraft fire from shore batteries and ships, but it was ineffective and the planes proceeded onward. Soon afterward they saw they had company—two Oscar fighters were trailing them from behind, but did not press in for an attack. Soon another pair in front of the American patrol bombers joined the other two fighters. On board the patrol planes the men manned their guns.

Near Singapore a fighter peeled off and went for Mears, scoring hits with 20-millimeter cannon fire on the Privateer's number three engine. The Oscar broke away, but was hit by Heyler's gunners, and it went down into the water. Mears' men tried to ward off the attack but were unsuccessful. The Privateer's engine caught fire and the plane began to lose altitude. The Oscars came back and went after the damaged bomber, only to be beaten back by Mears' and Heyler's combined firepower.

Mears went on the radio and in a calm voice told Heyler, "I'm afraid I'm going to have to ditch." The Liberator's pilot reduced speed to stay with the crippled PB4Y-2 as Mears prepared for ditching.

A few minutes later the flames appeared to go out and Mears felt better. In fact the fire had not gone out, and was eating away the interior portion of the wing. The fire blossomed again and he told his wingman, "I'm sorry, but I am going to ditch. Thank you for the way you stuck with me." It was his last transmission, as the number four engine went out 1,000 feet above the water. The Privateer banked sharply and the starboard wing broke off between the engines 300 feet from the water. The Privateer flipped on its back and went into the water nose first, killing all on board.[5]

The following are a series of photographs captured by Staff Sgt. George D. Hayball with a K-17 aerial camera while aboard a VPB-111 PB4Y-1 Liberator on 1 June 1945, showing the final minutes of Cdr. Pappy Mears' PB4Y-2 Privateer Bureau Number 59563 before it plunged into the water off Malaya. *All images courtesy of the NARA*

The two planes approach the coast of Malaya with "Pappy" Mears' Privateer in the lead moments before Japanese fighters began their attack against the Privateer.

Flames erupt and trail behind the number three engine after being hit by 20 mm cannon fire from an Oscar fighter two minutes after the attack began.

Smoke pours from the wing's leading edge while Lt. (jg) Heyler tries to keep his Liberator from overrunning the Privateer by using full forty degree flaps and minimum power.

The fire appears to have blown itself out, but close inspection reveals the aluminum skin behind the number three engine is scorched and damaged. Enlarging the image revealed that the top rear gunner and inside the navigator dome another crewman can be seen looking at the damage.

A gap of jagged metal behind the nacelle and the engine's attitude apparently shows the beginning of wing separation.

The Privateer continues losing altitude and is at 3,000 feet as it falls behind the Liberator as smoke reappears.

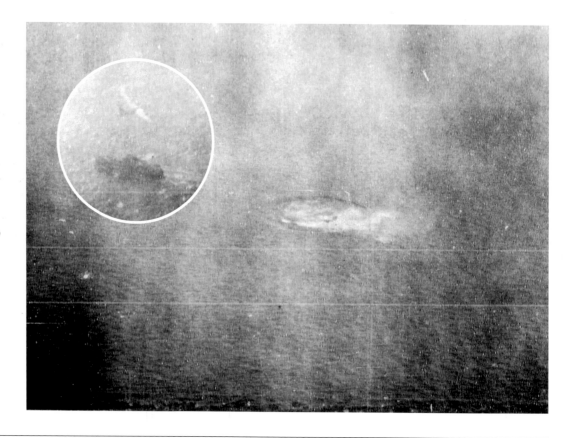

Barely visible from the Liberator due to haze, the Privateer passes over a cargo ship as "Pappy" Mears attempts to ditch the plane; the plane is at 300 feet. A moment later the section of the wing between the starboard engines separates and the Privateer turns over on its back and plunges into the water.

All this time the Oscars kept up their attacks. Seeing the Privateer go down, the Japanese fighter pilots tore into the lone Liberator, and for the next twenty minutes, twenty-eight separate attacks were counted. Heyler and his men fought bravely, turning back every attack without damage to their PB4Y-1. At one point the top turret gunner, Norbert James O'Rourke, ran out of ammunition, and while he fired one gun managed to reload the other gun with his other hand.

One Oscar was hit, then a second. One came within fifty feet and was hit hard by the bow, top, and starboard waist guns. Pieces of the fighter flew off, smoke belched from the engine, and it was not seen again. Heyler and his crew fought on, with the Liberator dodging in and out of cloud cover to break free from the attackers. In all, eight to thirteen enemy fighters pursued the bomber before most became discouraged, ran out of ammunition, or were low on fuel.

After fourteen hours in the air and after a running battle that lasted over an hour from altitudes ranging 11,000–1,000 feet, the Liberator landed at Palawan without any damage to the plane and no injuries to the crew. Heyler was awarded the Navy Cross, while the crew earned the Distinguished Flying Cross.[6]

Lt.Cdr. Egbert of VPB-111, piloting PB4Y-1 Bureau Number 38917, found a camouflaged river steamer along Borneo's east coast on 29 July 1945. It took twelve runs on the ship to finally sink it. *Courtesy of Peter P. Bresciano*

The following four images are of Combat Air Crew 12, led by Lt. Ken LaCount of VPB-111 flying PB4Y-1 *Reputation Cloudy* attacking a Japanese mine layer (first image) and two small freighters called Sugar Dogs. *Courtesy Ron LaCount, son of Ken LaCount*

Men were still being killed serving in VPB-106 and 111, and for what, some asked. A small minority of pilots and aircrews no longer believed in their mission. What was their purpose, they asked? There was not much left of the Japanese military—a few bypassed garrisons, a radio or weather station. Why risk lives? However, the majority still believed in the cause of total victory and felt they were playing an important part toward this goal. They continued to fly day after day and onward toward victory. While Navy Liberator and Privateer squadrons were fighting the Japanese in the Southwest Pacific, other such units in the Central Pacific were taking the war all the way to Japan.

Operational mishaps and the disappearance of an aircraft and its crew were the saga for VPB-111 13–20 June. On the sixteenth, Lt. (jg) Lou Bass went on patrol down the Makassar Straits and never returned—he and his crew just disappeared. On his first patrol, Lt. (jg) W. C. Brand ran out of fuel and was forced to ditch his Liberator in the Balabac Strait on the thirteenth. Nobody was hurt, but the plane was a total loss.[5] In the early morning of the twentieth, a PB4Y-1 raced down the wet airstrip at full power and crashed in the shallow water of the Sulu Sea. For one of the men killed (Lt. (jg) L. I. Israel) it was his first flight with the squadron—he had arrived only three days earlier.[6]

By late summer 1945, the Southwest Pacific had become the backwater of the Pacific War, with some men wondering if it was worth continuing risking their lives. The Philippines had been liberated and Okinawa vanquished. There were no more grand invasions, only armed reconnaissance missions to places like Singapore and Hong Kong to check on phantom movements of the Imperial Japanese Navy, which no longer existed. In the distance the invasion of Japan loomed ahead.

Lt.Cdr. Egbert standing by his aircraft 59876 *Lillie*. Note "The Boss" painted below the pilot's side window. *Courtesy of Peter Bresciano*

PB4Y-2 Privateer Bureau Number 59786 crewed by replacement Combat Air Crew One piloted by the VPB-111's "Skipper," Lt.Cdr. Egbert, who took over from Cdr. Barry in April 1945. The aircraft is parked on the ramp at Puerto Princesa Airfield, Palawan, PI. *Courtesy of Peter Bresciano*

8

Operations in the Central Pacific
October 1944–August 1945

By fall 1944, two Navy Liberator squadrons were stationed in the Central Pacific: VPB-102 and VPB-116. They were left on Tinian to continue strikes against the Japanese, mainly around Iwo Jima and the Bonin Islands, with occasional forays to bypassed islands in the Carolines and Marshalls. Both squadrons had suffered operational and combat losses since commissioning, with several crews being lost August–September 1944.

On 4 October, VPB-117 arrived at West Field, Tinian, under the command of Cdr. E. O. Rigsbee Jr. Both 116 and 117 would share the nickname the "Blue Raiders." For Rigsbee's group, they would become one of the finest PB4-Y squadrons in the Pacific and would be awarded the Presidential Unit Citation. In the months to come these squadrons and others like them would be used for long-range screening for the 3rd and 5th Fleets.

"Bud" Mills of VPB-111, who would shoot down two enemy aircraft while based in the Philippines during 1945, recalled the squadron's first base of operations upon arrival on 1 December 1944:

"By 1 December, we had moved to our forward operating location on the island of Tinian, in the Marianas, and proceeded to conduct combat operations on a daily basis. On Tinian was where the majority of the squadron's Liberators received their nose art. Our new assigned task was to conduct long-range reconnaissance in assigned areas over the Pacific and to prevent the undetected approach of the Japanese and destroy their shipping. We flew mostly single aircraft patrols, but on occasion we flew paired up. Mostly though we flew single ship sorties. In the Western Pacific and South China Sea the cloud coverage was usually 1,500–2,500 feet, so off came the oxygen masks, tanks, and other related equipment that made combat more difficult. Being able to move about more freely made for a much more tolerable flight, especially when they lasted over twelve hours. From our base on Tinian our search was usually North to Iwo-Jima and Chichi-Jima, an area where former President Bush's aircraft was shot down. We also flew south to Peleliu, in the Palau group of islands, where we were screening for the Pacific Fleet of Adm. 'Bull' Halsey. From mid-January, our orders were to

screen fleet movements from Tinian to Leyte, in the Philippines, then on down to Morotai, in the Dutch East Indies.[1]

"Every day crews took off on 600–1,100 mile searches north and west of Tinian. Increasingly, small shipping and enemy aircraft were encountered near Iwo Jima and the Bonin Islands. The Japanese were in the process of strengthening their position on Iwo Jima at the expense of Chichi Jima and Haha Jima by sending convoys of small ships—a junior version of the Tokyo Express. Most of the ships were slow, with an average speed of ten knots, weighing 70–100 tons, and were built of wood. Additionally, the Japanese sent out reconnaissance aircraft and stationed picket boats—these heavily armed vessels had to be destroyed."

The danger of attacking picket boats was illustrated on 4 October, when a VPB-116 Blue Raider Liberator flown by Lt. C. P. Cervone

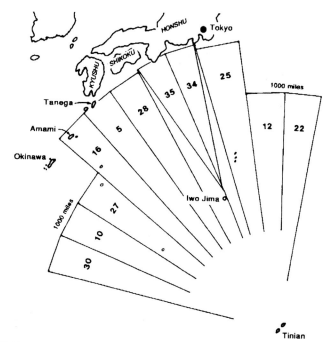

PB4Y Operations from Tinian during late 1944.

The Reluctant Dragon's Cdr. G. Russell "Pappy" Pearson stands beside Lt. Frank Burton's PB4Y-1 Liberator. *Courtesy of Navy Patrol Bombing Squadrons 102/14 Associations*

spotted one in the Philippine Sea. S. O. Melby, manning the port waist gun, spotted the ship through a break in the heavy clouds three miles away. Cervone circled, lowering altitude, as he closed in on the armed quarry. The ship spotted the Liberator and turned toward the potential attacker.

The Liberator's pilot descended to 400 feet and went in for an attack, only to be met by intense anti-aircraft fire. The rounds of

12.7 mm machine gun fire did not stop Cervone from continuing, even as his aircraft took hits. The first bombs missed and Cervone came around for another run. Closing in, F. X. Muth, ARM2c, looking through the bombardier's window below the bow turret, was hit in the face and shoulder by a 12.7 mm round. Unable to speak, Muth banged on the bow turret's hatch. The gunner, J. H. Bell, saw his wounded comrade and reported the man's condition. L. A. McCarthy, the plane captain, rushed to the crewmember's side, but there was no first aid kit and he had to rip a piece from a parachute to apply pressure on the wounds to stop the flow of blood. Muth went into shock after losing a considerable amount of blood. Cervone had to break off the attack and get the wounded man home. The trip back took six hours, and it was very doubtful the man would live, but through McCarthy's aid Muth did survive.

Combined Effort

A few days later two planes from VPB-102 and another pair from VPB-116 were sent out to look for and destroy a picket boat the Japanese had stationed some 1,000 miles from Tinian. Wayne Rorman, a member of 102, recalls the search:

"We were to leave on this mission early on the morning of 10 October 1944. It was a very big ocean out there and we were to seek out a relatively small ship. It could prove to be a long and difficult day. Our navigators would need to be accurate, as fuel consumption would be very important to our survival on such a long mission.

"Our planes were to communicate on VHF, and we were to fly wing on Lt. Jolly, who was also our executive officer. We planned to remain together until we reached the area of the ship. Then we would split up for our coordinated search. Lt. Jolly chose to carry two 500-pound bombs, while I chose to carry five 250 pounders (similar loads).

"We all took off at our scheduled departure time of 5 a.m. Our entire crew was really on edge, as this was our first attack on an enemy ship and the first time we were experiencing enemy return fire. We would certainly know more about ourselves at the end of this flight.

Outdoor movie theater on Tinian. *Courtesy of the VPB-117 Association*

Personnel from VPB-117 working on a PB4Y-1 bow turret. *Courtesy of the VPB-117 Association*

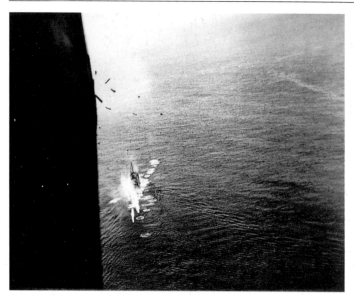

A Japanese lugger being strafed by Lt. John Adams of VPB-117. *Courtesy of the NARA*

Attack on Japanese shipping by VPB-117's Lt. G. B Squires. *Courtesy of the NARA*

"Just as we were about to turn on our cross leg, nearly 1,000 miles from base, we sighted the picket boat at the given position. It had apparently already sighted us, because they increased their speed to make it more difficult for our expected attack. The picket boat was approximately 150 feet long and thirty feet wide. We sighted a cannon on the bow of the ship and what looked to us to be several 20 mm guns and numerous smaller caliber machine guns along the sides of the deck.

"I called the planes from VPB-116 on VHF and they immediately headed to join us. Lt. Jolly and I prepared to make our attacks. We could not afford to wait for the 116 pilots to arrive because they might be delayed locating us and fuel would develop into a problem.

"We set up two 250-pound bombs with a fifty-foot spread. Tom Colley settled into his tail turret, while Dore and Smith manned the side guns and camera. Price stood by on the radio while Vince DeSousa opened the bomb bay doors and jumped the limit switch to make sure the bombs would drop. Ken Thoman in his bow turret and Lester Mumme in his deck turret opened fire with their .50-caliber machine guns. The muzzle blast from the deck turret jarred things off the cockpit ceiling. We were not prepared for this. We released our bomb and there was no skip; the bomb had fallen short. We were possibly a bit higher than we should have been at release point. We had more bombs left. We would drop one at a time until we had worked out our run. We certainly hoped the picket boat gunners were also having trouble with accuracy.

Some of the officers of VPB-117 from left to right: Sutton, Loesel, Studebaker, Currin, Sager, Long, and Golden. *Courtesy of VPB-117 Association*

Lt. Glenn Box of VPB-117 closes in on a Japanese Emily flying boat on 31 October 1944. *Courtesy of the NARA*

Fifty-caliber machine gun fire from the PB4Y-1 splashes around the Japanese flying boat. *Courtesy of the VPB-117 Association*

Smoke from the Emily's engine appears shortly before it crashes. *Courtesy of the NARA*

"Immediately after our first run Lt. Jolly made his attack. He set up two 500-pound bombs with the usual spread and started his run. The picket boat was still facing us and was not turned into Jolly's attack. He made a beautiful drop. There was a near miss, with one bomb exploding alongside the ship. His other bomb hung up and failed to release. They returned to altitude to stand by while we made our second run. The return fire from the ship was moderate. We circled, climbing higher to gain more speed. We set up one more 250-pound bomb. Here we go again!

"The deck guns sure did rattle our compartment. Thoman's guns were blazing. The return fire from the picket boat was moderate, but suddenly seemed much more real and threatening than it had when it was Lt. Jolly being fired at. Apparently our guns were doing their job. During our approach I saw a man on the deck of the ship that seemed to be picked up and thrown across the deck. I suddenly realized this attack involved real people; not just a ship made of wood and steel. We pulled up to clear the ship and released our bombs at the same moment. Again, the bomb did not skip and dug in short, but this time it exploded close enough to shake the ship.

"As we were circling for position we realized our bow guns were still firing every 10–20 seconds. Because the guns were overheated the shells were 'cooking off.' These shells firing before they were locked into the barrel caused the burned powder fumes to end up in the turret, causing problems for the gunner. We set up another 250-pound bomb. This drop was close and shook the boat again, but it was still alive and making knots. We found the return fire to be even less than before.

"Our set up was the same, but again, we gained altitude to give us more speed in our dive. We felt the last bomb had exploded under the ship, but the ship was still there; alive, only not quite so active.

The end of the chase as the Emily hits the water. *Courtesy of VPB-117 Association*

A ball of fire and smoke rises from the scene of the Emily's destruction. *Courtesy of VPB-117 Association*

There was also an oil slick showing. Thoman's guns continued to pop off. The picket boat continued to make headway! Again, we climbed back up to bombing altitude and started to circle the picket boat, preparing for our fifth and last run. The ship continued to fire at us using their three-inch guns and managed to keep the bow of the ship pointed at us as we circled.

"At this moment the two planes from VPB-116 arrived low on the water, coming in from the back of the picket boat. I do not believe they realized there were four B-24s involved in this attack until those two planes laid down their string of bombs. These bombs did not make a direct hit, but exploded right alongside the ship. Thoman remembers seeing the ship raise right out of the water on a wall of water and then settle back down again. Despite this the picket boat continued to move along in the water.

"At this point the other three B-24s in our team indicated their fuel supply was getting low and they needed to head back to base. I felt we could observe a bit longer. They all left, expressing concerns about their limited supply of fuel. This began to concern me. Had I calculated wrong? Were we also low?

"Within fifteen to twenty minutes, while we were still observing, the picket boat gave its last gasp, rose up on end, and sank. It was just like you saw in the movies. We were not able to get pictures of this event because we had used up all of our film early in the attack. We learned a good lesson about photography—close in and hold some film for the finale.

"We immediately climbed to 8,000 feet, set our heading for home, headed in the direction our navigator, Ensign Schuch, gave us, and put her in fast cruise mode. About halfway home we heard the others sweating their gas supply. We suggested we were making good time at altitude, but they felt they did not have the fuel to spare to climb up to altitude.

"Our arrival at Tinian was at least one hour before the VPB-116 planes and three hours before Lt. Jolly. Unfortunately, he had been given an erroneous heading. He spotted this in time to make a correction and they arrived safely, but landed with only vapors left in their fuel tanks. Nevertheless, the vapors were apparently good to the last drop, because they made it in safely.

"Our crew had performed very well, considering this was our first attack flight. Vince got a severe case of the shakes when it was all over, and I am sure everyone suffered some effects from the experience. Schuch had done his job well and we all appreciated that. It had been a long, stressful day [flight time 13.7 hours], but we had accomplished our goal. We had destroyed our target. Upon inspection of the plane we found a bullet hole about two feet below my seat. I wonder why they were mad at me!"[2]

Zekes versus Privateers

On the eleventh, Lt. Stimson of 116 was lost near Iwo Jima. The Japanese fighter group 252 Ku damaged him, but did not see him fall. However, he did not return. The following morning at 0858, 252 Ku was sent up again after radar detected two large planes.

PB4Y-1s *Dazy May* and *Tyn Yan Ty Foon* of VPB-116 were sent out to search for Stimson. Within a few minutes of their arrival near Iwo Jima seven Zeros went up and intercepted them. Several of the attackers dropped phosphorous bombs from above before making their gun runs. The ensuing battle lasted forty-five minutes while the Liberators dropped down to forty feet above the water to prevent the enemy from going under them. The patrol bombers flew together to concentrate their guns on the attacking fighters. One of the fighters, flown by Chief Petty Officer (CPO) Jinro Ishikawa, was hit and he bailed out, but was later rescued. An hour after intercepting the Liberators six Zeros returned to base, with two of the fighters flown by Lt. Shigehiro Nakama and CPO Ushio Nishimura being damaged. Both Liberators returned home relatively undamaged, with only *Dazy May* taking one 12.7 mm machine gun hit. In the after action report VPB-116 claimed to have shot down six of the fighters.[3]

Ensign Boss (front row/far right), wrote about the exploits of VPB-117 in an unpublished work titled, "Blue Monsters." *Courtesy of the VPB117 Association*

Crew 5 commanded by Lt. Glenn Box (middle/front row) that survived a ditching of their Liberator. *Courtesy of the VPB-117 Association*

Unidentified men stand next to VPB-117's PB4Y-1 Liberator Bureau Number 38740 *The Daring Dame* on Tinian circa November–December 1944. *Courtesy of the VPB-117 Association*

Zekes versus Liberators

The next couple days Liberators of VPB-102 struck the Bonin Islands, attacking shipping and shore installations. The fifteenth proved that the Japanese were still quite active in the area. Two Liberators on separate missions tangled with a heavily armed landing ship off Haha Jima, while the other bomber caught a convoy of ships off Kita Iwo Jima and in turn was attacked by two Zekes.

At Haha Jima, Lt. (jg) D. K. Close's bomb bay doors would not open on a bombing run just as every ship in the harbor, as well as shore batteries, opened fire on the Liberator. One round hit the tail turret's ammunition box, touching off a fire among the .50-caliber rounds. Gunner R. E. McCord received first and second degree burns putting the fire out. Then the number-two engine was hit three times while the bomber flew at 500 feet and began leaking gas and oil.

Since the bomb bay would not open, and now flying a damaged aircraft, Close got out of the harbor and began gaining altitude while the crew began throwing everything out of the plane that was not nailed down. The patrol plane commander feathered the engine and headed back to Tinian.

For Crew 11 of the Reluctant Dragons, they lived to fight another day. Earlier in the day, two other crews had a narrow escape off Iwo Jima. Lts. F. O. Burton and W. D. Rorman closed in on the volcanic island at 200 feet and found two ships five miles off the coast. Closing in for the attack, Lt. Burton realized the two ships were heavily armed landing ships. Patrol plane commanders were under orders not to attack such vessels at low altitude, so the Liberators broke off and headed for Kita Iwo Jima.

A small coastal vessel was sighted lying at anchor next to the remains of a similar vessel sunk in another engagement. Lt. Burton bombed and strafed the ship to pieces on the first run and was preparing to deliver his final attack when an enemy fighter was spotted flying toward them one hundred feet off the deck. The Liberators parted company, with each patrol plane commander

heading to opposite ends of the island. Six more coastal vessels were spotted, as were five enemy fighters covering them at 1,200 feet. Burton and Rorman pushed power to full throttle and roared in for the attack despite the presence of enemy planes.

The fighters, now identified as four Zekes and one Hamp, did not interfere with the Liberators' attack until after the second run and after two of the vessels had been severely damaged. The Hamp came in toward Rorman's bomber, only to have the Liberator's bow and top turrets open fire when the fighter was only 500 yards away. Fifty-caliber machine gun rounds found the fuselage of the Hamp; and trailing smoke and losing altitude, the fighter headed toward Iwo Jima. Even during the attacks Burton and Rorman managed to continue attacking the coastals, leaving several sinking. The fighters broke off their attack and the Liberators headed home unmolested.

While combat patrol squadrons were ferreting out the enemy on Guam, the ShutterBugs of VD-4 led by Lt.Cdr. Charles Clark continued with their primary role of aerial photography. On 7 November 1944, the squadron was assigned to cover Iwo Jima to obtain high-resolution photographs before the invasion. Flying at 20,000 feet under the leadership of Clark, the six planes were jumped by ten enemy fighters as they approached the target.

Lt. Richard Mather's Liberator became the focus of an attack by two fighters. Harold Hedberg (ARM2c) damaged one of them, but not before tail turret gunner George Lockos was killed. Mather's plane returned to base with twenty-two holes in the tail section. Meanwhile, the rest of the formation battled the Japanese fighters across the island and out to sea, as three more enemy planes were brought down before the engagement was broken off and the VD-4 Liberators headed back to Guam.

Crew Five Goes Down

On 16 November, a VPB-117 PB4Y-1 commanded by Lt. Glenn Box took off for a routine patrol and reconnaissance of a Japanese-held island; the patrol would not be ordinary or routine. Box had a long background in the regular Navy, serving mostly in the aviation

A Japanese air raid against Tinian on 2 November 1944 damaged *The Daring Dame* beyond repair. *Courtesy of the VPB-117 Association*

branch. He was an old aviation pilot enlisted man who flew and wore Navy wings without a commission. He was also a Mustang—an enlisted man who accepted a commission. Glenn flew for the enjoyment of flying. . .it was his job and his life. Box and crew went out to check out whether a Japanese radar station they had put out of action in a previous engagement was still inoperable.

This time the Japanese were ready and almost blasted the blue Liberator out of the sky. You could walk on the flak and the number one engine stopped. Box lost no time getting out of there and found a hell of a job on his hands. The shell had bent the prop and it would not feather. The engine threatened to vibrate and tear off its mounts. It was a hell of a spot to be in almost 1,000 miles from home and with night coming on. Both pilots held rudder as the drag of the windmilling prop and loss of power added additional towage. Higher power settings had to be used on the other engines and 773 had a hard time maintaining flying speed. It was going to be a tough, long haul home, and Box knew things had to go just right for the remaining fuel to last. No matter what he did the bomber was determined to lose altitude. The crew lightened the ship and everybody prayed.

Night came and Box feared the gas would soon be exhausted and he would have to set her down in the black water. From past experiences on the part of men who had to ditch, a Liberator with no power, at sea, and in the dark was not a pretty picture. A PB4Y was not built to land at sea and showed a tendency to break up upon hitting, trapping men. The best odds showed a fifty-fifty chance that half of the twelve-man crew would survive.

Box called all hands: "Men, we better prepare for ditching. You all know your stations and what equipment you are responsible for. Okay, I'll give the word when and if the time comes. Good luck."

Each member of the crew had his own place to lay and was instructed to brace and pad himself to soften the shock when the plane crashed. In addition, each one had some pertinent survival equipment to take with him. All wore "Mae West" life jackets that immediately inflated when the CO_2 bottle was broken. Life rafts, food, and water were ready to be pressed into immediate use. The crew was ready and knew Lt. Box would effect the best ditching possible under the circumstances.

The bow turret gunner screamed, "I see lights due ahead. Please say I'm right." All eyes that could be brought to look directly ahead strained for those life-giving lights, and sure enough they were there; it was home, as that was all it could possibly be. The base was the only island in more than 700 miles, and there she was. Without warning the Liberator quit her life's blood censured. She plunged downward. Box flew her all the way down and stalled her out just as the waves washed her belly. PB4Y number 773 went in and started toward her watery grave.

It was over in a flash. The three pilots did not know how they got out. The forward section of the flight deck must have torn off and thrown them into the ocean. Box felt a sharp pain in his right

Shrapnel holes in the fuselage show where Rudolph Tonsick (ARM2c) was mortally wounded on 15 December 1944. *Courtesy of the VPB117 Association*

leg, which turned out to be broken. They swam together, realizing they must not be separated again. Box found the copilot; he was stunned and racked with pain. He could not localize it, as his whole body was in torture and agony. His life jacket was torn open and useless. Box held him up, aided by a piece of wreckage.

Other members of the crew swam up. One of them could not stand the suspense before crashing; he had to see how close they were to the water. He had just reached the starboard waist hatch when they hit and was mercifully thrown clear of the plane, suffering no injuries. After a few minutes three more of the crew were located. The radar man was badly injured, and all through the night one of the officers held him up as he slipped in and out of consciousness.

The following day the Reluctant Dragon's commanding officer, Pappy Pearson, was on a routine patrol when he spotted them. He had the crew drop smoke flares and dye marker to mark the spot, circled again, almost touching the water, then dropped a seven-man life raft and reported his position for the rescue. Exhausted after being in the water all night, the men managed to climb into the raft, and several hours later they were picked up by a PBM. Seven men saved and five lost.[4]

Photographic Operations November 1944–August 1945

PB4Y-1Ps of Navy Photographic Squadron Five (VD-5), led by Commander A. D. Fraser, arrived on Guam 15–20 November to replace the "Shutterbugs" of VD-4. Armed photo reconnaissance operations commenced on 25 November, with six PB4Y-1Ps escorted by seven B-24s of the 11th Bombardment Group conducting a mission over Chichi Jima, Haha Jima, and Iwo Jima. November 1944–May 1945, squadron Liberators flew 122 missions and 277 sorties before being relieved by Lt.Cdr. J. C. Hutchison's VD-1 on 18 May 1945. VD-1 continued operations from Guam with advanced echelons conducting reconnaissance missions of the Japanese home islands from Iwo Jima and Okinawa.

Navy Photographic Squadron VD-5 Crew One consisted of (L to R) J. F. Rankin, PheM3c; C. E. Brown, AMM3c; H. M. Rogers, ARM1c; J. A. Carlson, AMM2c; Ens. L. E. Dunlap; Cdr. A. D. Fraser; Lt. (jg) J. R. Roberts; D. A. Bisignano, ARM3c; J. D. Evans, ADM2c; C. T. Carey, AMM1c (not related to the author); and L. J. Bodkin, PhoM1c. *Courtesy of the Tailhook Association via Mahlon Miller*

VD-5 Crew Four consisted of (front row, L to R): J. L. Hawley, PhoM2c; C. C. Greenhoe, PhoM2c; F. R. Marrone, ARM3c; and D. C. DeButts, AMM1c. Back row (L to R): S. A. Norman, AMM2c; Ens. D. R. Sparks; Ens. C. J. Collins; Lt. G. H. Conover; H. R. Kriser, AOM2c; R. C. Bishop, AMM2c; and C. E. Swecker, ARM2c. *Courtesy of the Tailhook Association via Mahlon Miller*

VD-5 Crew Five consisted of (front row, L to R) J. R. Martin, PhoM2c; P. C. Fajardo, ARM3c; N. Lagow, AMM2c; R. A. Hill, AMM1c; Lt. M. R. Cooper; and H. A. Billerback, CPhoM. Unfortunately, at the time of publication the rest of the crew are unknown. *Courtesy of the Tailhook Association via Mahlon Miller*

VD-5 Crew Nine consisted of (front row, L to R) E. J. Moser, ARM1c; G. Dobrowolski, AOM2c; G. R. Rullen, PhoM3c; and B. W. Zukowski, PhoM3c. Seond Row: R. D. Hansen, AMMf1c; A. D. Moti, AMMf2c; D. L. Gibbs, PhoM1c; Ens. O. R. Toon; Lt. C. M. Witt; Lt. (jg) C. H. Hunter; R. A. Trentham, AMMf2c; and J. P. Cotter, ARM3c. *Courtesy of the Tailhook Association via Mahlon Miller*

Maintenance being performed on a VD-5 Erco bow turret.

Loading ammunition in the tail guns of a VD-5 Liberator.

Engine maintenance on a VD-5 Liberator.

Tinsmiths at work on a PB4Y-1.

Admiral Chester Nimitz inspecting photographs at the VD-5 lab. *Courtesy of the NARA*

Riveting a piece of aluminium on to a VD-5 Liberator.

Interior view of the waist section.

A waist gunner aboard a VD-5 Liberator.

9

Tinian Operations
The Arrival of VPB-118 and the PB4Y-2 Privateer
January–June 1945

January 1945 brought the arrival of the Navy's first PB4Y-2 Privateer squadron, with aircraft from VPB-118 landing at Tinian on 6 January. Nicknamed the "Old Crows," like some of her counterparts, the squadron began its life as a PBY-5 squadron under the designation VP-71 and was in the Solomons at the time of VB104's first tour. The commanding officer was Kelly Harper, class of 1934 and former leader of VP-71.[1]

The new aircraft and the amount of fire power and electronics gear they possessed dazzled the men of VPB-102 and 116. They could not wait to trade in their Liberators for the Privateer. However, they would have to wait; "Pappy" Pearson's group would not get a PB4Y-2 until late July.

The Tinian-based squadrons continued searches north and west of Tinian at distances of 600–1,000 miles. For 102, the squadron conducted successful strikes, resulting in the Japanese losing a number of coastal vessels. Although not involved in the more glorious role of carrier-based strikes or the strategic bombing of Japan by B29s, the Navy Liberator and Privateer squadrons played a valuable role. They were able to reduce the amount of equipment and manpower sent to reinforce Iwo Jima and to block Japan's capability of communicating American fleet movements with the destruction of picket boats.

Two Privateers flown by Lts. Farwell and Serrill conducted the first patrol for 118 on 13 January. The 1,000-mile search was routine. The dry spell ended for 118 on 23 January, when Lt. Binning and crew heavily damaged a 300-ton cargo ship off the Bonin Islands.

In contrast to the month before, when there were few enemy contacts made, February was a busy operational month, with the Tinian squadrons running reconnaissance missions to Truk and Marcus Island to check for signs of Japanese movements during the invasion of Iwo Jima. Picket boats that plowed the waters off Japan to alert the mainland of impending B-29 raids also continued to be targets of Navy patrol squadrons. In addition, the squadrons were assigned barrier patrols for Task Force 51, which was heading for Iwo Jima. Later in the month Liberators and Privateers would be

Cdr. Cecil Kelly Harper and Combat Aircrew One of VPB-118—assembled by Bureau Number 59404 *Pirate Princess*—consisted of (back row, L to R): Charles L. Eberle, ACMM; Lt. (jg) Charles R. Peterson; Cdr. Cecil K. Harper; Lt. John M. Eaton Jr.; and Tom (?). Front row (L to R): Harry F. Owens, ARM2c; Robert W. Wilson, ARM3c; Leslie E. Levie, AOM3c; (?) Bull; Vern A. Amick, AMM3c; Robert M. Gerhard, AMM3c; and Thomas L. Kelecy, ACRM. Note: Two men identified as crewmembers are named Harold A. Taylor, AMM3c, and Theodore J. Wilson, ACOM. *Courtesy of Richard Peterson*

assigned to screening missions for Task Force 58 before its first strike on the Japanese mainland.

On the first day, Lt. Finley of 118 attacked a 1,200-ton freighter off Iwo Jima. Anti-aircraft was intense and Finley was hesitant to go in for a bombing run; instead, his gunners strafed the ships, resulting in serious damage. Cdr. Harper's crews were new, inexperienced, and unsure of their new plane's capabilities. Over the next few weeks the Old Crows would gain experience and fully realize the Privateer's capabilities.

A VPB-118 PB4Y-2 Privateer (Bureau Number 59380) *Navy's Torchy Tess* with engines running, possibly on Tinian. *Courtesy of Davis McAlister*

Close up of *Torchy Tess* nose art. *Courtesy of Davis McAlister*

The arrival of the PB4Y-2 Privateer to the combat zone in the same period as a major amphibious landing triggered concerns among VPB-118 that their aircraft might be misidentified and shot at by friendly forces, so the squadron flew recognition flights over the invasion fleet to head off such an incident. However, it was not one hundred percent effective, as Lt. August M. Lodato found out on the tenth. While effecting a rescue operation for a crewman of a downed Army B-24 the plane was shot at by the tail gunner of a PBM rescue plane. Fortunately the plane was not hit.

The month also marked the arrival of another Navy squadron and a change of command for VPB-102. On the twenty-second, Cdr. Louis P. Pressler assumed command of VPB-102 and would remain in command until the closing days of the war. Cdr. W. S. Sampson and VPB-106 (Wolverators) began arriving at West Field, Tinian, 10–16 February, and would remain until May. Sampson's squadron had the distinction of having the first operational loss of a PB4Y-2 Privateer. It also suffered an operational loss in December 1944, when one of its PB4Y-1 Liberators was forced to ditch 240 miles off Oahu, killing six of the fifteen men on board.

As the invasion of Iwo Jima neared attacks on enemy shipping intensified. On 15 February, Lt. "Horse" Thompson, a combat veteran of VB-104, was the first to hit a picket boat while flying fleet protection, and in the process he had the distinction of being the first patrol plane commander to have a plane damaged by enemy fire.

The attack occurred some 175 miles off the island of Muko Jima. The weather was terrible, with low visibility, when the radar operator picked up a blip. The vessel was directly ahead of the task force, so Thompson went down to make sure the ship was not friendly. The picket boat identified itself by firing 20 mm and 12.7 mm guns at the Privateer. The patrol bomber took hits in an engine cowling from a 20 mm round and a 12.7 mm round to a propeller.

Invasion of Iwo Jima taken by a VD-5 Liberator on 20 February 1945. *Courtesy of the NARA*

Thompson went in at minimum altitude with his gunners strafing and his bombardier, Ski Kwiatkowski, dropping incendiary bombs. The bombs caused slight damage and .50-caliber machine gun fire managed to silence the vessel's guns. Thompson then radioed his position to the fleet for carrier planes to finish the job. Later in the evening, Lt. Cdr. Farwell attacked and damaged a Zeke while the fighter was landing at Iwo Jima. Seeing the brazen attitude exhibited by the American plane, the Japanese sent up anti-aircraft fire from 90 mm guns, with six shells bursting around the plane. Farwell decided to leave. While flying through heavy overcast the plane picked up blips on radar. Eight miles ahead were three 100–175-ton freighters each armed with 12.7 mm and 20 mm guns on their aft sections.

Farwell immediately went in for an attack on the largest of the three ships. A 20 mm gun on the ship began firing but the Privateer's gunners killed the gun crew, though not before they inflicted some damage to the bomber's port wing. Breaking off the attack, the Privateer's pilot aimed for another ship. During the attack seven bombing and strafing runs were delivered and the ship was left ablaze and sinking.

With the invasion of Iwo Jima patrols around the island were concluded. The island, with which the men of Navy squadrons had been in frequent contact since VB-109 Cdr. Norman "Bus" Miller's attack on 14 July 1944, was invaded on the nineteenth. The battle would prove to be the costliest the Marines had ever undertaken. Nevertheless, for their sacrifice a new air base would be gained and the lives of hundreds of airmen would be saved. On the twenty-sixth,

VPB-102's Lt. Morgan had the distinction of being the first to land a four-engine bomber on Iwo Jima while the battle was still being fought.

VPB-121 on Eniwetok

In another part of the Central Pacific, Lt.Cdr. Raymond Pflum's VPB-121 arrived on Eniwetok. Pflum was a combat veteran of VP-1, a Coronado (PB2Y-3) flying boat squadron that served in the Solomon Islands. Additionally, Liberator veterans of VB-110, a Navy Liberator squadron that had served in Europe, joined the squadron. VPB-121's arrival in the Pacific was not without incident, with a ditching of a Privateer off California on 11 January, but there was no loss of life. Billy Buckley was a crewmember aboard the aircraft:

"The squadron was to fly to Kaneohe Bay, Hawaii, in January 1945, for further deployment in the Pacific. I believe it was to be two six-plane flights, with the exec leading the first and the skipper leading the second a day or two later. We were in the first flight.

"All flights from the mainland to Hawaii were night flights at that time, so we took off from Camp Kearney (later NAS Miramar, just outside San Diego) late in the afternoon. We had one engine running slightly rough, but I guess the pilot and mechanic thought the mag drop was not excessive, so we kept going.

"There are three points to be plotted on a TransPac flight: the equi-distance point, the equi-time point, and the point of no return. We had not reached any of these points when we lost two engines about 800 miles into the flight. The pilot turned back to return to San Diego. The plane had extra bomb bay tanks installed for the fuel needed for the long flight and was still heavy at that time. There were also carriers installed in the bomb bays loaded with our personal effects. PPC Lt. Leary ordered the crew to lighten the ship by throwing everything not essential over the side. We dropped the bomb bay tanks and carriers and all non-essential equipment.

"When the engines quit I was on the radio watch and sent the distress message. The pilots had feathered three of the engines, but

Bureau Number 59481 was part of VPB-121's inventory; it is unknown whether it sported any nose art. *Courtesy of Steve Hawley*

This VPB-121 crew was shot down over Wake Island. *Courtesy of Richard Jeffreys Jr.*

R.F. Jeffreys (Back row/far right) served two tours with PB4Y squadrons. *Courtesy of Richard Jeffreys Jr.*

kept number three windmilling so we could have power for the lights and radio. I stayed on the radio circuit until shortly before we hit.

"When we reached a point about 500 miles from San Diego all four engines quit. We were at about 8,000 feet and it was dark. Lt. Leary made a great dead stick landing in the water and all hands got in rafts, including Turbo the dog. About six hours later we saw the first search plane. It just kept going. A few minutes later we saw another and it turned toward our rafts. It was a great feeling.

"We were picked up by a Coast Guard PBM using Jato bottles and flown back to San Diego NAS at North Island. We got back to Kearney that night owning nothing but the flight suits we were wearing. We were met by the captain, who said we had liberty if we could borrow a uniform. He seemed to be looking at me when he said it. I had to go before him at captain's mast a few days earlier for some infractions of rules and he had restricted me to the base

until we left, so I figured he had lifted my restriction. Our crew was given a new plane and we made another try without incident. It was never determined why all four fans quit at one time."[2]

During the next five months the squadron carried out harassing raids on bypassed Japanese garrisons on Wake and Ponape. The Japanese on these islands were isolated and subsisted on a near starvation diet. Supplies, when they came by submarine, were inadequate, and the men had to supplement them by catching fish and rats. Still, they had enough strength to fend off enemy air attacks. For VPB-121, the tenacity of the Wake Island garrison was tested on 7 March.

During pre-dawn hours, five Privateers took off from Eniwetok with Cdr. Pflum leading one section, while Lieutenant J. B. Rainey led the other. Along the way to the target one plane had to return to base after radar failure. The four remaining bombers hit the island just before dawn from 4,000 feet. Individually, the Privateers roared

Bureau Number 59409 *Come 'N Get It* **belonged to Central Pacific-based VPB-121.** *Courtesy of Steve Hawley*

Bureau Number 59617 *Miss Milovin* **of VPB-121 appears to have mottled blue-gray fuselage coloring.** *Courtesy of Steve Hawley*

PB4Y-2 Bureau Number 59564 *Ol Blunderbuss* and unidentified members of VPB-121 circa mid-1945. *Courtesy of Steve Hawley*

VPB-121's PB4Y-2 Bureau Number 59584 *Lotta Tayle* named for the scantily clad nose art and for the aircraft's tail vertical stabilizer. *Courtesy of Steve Hawley*

over the island dropping 500-pound bombs among barracks that dotted the shoreline between Peale and Wake. The Japanese did not open fire until the third Privateer came over.

After unloading his 500-pound bombs, Lt. William McElwee Jr. came back around to drop a load of fragmentation cluster bombs. He did not get the chance, as his PB4Y-2 was hit by 25 mm cannon fire and the plane burst into flames. Trailing smoke and fire, the bomber crashed into the lagoon off Wilkes Island. As the crews of the remaining three Privateers headed home they looked back and saw the glow of McElwee's burning plane. A rescue PBM was sent

out to search for survivors after daylight, only to find the Privateer broken in two pieces, floating in the middle of an oil slick. There were no survivors.

Pflum's crews continued this type of harassing raid supplemented with anti-submarine searches which proved fruitless. It was a tedious time for the squadron, often involving 12–15 hour "whitecap" patrols. The men were eager to get into the "real war," the war other squadrons such as theirs were fighting in the Mariana and Bonin Islands.

VPB-121 would have to wait—wait for the "real war"—which would cost the lives of more squadron members. Their time would

Crewmembers standing next to VPB-121's Bureau Number 59450 *Aboard for Action*. Courtesy of Steve Hawley

This is the squadron insignia of VB/VPB-102, the "Reluctant Dragons." Courtesy of Al Marks

This is the squadron insignia of VB/VPB-115. *Courtesy of Al Marks*

come when sister squadrons began losing aircraft and men as Navy Liberator and Privateer squadrons pressed onward toward Japan, and finally victory in the Pacific.

Fox Tare Dog Bites

For the Tinian-based squadrons March was relatively calm, except for a relentless war on Japanese picket boats as American forces prepared to invade Okinawa. These ships were the eyes and ears of the Japanese Navy, and they had to be eliminated at all costs.

On 5 March, Iwo Jima's airfield was operational and allowed planes from VPB-116 to become the first PB4Y squadron to stage from the island. Japanese snipers were still active on the island and Ensign R. H. Rupkey was wounded by a Japanese machine gun round. He survived, but knowing that you could be shot just by standing next to your plane, helmets became the head cover of choice.

Although somewhat dangerous to fly into at the beginning, the airfield on Iwo Jima would become a safe haven for battle-damaged B-29s that could not make it back to Saipan. Two days after 116's arrival a Liberator and her crew from 102 also found it a welcome sight. On 7 March, Lt. (jg) C. T. F. Capdevielle and Crew 18 of

Some units had patches made for their flight jackets. Here is the squadron patch of VPB-117, the "Blue Raiders." *Courtesy of Al Marks*

The squadron patch of VB/VPB-116, the "Blue Raiders." *Courtesy of Al Marks*

VPB-102 took off from Tinian on a 1,200-mile search north of the island. Before it was over they would have to land on Iwo Jima, where the Marines were mopping up remnants of the Japanese garrison. Capdevielle recalls the mission:

"At 1215, at the end of our first leg, we spotted two small craft dead in the water. We did not pick them up on radar, although they were only five miles away. On closer observation we discovered they were typical picket boats (one FTD and her escort). We circled them and radioed for permission to attack. In time, permission was granted. [Fox Tare Dog was the military term for a Japanese coastal freighter with a tonnage of approximately 800–1,000 tons.]

"When I turned into the ships, the escort closed in on the FTD and stopped not more than fifty feet behind. I started my run in on the starboard quarter of the escort, lining up the two ships. Both ships started firing while I was still out of range, and while most of it was machine gun fire, some was thought to be 20 mm or larger. Two large guns, possibly three-inchers, were seen on the bow and stern of the freighter transport, but they did not fire and did not appear to be manned. The ships threw up a large volume of fire as I pulled into range. We were making a low-level attack on these ships, strafing and skip bombing them.

"On this run we were hit in the port accumulator, which is situated below the pilot's feet underneath the flooring, and I became covered with red hydraulic fluid. My copilot, Robert Lomasson, who had been riding the controls with me, took over the controls and helped me recover. I could not see because the hydraulic fluid splashed into my eyes. By this time we were heading for the ocean. The crew was strafing and it was time to drop my bombs. I pressed the pickle twice rapidly, but the second string of three bombs went over the FTD. I had to do it because the only pickle switch is on the pilot's yoke. Due to skidding and slipping and because I could not see, the first string of bombs fell to the right of the escort. Lomy took control of the airplane at this point and recovered. We flew right over the ships and the crew was still strafing. One of our crewmembers commented he saw men jumping into the water.

"We immediately contacted the base, explaining our condition. Plane Captain Ed Pagel surveyed the damage and advised me that we had no brakes and were low on fuel. Ed also advised me that he thought he could fix the accumulator. He found a 12.7 armor piercing slug had pierced it and he plugged the hole with a dime. He did not know if the brakes would hold. We needed to replace the lost hydraulic fluid to attempt to make them hold. We put in every kind of fluid we could find: juice, drinking water, coffee, and even urine. Of course there was no way to test the brakes to see if they would hold.

"When we again contacted our base about our condition I mentioned we were low on gas. I then asked Ed if he thought we could make Saipan, which was closer to us than our base on Tinian. He advised me that we had used too much gas making our attack to be able to make it. The base advised us to land at Iwo Jima. I was stunned at these instructions, because there was a fierce battle still going on there.

"While on our way to Iwo we jettisoned everything we could, including our bomb bay tank. When we were within radar range we were told to go south of the island and make a right turn for our landing. At just about that same moment Navy fighters intercepted us. They led us to the western end of the island to make a left turn on to the landing strip. As we approached the fleet that was bombarding the island ceased firing so as not to hit us.

"While all of this was going I had my waist gunners attach parachutes to the gun mounts. They were to open them as we touched down to aid in stopping us in case the brakes did not work. There was a control jeep—there was no tower—running up and down the runway. He instructed us that the last 500 feet of the runway had not been 'de-mined.' That was when they chose to tell me to land on the south end of the runway so as not to approach over the battle lines and over the runway that still had mines in it.

"It was easy to tell which way the wind was blowing by the volcanic ash that was over the water. This day the wind was from the east, and Mt. Surabichi was blocking it from blowing over the runway.

"Although I was not a carrier pilot, my Navy training techniques were very helpful. As I was on final approach I had unnecessary crewmen go aft. I stalled the aircraft so it began to shudder. I landed on the very end of the runway, on the main mounts and the tail scag, at the minimum safe air speed. Once I touched down I rolled the trim tab back and Lomy and I held the yoke in our guts to keep the nose high.

"On touchdown two crewmembers at the port and starboard waist hatches released the parachutes. One held, but the other ripped open. These parachutes were not designed for this kind of use. Two factors helped in slowing us down: a slight rise in the runway and the friction of the volcanic ash as soon as the nose wheel touched down. Due to the loss of speed I applied the brakes and kicked hard rudder just as we were running out of runway. The brakes held momentarily, then they were gone.

"On touchdown I cut the engines and opened the bomb bay doors. I applied the brakes again and there was nothing. We were now heading for the ocean, rolling along the parking mat between two rows of carrier planes. The jeep was now riding along beside us, on my side of the plane, so I opened my window and advised him that we had no brakes. Two men immediately jumped out of the jeep and chocked our main mounts and we came to a stop. Our crew then deplaned.

"As soon as we touched down the bombardment began again, even from the coastline where we were headed before the wheels were chocked to stop us. A row of howitzers was firing from this coastline, as well as the ships offshore.

"We immediately advised the operations officer of our problem, and he sent some of his mechanics to help Ed repair our hydraulic system. He also gave us enough fuel to get to Tinian. This fuel had to be pumped into our tanks from fifty-five gallon drums.

"The repairs and gassing were taking a long time and night was approaching fast. I became very impatient. I had to consider how I was going to take off. Operations offered us a night's lodging aboard one of the ships offshore. When I found out we would have to ride to the ship in a dinghy through an area that was often under fire and would have to listen to shelling all night I decided to try for the takeoff.

"Eventually we were ready. Ed thought we would have some brakes on arrival in Tinian if I did not have the use of them on takeoff. He felt the repair would hold, and the fluid was now real hydraulic fuel instead of the mixture we had used on landing.

"I do not recall how long the runway was, but I do remember it was uphill, a fighter strip, and the last 500 feet could well be mined. I could not see how I could make such a short-field takeoff without holding the aircraft back with my brakes until my engines were fully revved up. In addition, I had to use the brakes to taxi into position for take-off.

"So we loaded up and started the auxiliary generator. Eventually we started all of the engines and taxied out to the end of the runway. So far the brakes held. We went through our take-off checklist and were ready to give it all the coal. If the brakes did not hold we would end up in the minefield.

"Now, when we asked permission to take off, we were reminded to make a right turn immediately after takeoff and to stay close to the deck until we were well clear of the island, on the eastern side. Only then would it be safe to climb. Of course all of this was because of enemy fire.

"We were at the very end of the runway when I pressed down on the brakes and gave her the coal. I was relieved the brakes were holding. When I attained the power we needed I released the brakes. Off we went in a cloud of dust.

"When I arrived at the point where I thought the minefield started I pulled back on the yoke and we were airborne. Lucky for us, my judgment call of where the mines started was correct. I barely cleared the terrain when I was over water and was able to begin my climb. The short time we were over the lines we were conscious of small caliber ammunition striking the fuselage.

"We had just flown over the lines during a war! The terrain looked like something out of a horror movie. Some of our guys wanted to strafe, but I could not let them because we could not tell the good guys from the bad guys. There was no defined front.

"The flight back to Tinian was uneventful and we made a normal landing. Despite our delay at Iwo we arrived back before dark. We were all glad to be home and relieved. Upon inspection of the plane we counted over fifty small-caliber holes in the fuselage and several larger ones that were the result of our attack on the ships."[3]

Wolverators and Old Crows

For the Wolverators, encounters with the enemy over the next few days proved costly. On 9 March, Lt. Edward Ashley and a crew of fifteen, with three passengers, took off on a flight to Japan and were never heard from again. Ashley and crew had been the first to conduct a combat mission against Japanese picket boats on 26 February, but became the squadron's first casualties during a similar encounter off Honshu while attempting to photograph enemy naval vessels in Tokyo Bay. Twelve crewmen of Crew 15, commanded by Lt. (jg)

Edward Ashley, and three passengers boarded PB4Y-2 Bureau Number 59497 at Iwo Jima for a 760-mile flight. The passengers consisted of observer Marine Corps 1stLt. Robert N. Williams Jr. and two plane captains assigned to other flight crews (AMM1c Jerome O. Campbell and AMM1c Joseph W. Schroder).

Ashley kept an altitude of fifty feet to avoid enemy radar and successfully found the ships in Tokyo Bay, but the plane's approach was observed, and according to starboard waist gunner S1C Charles W. Reddon, "When we finally did see the fleet, they shot everything they had at us. Airplanes, land-based [guns], ships. We were really blown up in the air."

He hit the turret's emergency release. "No. 3 engine was on fire. I pushed my emergency release on the turret. . .and it dumped me inside the plane. There was a huge hole right behind me, it must have been made by a 20-millimeter [shell]. When I saw that it was only about two seconds before we hit the water."

Reddon and tail gunner Raymond Gray Jr., the only other survivor, were fished out of the water by Japanese sailors and sent to Ofuna POW camp, where they spent the next six months malnourished and enduring torture before being set free upon Japan's surrender.[4]

On 14 March, VPB-106's J. F. Huber Jr. and J. F. Ripplinger teamed up with two rocket carrying PV-1 Venturas of VPB-151 to destroy two picket boats. Huber's plane sustained serious damage to its control cables, and first radioman and forward top turret gunner J. E. Mullen (ARM2c) was seriously wounded in the legs by a cannon shell.

The squadron patch of VPB-118, the "Old Crows." *Courtesy of Al Marks*

Lt. Thomas "Totterin Tom" Dodson and Crew Two of VPB-118 assembled next to Bureau Number 59410 *Miss Lottatail* consisted of from (back row, L to R) James K. Wahl Sr., AMM3c; Paul H. Crowley, AMM2c; Lt. (jg) Richard E. Carmelich; Lt. Tom L. Dodson; Lt. (jg) Robert J. Berens; and Walter M. Johnson, ARM2c. Front row (L to R): Joseph C. Tortorice, AOM3c; Poon Sung Lieu, AOM3c; Tom L. Bay, AMM1c: Amos A. Price, AMM3c; Harold A. Peterson, ARM1c; and John H. Seddon, ARM3c (not shown). The crew was nearly lost on a mission over Shantung Peninsula, China, on 27 July 1945, when the No. 1 engine was damaged and the plane was pierced by one hundred holes. Dodson aborted the mission and ordered the crew to throw overboard all non-essential gear; they landed safely three hours later. *Courtesy of Richard Peterson*

Since the fall of Iwo Jima encounters with enemy aircraft had become almost nonexistent. As PB4Y search planes headed closer to mainland Japan these types of encounters intensified. On 11 March, a Privateer flown by 118's Lt. (jg) N. M. Keiser encountered fourteen Japanese aircraft in fifteen minutes. A little before 11:30 a.m., two Emily flying boats were spotted 7,000 feet above the Privateer, being escorted by seven Nicks. They were too far away so Keiser did not pursue. Four minutes later three more Nicks were spotted as they approached, but none of them attacked.

Another four minutes elapsed before a single Emily was sighted 3,000 feet above the Privateer. Seeing his chance, Keiser pushed the PB4Y-2's throttles forward and headed for the enemy. The Japanese plane was taken completely by surprise as the Privateer's bow guns opened fire at maximum range and the first rounds chewed off pieces of the plane's tail. Seeing he was being pursued the Emily's pilot nosed his plane down, turning to the right.

The enemy plane fought back by firing one of its waist guns to no avail, as the combined fire power of the Privateer's bow, top, and starboard waist turrets sent back a stream of machine gun fire, knocking out the port waist position. The plane went into a steep glide from which it never recovered, hitting the water and exploding, and sending a thick column of black smoke 5,000 feet into the sky.

During the fourteenth and fifteenth, VPB-118 also took on enemy shipping as the squadron ventured closer to mainland Japan. Lt.Cdr.

Farwell was the first to hit shipping with an attack on six fishing trawlers just before noon on the fourteenth along the coast of Kyushu. After sinking four of the boats and causing another two to beach themselves Farwell went looking for more targets. He did not have long to wait, as a small cargo ship was sighted twenty miles from his first attack. After fifteen minutes of strafing and bombing the vessel the Privateer left it burning. Two hours later, Lt. Montgomery encountered two picket boats off Japan. During the battle between patrol plane and picket boats the Privateer took hits from 12.7 mm fire, with one round narrowly missing the tail turret. Conversely, the Japanese craft had some casualties among her crew but was not sunk.

A day later, VPB-118 tangled with small shipping at Truk. Besides submarines, the small, wooden vessels were the only available means to ferry soldiers and supplies from island to island. Unfortunately for their crews, land-based squadrons would not leave them alone. At Truk, Lts. Serrill and Thompson approached the atoll from the northeast at 1,500 feet. In the lagoon seven small boats 40–60 feet long, consisting of luggers and sailboats, were spotted; five men on the sailboat leaped overboard as the Privateers came in with machine guns firing. The crews never had a chance, as Serrill's and Thompson's crews expended 5,500 rounds of .50-caliber machine gun bullets at the wooden vessels. For the unfortunate crew who decided to leap overboard, a 250-pound bomb was dropped amid them and exploded, and there were no survivors.

During the remainder of March VPB-118 crews encountered more shipping, but were for the most part unsuccessful in their attacks, except for Lt. Dodson on the twenty-eighth. His PB4Y-2 was on its outbound leg of the patrol above the Philippine Sea when a target was spotted on radar at twenty-five miles. Getting a closer look, Dodson

Lt. (jg) Hooper of VPB-102 attacked Japanese picket boats some one hundred miles off the Japanese coast on 23 March 1945. His PB4Y-1 was struck several times by 20 mm cannon fire and had to divert to Iwo Jima, where he landed safely even with damaged flaps. *Courtesy of the NARA*

realized they were well-armed picket boats and decided to send a call for PVs. The Privateer and her crew circled for a half hour waiting for reinforcements to arrive. They did not arrive, so Dodson went down alone at masthead height and attacked the ships. Diving at full speed, his gunners began firing when they were 600 yards from both ships. The gunner's .50-caliber fire raked the decks from bow to stern as Dodson dropped two bombs, but before one of them hit the smallest ship exploded. Swinging back for the second target, another strafing run caused the vessel to explode and break in two. The Privateer's crew watched as the aft portion of the ship slid beneath the water, leaving only the tip of the bow bobbing on the surface.

On 3 April, Cdr. Harper's radar picked up targets twenty-two miles distant which turned out to be two picket boats spread one hundred yards apart. He called in PV-1 Venturas from VPB-133, based at Iwo Jima, which arrived an hour and a half later. The Privateer's crew watched as the three aircraft fired twenty-three five-inch rockets and strafed from 3,500 feet. The rockets missed, but the ships took hits from the .50-caliber nose guns of the Venturas. Harper followed in forty-five seconds later and missed with three bombs as his gunners raked the bow and deckhouses of the vessels. The picket boats responded to the attack by sending up accurate fire from 12.7 mm machine guns. The plane took thirteen hits to the port wing and fuselage, knocking out the number two engine. Harper broke off the attack while the Venturas continued theirs. They, too, were unsuccessful in sinking either ship, and all three PV-1s were seriously damaged by anti-aircraft fire.

VPB-108 on Tinian

While the Tinian-based squadrons ferreted out Japanese forces in their assigned sectors, another squadron reported for duty with Fleet Air Wing 1. Between 6–21 March, VPB-108 began arriving at Peleliu under the leadership of Lt.Cdr. Muldrow, a veteran of the squadron's first tour.

Living conditions on the island were deplorable, with personnel living in tents, menaced by a variety of insect life, a lack of fresh water, and food comprised of K or C rations. During their brief stay on the rain-soaked island, the squadron managed to carry out thirty anti-submarine patrols and twenty-one long-range searches to the Philippines.

Muldrow's squadron made a name for itself through the ingenuity of one man: Lt.Cdr. Robert C. Lefever. He was the first to install fixed forward-firing 20 mm guns in his Privateer. Testing them on the enemy proved successful enough that other PB4Y-2s were fitted with the cannons. During his crew's combat tour they destroyed twenty-six ships, sixty fishing boats, and numerous land installations. Lefever also had the honor of being the first to make a strike against the enemy. On 4 April, he attacked anti-aircraft positions on Babelthuap, in the Palau Islands. By early April, VPB-108 had arrived on Tinian with their Privateers.

On 5 May, Lt. Ebright tangled with an enemy APD (destroyer-type transport) and nearly came to grief as a result. Shortly after he started a routine sector search northeast of Iwo Jima he was ordered to attempt to locate an APD reported to be northeast of the Bonin Islands. He soon found the enemy ship and kept it in sight while he homed in six P-51s that had taken off from Iwo as soon as his contact report was received. The Mustangs made rocket attacks on the APD without much success, but since their strafing seemed to clear the decks Ebright decided to follow the last of the fighters for a low-level run.

Coming in, accurate strafing by his forward-firing 20 mm cannons and .50-caliber guns, and a near miss with a 100-pound bomb caused slight damage to the ship. As the Privateer passed over the APD at masthead height it was hit between the number three and four engines by a 4.7-inch shell. The number four engine was put out of operation immediately, the number-three engine was damaged, and later the propeller had to be feathered. One hour after the attack, finding that he could not maintain course and altitude with two engines out on the same side, Ebright was forced to ditch the plane a few miles west of Hama Jima.

Fortunately the sea was calm and the ditching was successfully carried out, although the plane was difficult to control with only two engines on the port side functioning. Most of the crew sustained minor injuries, but all got out of the plane easily in to two life rafts. Another VPB-108 Privateer had contacted Ebright soon after the latter's plane was hit and orbited the rafts until relieved by a B-17 and a B-29 Dumbo from Iwo. After some four and a half hours in the rafts, the men were picked up by a destroyer and returned to base. Plane Captain E. F. Vodicka, AMM 1/c, was out of action for several weeks, but the rest of the crew, whose injuries were minor, returned to the squadron before the end of the month.

Crew 15 of VPB-106 (next to PB4Y-2 Bureau Number 59391) was lost in action on 9 March 1945. The original crew seen here consisted of Pilot Lt. (jg) Edward W. Ashley, USNR; Ens. Robert M. Castiglia; Ens. R. C. Goldthwait; Frank B. Blake, AMM2c; Warren Kish, ARM1c; Beauford J. Grothe, AOM2c; Raymond W. Gray Jr., S1c; Charles W. Reddon, S1c; Orin L Hackett, AOM2c; Bertram Brown, ARM3c; Gonzalo Mireles, S1c; and Francis O. McLaughlin Jr., AMM1c. Ens. William G. Benes Jr. replaced Goldthwait. *Courtesy of Richard Peterson*

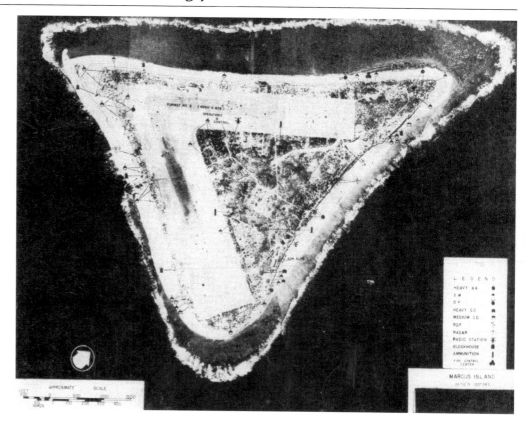

A PB4Y-1P Liberator of Navy Photographic Squadron One (VD-1) took reconnaissance photographs of Japanese-held Marcus Island, revealing the island's defenses and radar/radio structures. *VD-1 Cruisebook*

The Marcus Island Raid

For several days, and for all units attached to the Navy Search and Bombardment Group, Tinian had been on a one-hour alert status. This situation was the result of intelligence reports that the enemy might attempt to stage a number of aircraft through Marcus and Truk, possibly hitting B-29 bases in the Mariana Islands en route, with the final objective of attacking dry docks and warships at Ulithi. On the afternoon of 8 May, a submarine off Marcus reported sighting several unidentified twin-engine planes landing on that island. The order for the strike of 9 May came in a secret dispatch.

VPB-108 was instructed to cover the east-west runway at Marcus and VPB-102 the north-south runway, with the primary target being enemy aircraft on the runways or in nearby revetments and parking areas. All planes carried 3,100 gallons of gasoline and twenty 100-pound bombs fused at four to five seconds delay.

Between 0200 and 0100 hours the morning of 9 May, three planes from 108 took off from West Field, Tinian, for the Marcus strike. Following forty minutes later, planes from 102 left the airfield. Weather conditions for the takeoff were terrible, with heavy rain making visibility almost zero.

Lt.Cdr. Muldrow, who was the first airborne, circled soon after takeoff and turned on his landing lights to give his two other Privateers, piloted by Hartvig and Panther, an opportunity to rendezvous with him. The three planes stayed together in a loose V formation all the way to the target, flying first at 12,000 feet and then down to 1,000 feet.

The weather improved all the way, with heavy rain being followed by intermittent squalls and low clouds. High power settings were used in an attempt to reach Marcus before daybreak. Muldrow led the section with Panther to his port and Hartvig to his starboard. The latter fell slightly behind when a detonation in the number two engine forced him to throttle back to lower power settings.

About 150 miles out the planes dropped down to 200 feet, and at seventy miles they went to one hundred feet. At sunrise they still had some distance to go. They could see a PB4Y-1, later identified as Lt.Cdr. Pressler's plane, ten miles to starboard, flying a parallel course. Pressler did not attempt to join them and flew straight toward the island, making his run at about 0715 over the assigned target area—the north-south runway—and destroying two aircraft he caught at the junction of the two runways, apparently about to take off.[5]

Muldrow, Hartvig, and Panther proceeded on a course which took them about twenty miles to the west of Marcus. From that distance they saw the smoke of the aircraft set on fire by Pressler, so they immediately turned and headed for the island on a bearing that would take them directly over their target. About three miles out they were subjected to intense and very accurate heavy anti-aircraft fire, the first burst coming quite near them. At this point they commenced mild evasive tactics which became violent during the final approach to and into retirement from the island.

Since the ceiling and visibility were unlimited, they could see the island quite clearly before they passed over it. The only planes they could spot were the two Pressler had attacked which were already burning fiercely, with dense smoke rising high in the air. Since this smoke offered a chance for partial concealment they headed directly for it.

Sand can be seen kicking up around structures from the impact of machine gun fire by an attacking VPB-108 Privateer on Marcus Island during the disastrous attack of 9 May 1945. *Courtesy of the NARA*

Muldrow's plane was hit before it crossed the reef and was soon hopelessly shot up. The number three engine was knocked out, the number four engine was torn completely off the wing, some of the tail surfaces were blown away, and there were fires in the forward section. One shell tore off the back of the plane captain's head. The Privateer swerved to port, passed over the island at one hundred feet, and crashed into the sea about half a mile offshore.

Panther and Hartvig made their runs at twenty-five and seventy-five feet, respectively, bombing and strafing gun positions, airfield installations, and personnel along the east-west runway. A 40 mm shell tore an eight-inch hole in the aft section of Panther's plane, struck an ammunition box, and started a fire, which with the prompt action of Plane Captain VS Hargraves, AMM2/c, was kept under control.

Three aircraft of VPB-102 hit the island soon afterward; one was shot down in flames. One was so badly damaged it had to be surveyed, and the third was hit repeatedly and brought back to base with difficulty. Immediately after the attack Hartvig and Panther rendezvoused near Muldrow's crash and began to circle just out of anti-aircraft range. They were on the alert for a possible aerial attack, since Pressler contacted the other aircraft that he thought enemy fighters were following him. Pressler was circling the island, waiting for the other planes of his squadron to come in for the attack. Since he was the senior officer present and since one of his planes, piloted by Lt. Holahan, had crashed into the sea in flames in the same general vicinity, he took charge of the reports and search operations.

After remaining in the area for another half hour Panther and Hartvig climbed to 6,000 feet and headed for Tinian. The latter was low on fuel, so he decreased power settings and fell behind Panther. On the way he was in constant contact with Barnes and Goodman

of VPB-102, whose planes were badly damaged in the Marcus attack. Since both men were having communications difficulties he relayed messages from them to base and assisted them in staying on the submarine USS *Jallao*, which was in the area.

The Commander Air Sea Rescue Unit, Saipan, ordered a B-17 rescue plane equipped with a motor whaleboat and a PBY-5A Dumbo plane to proceed to the scene of the reported sighting. Lt. Charles Baumgartner of VPB-108 was sent out from West Field, Tinian, to orbit the rafts and cooperate in rescue work if necessary. At 1830, he reported that the submarine had rescued two officers and three enlisted men. A dispatch from the *Jallao* at 0407 hours

Bomb blasts and a burning Japanese aircraft clearly show the altitude of an attacking VPB-108 Privateer. Bursting flak is in the top center of both images, as well as ejected shell casings from the aircraft's tail turret. *Courtesy of the NARA*

on the tenth confirmed this statement, giving further information that all five survivors were wounded—two seriously.

One of the survivors, Lt. Wallace, recalls finding himself fifteen to twenty feet under water and swimming toward a bright spot above that proved to be the surface. The tail gunner locked himself in the tail turret just before the crash and had no idea how he escaped. When he came to, he discovered he was caught on a piece of the wing that was floating upright with his clothing in shreds, while Ensign Palma was dazed from a severe gash in his head. Somehow one of the plane's life rafts was floating on the water. Wallace swam to it and inflated it in an inverted position, and Palma, though badly hurt, managed to turn it over. As soon as all five survivors either climbed or were hauled into the raft the oars were broken out, and those who could took turns rowing to get away from the island. The men spent seven hours in the raft awaiting rescue.

After the crash the men had a narrow escape from capture and probably certain death. A sampan sent out from Marcus to search for them came dangerously near and an enemy plane flew directly overhead without sighting them. As they were being transferred to the *Jallao* shore batteries on Marcus opened on them, one shell landing exactly on the spot where the submarine had been a few seconds before it crash-dived.

For the men of VPB-102 and 108, they considered the strike a suicide mission which had taken the commanding officer of one squadron and other good men. Muldrow, Hartvig, Panther, and Hartgraves were all awarded the Navy Cross, every man who participated in the raid was awarded the Distinguished Flying Cross, and thirteen Purple Hearts were awarded, eight posthumously. Lt.Cdr. Lefever, the ingenious man who put 20 mm cannons on his Privateer, became 108's new commanding officer, while Lt.Cdr. Ackermann became executive officer. On 19 May, Lt. (jg) Bezursik and crew reported to the squadron as replacements for Muldrow's crew. For the Tinian-based squadrons, they would continue to be on alert status for the rest of the month, raising tension and uncertainties as to whether they would have to be called again to take on such a mission.

Though creating continuous tension and uncertainty, fortunately for VPB-102 and 108, the squadrons were not called upon for another semi-suicidal attack like the Marcus strike of the ninth. Every day searches were flown to the north and west of Tinian, some 2,000 miles long. On 27 May, VPB-108's Lt. Hazlett orbited for three hours over a survivor in a life raft about 120 miles southeast of Iwo Jima. The man was later identified as B-29 copilot 2nd Lt. Dale B. Ellis of the 40th Group of the 50th Bomb Wing. He was the only survivor of a crew that had participated in a major strike on Nagoya and had been adrift in a one-man life raft for fourteen days.

For the remainder of the month, the squadrons flew several sorties to Truk to check on the airfields. The Reluctant Dragons paid visits to the atoll on 11 and 15 May, while 108 made checks on the thirty-

A crewman aboard a VPB-102 Liberator took a photograph displaying two plumes of black smoke rising from the ocean, probably showing the crash sites of the VPB-102 Liberator and the VPB-108 Privateer lost during the Marcus raid. *Courtesy of the NARA*

Lt. Donald Hartvig receiving the Navy Cross from Rear Adm. Leslie Genres for his actions during the Marcus Island raid as a patrol plane commander with VPB-108. Hartvig was only twenty-three years old at the time. *Courtesy of Donald Hartvig*

The squadron patch of VPB-122. *Courtesy of Al Marks*

VPB-124 Squadron insignia. *Courtesy of FT Pierce*

first. Small shipping was encountered and airfields were bombed. The Japanese still managed to send up a fighter or two and anti-aircraft fire, but the attacks were weak and ineffective. For 102, Lts. Morgan and Stillman attacked and sunk small shipping in Truk Lagoon on two different occasions. There was very little left in the Caroline Islands to attack, so a majority of searches centered on Japan.

Hal Olsen's Nose Art
By June, Tinian was in full swing as a B-29 heavy bomber base with a secondary role as a rest and relaxation facility for forward-based squadrons. While on Tinian for R&R and before moving back to the forward area, PB4Y squadron personnel had the time

WWII nose artist Hal Olsen is seen painting *Redwing* at Tinian during 1945. *Courtesy of Hal Olsen*

Hal Olsen (left) painted the nose art on this Privateer *Indian Made*, which is probably VPB-121's Bureau Number 59491 and sports the same Native American woman as VPB-123's *Redwing. Courtesy of Hal Olsen*

Hal Olsen's *Call House Madam.* She decorated a PB4Y-1 Liberator belonging to VPB-116. Navy nose artist Tinian, 1945. *Courtesy of Hal Olsen*

Hal Olsen's *Pistol Packin' Mama II.*

to have their aircraft decorated with nose art. One of the artists on the island was Hal Olsen. His Navy rating was Automatic Pilot Specialist (AMM-2c) assigned to Instrument Trailer Group (ITG-31, Carrier, Aircraft Service Unit (CASU-44)).

While his shipmates bought whiskey and cigarettes, he stored oil paints and brushes in his locker before leaving California aboard a Liberty ship with intentions of painting scenery of the islands in off-duty time, but soon found a demand for nose art paintings on planes. A couple weeks after his arrival the Japanese managed to stage an attack on Tinian, resulting in the destruction of a Navy paint locker. Hal Olsen recalls this event as the catalyst for going into the nose art painting business:

"Nobody was on duty that time because it was during the midnight hours. It rocked the whole area. Therefore, eventually, I went down to check it out in the morning. They told me a guy who was doing nose art on the bombers stored his paint supplies in the locker that was destroyed—he was now out of business.

So I said, 'I'll try that.' He was getting fifty dollars. In those days it was close to five or six hundred dollars in real money today. So he was getting fifty dollars for every one he did. So I watched, and I talked with people that he worked with, and actually the guy came out and helped me on the first one. I got up on an oil drum, and I used the calendar from the pinup girls that were popular during the war. I made a pencil grid on the calendar, then went and chalked proportionate to the life-size of the girl on the side of the plane.

"There was a new squadron of PB4Y2s arriving. The first thing these squadrons would do they would get their bunk, and then they'd come down and look for the nose artist because they wanted to look salty. I had ten people waiting for me to do nose art on their planes. I was so busy. I worked as soon as it got daylight. I went out and worked from then until about noon, when my Navy job took over, and I worked until midnight on my Navy stuff in the trailer or on the field."[6]

Hal Olsen's *Lady Luck III.* She was a VPB-111 PB4Y-2 Privateer. Tinian, 1945. *Courtesy of Hal Olsen*

Artist and *Accentuate the Positive.* Navy nose artist Tinian, 1945. *Courtesy of Hal Olsen*

"In the Pacific there was no military commander assigned to oversee nudity. Nose art for the crew was a personalized reference to a piece of military hardware. You trust your life to the plane to get you back safely. Nose art brought the crew together."[7]

During his assignment on Tinian Hal painted nose art for such squadrons as VPB-102, 108, 109, 116, 121, 123, and 124. His last painting was "Up-an-Atom" on a B-29 that participated in the atomic bombing missions against Japan. After the war he studied art at Boston Museum School of Fine Arts and became a technical illustrator for the Los Alamos National Laboratory.

VPB-108's Bureau Number 59441 *Accentuate the Positive* crashed on landing and was stripped of useful parts, such as the forward top turret and window glass. *Courtesy of Bob Baird*

Hal Olsen's *La Cherie*. Navy nose artist Tinian, 1945. *Courtesy of Hal Olsen*

Hal Olsen's *Easy Maid*. Navy nose artist Tinian, 1945. *Courtesy of Hal Olsen*

La Cherie belonged to VPB-121 and VPB-108. *Courtesy of Bob Baird*

VPB-116's PB4Y-1 Bureau Number 38923 *Easy Maid* was a J-model B-24 Liberator adorned with Hal Olsen's nose art. The aircraft didn't survive postwar scrapping, but the nose art did and is now displayed at the Commemorative Air Force's Museum in Midland, Texas. *Courtesy of Bob Baird*

10

Iwo Jima Operations
March–August 1945

By late March and early April, advanced sections of VPB-102, 108, and 116 began staging from Iwo Jima. Search sectors covered Kyushu, Honshu, Okinawa, and the Bonin Islands. Small shipping was encountered and attacked, as were bypassed Japanese garrisons at Truk and the Bonin Islands.

On Iwo Jima living conditions, in the report of three patrol squadron commanders, were, "miserable beyond the point of justifiable excuse." There was little water for drinking or bathing available in the living area. For bathing, saltwater showers a quarter mile away were turned on at 1600 and off at 0900 hours. Drinking water and liquids were generally rationed in the mess hall to one cup per individual per meal. Water was available with flight rations for flights only by a chit from the executive officer of CASUF 52. With Iwo Jima's heat and constantly swirling dust such was hardly a livable minimum, and only the generosity of a naval construction battalion five miles distant made life tolerable. Neither electricity nor lanterns were available. Sanitary facilities were utterly lacking, with only one head (capacity eight) a quarter of a mile away serving all patrol squadron personnel.[1]

The Reluctant Dragons versus Picket Boats

During March, VPB-102 began losing planes through aggressive attacks on shipping. For Lt. Rorman, the danger of attacking enemy shipping at low altitude was experienced first hand on 12 March, when his Liberator was severely damaged 200 miles off Okinawa. Flying outbound in his search sector from Iwo Jima, he sighted a picket boat and a freighter separated a quarter of a mile apart. Seeing the picket boat dead in the water, he dove down and attacked this vessel. Rorman's top and bow turrets targeted defensive fire from 20 mm guns aboard the vessel as the pilot pickled off four 100-pound bombs from one hundred feet. Two of the bombs were direct hits, and the picket rolled over on her port side and sank stern first. Knowing that his ship was the next target the freighter's captain turned away.

The Liberator began taking hits from anti-aircraft fire, with one 12.7 mm round hitting the bow turret, temporarily stunning gunner K. F. Thoman. The round then went through the aircraft, slicing through wiring before wounding copilot Richard Silzer. The top and bow turrets continued firing, and suddenly the stern of the ship blew up and disintegrated—apparently it had been carrying ammunition.

VPB-116's Bureau Number 38960. *Courtesy of Bob Baird*

Close up of *Worrybird* nose art. *Courtesy of Bob Baird*

Members of VPB-116 taking the protective canvas cover off the bow turret of PB4Y-1 (B-24J) Bureau Number 38953. *Courtesy of Bob Baird*

The Liberator shook violently from the concussion as Rorman instinctively turned away from the explosion. It was too late and debris hit the plane. After a successful landing at Iwo, an inspection of the damage revealed a piece of the ship's planking embedded in the number one engine. The plane never flew again.

Less than two weeks later, another VPB-102 plane belonging to Lt. K. C. Hooper and Crew 15 attacked a picket boat only one hundred miles from mainland Japan. Coming in at one hundred feet preparing to bomb the ship, the power to the bow turret went out, making it all but useless in suppressing the vessel's defensive fire. Just as bombardier J. A. Feetham was about to release the bombs, a 20 mm shell came through the bombardier's window under the bow turret. The round went past his left shoulder, jerking his head set off, destroying the interphone junction box, and ripping out the bomb release panel. Without communication there was no way to tell the pilot he could not drop the bombs. The Liberator took two more cannon hits that blew off four square feet of the port wing's upper surface and damaged the aileron, while another round damaged the starboard horizontal stabilizer.

Heading back to Iwo Jima, the controls were stiff and the flaps could not be lowered. He made a no-flaps landing without any injuries, but the bomber was a total wreck from the damage. Two days later another crew went out to attack the well-armed picket boats; this time they would not be as lucky as Hooper.

Seeing that Liberator and Privateer squadrons were getting abused by the picket boats, Fleet Air Wing One devised a plan where rocket-equipped PV-1 Venturas would team up with the heavy bombers to attack such vessels. When a Liberator or Privateer crew spotted a picket boat they would call in the Venturas to attack.

In theory, and in practice, it was a sound plan. The twin-engine Venturas could fire their rockets at a safer distance than a patrol bomber coming in for a strafing and bombing attack. However, if PV-1s were unavailable the patrol plane commander could attack alone. For the Reluctant Dragons' Lt. Otis C. Andrews and crew, this was the plan they followed on 25 March.

After spotting two picket boats and waiting forty minutes for Venturas to arrive, Andrews decided to attack the vessels alone. The ships were waiting for him when the Liberator came into range. Coming down through cloud cover the plane began taking hits. The fire was so intense that the pilot turned away from the ships, but not before a 40 mm shell tore through the plane's waist. Daniel B. Walland was hit in the abdomen, with shrapnel piercing his intestines, while William F. Janssen took hits to both legs and an arm. First aid was administered and the Liberator headed back and landed at Iwo. The wounds to Walland were too severe and he later died. For Janssen, his wounds proved to be a ticket back to Pearl Harbor.

Rorman's Close Call
Lt. Rorman had another narrow escape with picket boats two days after Andrews' incident, and in the process wrecked his second Liberator in two weeks. On this mission he was joined by three PV-1s from VPB-133. Rorman looked for and found enemy picket boats operating between Honshu and the Bonin Islands. After watching the Venturas make several runs the lone Liberator joined in. As the patrol bomber approached, Rorman noticed the ship was heavily armored with four turrets and numerous machine gun positions.

A proud looking Lt. Gudka of VPB-102 showing off his unnamed nose art on PB4Y-1 Bureau Number 38819, which would be stricken from the squadron's inventory in April 1945. *Courtesy of the Navy Patrol Bombing Squadrons 102/14 Association*

One of the men shown in this photograph is Lt. Don Strange of VPB-102 with PB4Y-1 Bureau Number 38783 *No Strain II. Courtesy of the Navy Patrol Bombing Squadrons 102/14 Association*

PB4Y-1 Bureau Number 38734 *Dazy May?* **was the primary aircraft of Lt. Bill Alleman's Crew 17 of VPB-102, and may have also seen action with VPB-116.** *Courtesy of the Navy Patrol Bombing Squadrons 102/14 Association*

Rorman's top and bow turrets opened fire, only to see the rounds bouncing off the hull. When the Liberator was within 400 yards, every gun on the ship opened fire at the same time. The bomber took three hits, with one blasting the starboard horizontal stabilizer to shreds. Despite the intense barrage, Rorman went in one hundred feet off the deck and released four bombs. The first bomb hit the bow, bounced off, hit the water, and exploded alongside the vessel. The other three were direct hits and blew the superstructure off, splitting the ship in two.

Suddenly there was a loud bang, and the plane shuddered as an explosion hurled Rorman's plane over 300 feet in the air. The plane stood on its tail with the bow straight up and it began to fall over on its back. Realizing what was happening, Rorman and his copilot pulled on the yoke as the Liberator fell over on its left wing and went into a dive. They pulled the yoke back to their chests with their feet bracing the instrument panel, trying to regain control. The plane pulled out of the dive less than one hundred feet above the water, only to go into a vertical climb.

The pilots pushed the yoke all the way forward and the copilot held it with his feet, but they could not get the nose down until it stalled. Again, the Liberator went into a vertical dive and then out again. For more than an hour the pilots battled the bomber to keep it in the air. The pilots were joined by navigator Ensign R. F. Silzer, Plane Captain V. B. De Sousa, and first radioman H. E. Price, who assisted the exhausted pilots with the controls. In the rear of the aircraft, Tom Colley climbed out of his tail turret to see what had happened:

"As I got out of my turret, my first sight was of the large hole in the after station bottom entry hatch. Looking forward, I saw that two of the control cables in the overhead, which ran to the elevators, had been severed in the explosion. However, the electrical wires that ran in the overhead adjacent to the control cables to the Servo Booster Unit in the tail section were not severed.

"Going forward and carefully stepping over the damaged hatch, I saw Smitty [James L. Smith], Vince [Vincent DeSousa], and E. B. [Edwin B. Dore] lying on their backs in the after station. A waist .50-caliber was lying across them and the other .50-caliber was out of its mount and on the deck beside them. I threw both .50-caliber guns out of the waist hatch without disconnecting the belts. Both guns cleared, so I guess a link in the belts must have given up. The adrenaline was flowing, because I don't believe I could have normally lifted a .50-caliber alone.

"E. B. was on the starboard side. He had a scalp wound. Vince's head was on Smitty. Both were lying on the port side. Vince's face looked like it had coarse black pepper sprinkled on it, with some spilling on Smitty. I looked at E. B's scalp and applied pressure to the wound. He was moving and coherent by then. Fortunately, the black spots on Vince's face were nothing but burned powder residue from our .50-caliber ammunition that had been hit by the exploding shell, so we brushed him off. There were no burns or visible marks. The three of us then threw out the two tail turret ammunition boxes to lighten the plane as much as possible. We then stripped out the ammunition in the two chutes and troughs that fed the tail turret. This lightened the plane by several hundred pounds.

"An inspection was made for damage, and we discovered that one 250-pound bomb was still hung up in the bomb bay. The lower bomb, on the starboard, forward bomb rack, was hanging by the rear shackle. The front shackle had released and the arming wire was pulled out, but the propeller was not spinning. I did not know if the bomb was armed or not. Vince crouched in the small space immediately after the flight deck. I sat on the bomb bay catwalk with my legs wrapped around the vertical bomb rack and lifted the front end of the bomb. Vince manually operated the hydraulic bomb bay door handle at the front of the bomb bay bulkhead and someone released—either manually or electrically—the shackle and the bomb fell free. I knew there was only one bomb, and I expected Vince to only partially open the bomb bay doors, but he opened them all the

VPB-116 replacement crews began arriving with the PB4Y-2 Privateer in mid-1945, such as Bureau Number 59760 *Cover Girl*. *Courtesy of David Smith*

Putting protective canvas over a VPB-116 Privateer. *Courtesy of David Smith*

way and scared me to death. I suppose there was interlock that would prevent any release unless the doors were fully open.

"I went aft, and everybody was getting his parachute harness on. I realized my parachute was on the port side, aft of the damaged hatch, by the tail turret. I carefully found my way back and retrieved the chute and returned, just as carefully, to the area of the waist hatches. I got a harness, sat down on the step between the radome platform and the waist hatch, and suddenly realized we had a chance of making it home. I became so weak I could not buckle the harness, and then proceeded to throw up all over the waist hatch area."

Only after the damaged skin from the stabilizer blew off were the pilots able to gain some control of the bomber. At the end of a three-hour flight Rorman made a perfect landing back on Iwo Jima.

Freighters, Pickets, and Nicks

VPB-118's Lt. Keiser, staging through Iwo Jima on 10 April, picked up targets on radar that turned out to be a destroyer escort and a 2,800-ton freighter transport northwest of the Bonin Islands. The Privateer's pilot decided to continue searching. On the return leg of his search, Keiser was flying at 3,500 feet above a solid wall of clouds. Radar picked up the same two ships and homed in until the patrol plane was a mile away. The ships were in column, with the escort ahead of the freighter, as Keiser made a run on the merchantman.

The target increased her speed as the escort turned toward the attacking plane. Every gun on the Privateer, with the exception of two stations, opened fire at the freighter, while the starboard waist guns and the forward top turret fired at the escort. When the plane was 500 yards away and only five seconds from bomb drop, a 20 mm round exploded next to the bow turret, shattering the turret and wounding gunner William Arnold (AOM2c). The bombs were released and exploded near the ship, but damage assessment could not be made because Keiser had to get the wounded gunner back to base.

On 13 April, service men and women throughout the Pacific received word of President Franklin D. Roosevelt's death and the swearing in of Harry S. Truman. It was a somber time for many, but the pace of war never faltered, as Navy squadrons throughout the Pacific continued patrols. On the day of the announcement, Lt. W. N. Lloyd of 118 attacked and sank two small cargo ships south of Iwo Jima, while VPB-102's Allen C. Morgan and S. Oset attacked a weather station on the Japanese coast.

Continued attacks on picket boats, fishing boats, and small cargo ships continued, with Lt. Keiser of VPB-118 making an attempt on two of them on April 16. He tried to have other patrol planes rendezvous with him and coordinate an attack but it never materialized, so Keiser went in alone.

The ships were well armed with duel-mounted 20 and 40 mm guns fore and aft, and they were waiting on the Privateer to come on in. Both plane and ships opened fire at the same time, with the Privateer being hit twenty seconds later. Keiser broke off the attack as rounds raked the plane from the wings to the tail; a fire broke out in the cockpit but was quickly extinguished. The aircrew learned a valuable lesson—never attack picket boats without the element of surprise or with a coordinated attack by more than one aircraft. Keiser and crew did not make the same mistake twice.

While most of the squadron aircrews were engaging the Japanese, a Reluctant Dragon crew decided to take on the American submarine force. On 19 April 1945, a VPB-102 PB4Y commanded by Lt. Thomas F. Copeland attacked a submarine along the Japanese coast that was near a convoy. They thought it was Japanese and attacked it. As it turned out, the sub was the USS *Pogy*, which was about to make a surface daylight attack against the convoy. Luckily they were not damaged and managed to escape the Japanese escort, but the skipper of the submarine was livid.[2]

The Reluctant Dragons had been lucky for a while, with no deaths and few wounded in months of combat. On 23 May, the safety record ended when R. A. Buscher's Liberator crashed five miles off Iwo Jima, moments after leaving the field. Only three of the crew survived. There was a kinship among squadron personnel, a special bond that brought out the best in people. There was always someone willing to step forward in a time of need. When Buscher went down someone had to take over his search sector. Lt. Stanley Oset stepped forward and volunteered to fly, although he and his crew had flown to and back from Honshu the previous day. There was no other crew available, with all operational aircraft and crews already flying.

The crew took the only plane available and pointed her toward Honshu. Some ten hours later the landing gear of Oset's Liberator touched down on Iwo's runway, and as the plane slowed men standing nearby could see several holes from enemy gun fire that had pierced the skin of the plane's tail. It had been an interesting day for the crew, beginning with the sinking of a net tender and a cargo ship. The first was destroyed by two 100-pound bombs, while the second was blown out of the water by strafing.

Later a convoy of seven transports, a destroyer, destroyer escort, and three patrol boats was sighted. Oset flew around them, trying to figure out the best plan of attack, as the ships, guessing the Liberator's intention, sent up a stream of anti-aircraft fire. Two Nicks came in and any chance of attacking the ships was abandoned in favor of survival. Oset increased power and headed toward the deck with the fighters following. Coming in from behind at five and seven o'clock, one of the fighters took hits from tail gunner Weimer. The Nick's starboard engine burst into flames and it was last seen heading toward the coast. The other Nick made one more attack, but was driven off. The Liberator survived with holes in its skin but none in the men.

During the next two months the squadrons on Iwo Jima would continue anti-shipping strikes, but a new mission would soon materialize by late June: providing fleet barrier protection. Enemy contacts were frequent in June, averaging about one a day. On 11 June, VPB-108's Ensign Moore threw everything in the book at a large transport just southwest of Choshi Point without sinking it. He made ten runs on the tanker at low altitude—some with half flaps—expending five 250-pound bombs, 4,000 rounds of .50-caliber, and 200 rounds of 20 mm ammunition, but the ship would not blow up. The same day, some one hundred miles to the west, just off the coast of Honshu and south of Hamamatsu, Lt. Hazlett of VPB108 had trouble with a ship that exploded too easily.

While directly over a medium-size cargo ship, on his second run the ship blew up and engulfed the plane in a wall of fire and cascading debris. The explosion lifted the Privateer nearly 500 feet into the air; pieces of the ship hit all parts of the plane, including every propeller and engine. There were between ninety and one hundred dents and holes; pieces of plank, rope, and debris, one or two spikes, and a large section of wire cable were lodged in the plane. The concussion blew out three of the four bombs in the rear bomb bays and nearly got the plane captain, who was thrown violently across the catwalk. None of the crew was injured,

"Big Snow Propaganda." A VPB-116 Privateer with loudspeakers in her bomb bay was used to harass Japanese troops on bypassed islands. *Courtesy of David Smith*

Ens. Elmer Moore of VPB-108 left Iwo Jima in heavy rain and poor visibility at 0700 hours on 24 April 1945, to ferret Kyushu. This surface vessel was picked up by radar at Tosa Bay and was left sinking after a strafing and bombing attack. *Courtesy of the NARA*

Lt. Allen Morgan (standing, second from left) and crew beside their primary aircraft, PB4Y-1 Liberator *Cuntry Cuzin. Courtesy of Allen C. Morgan via Joseph Morgan*

and although the number three engine was vibrating considerably and the controls were sluggish, the plane was kept in the air without much difficulty.

In fact, immediately after this narrow escape Hazlett joined Lt. (jg) Hill, who was flying with him, in two coordinated attacks on a tug and two luggers nearby. Hill proceeded to sink a wooden sea truck and then escorted Hazlett 600 miles back to Iwo Jima. After getting his landing gear down only with difficulty, Hazlett brought the battered plane down safely. Only then was the full extent of the damage realized; *Lady Luck II* had made her last flight and was immediately surveyed.

A peculiar mission unfolded at Iwo Jima on 16 June 1945, as VPB-102's Lt. (jg) Allen Morgan decided enough was enough, and he and a volunteer crew were going to end the war and avenge the death of his friend, Ensign R. L. Schile, by bombing the Emperor of Japan's Imperial Palace in Tokyo. Schile was Commander Pressler's bombardier/navigator who was killed on 10 June by a 20 mm cannon round during an attack against an enemy patrol boat off Honshu. Seven men volunteered to join Morgan on the monumental mission comprised of Leo H. Lentsch, George K. Kratochvel, Carl E. Otis, Barton Fitzgerald, William F. Venable, George A. Lauzon, and Joseph A. Roadenbaugh. Bombs were loaded aboard a PB4Y-1

Liberator and Morgan and crew departed Iwo by giving the airfield tower the code name "Victor Three," then headed toward the Japanese coast. Unfortunately, or maybe fortunately, the mission had to be aborted when a severe thunderstorm was encountered and they returned to Iwo, only to be greeted by a welcoming party of high-ranking officials. The men were sent back to Tinian and grounded for seven days for "flight fatigue."[3]

In July, the war was winding down in the Pacific and B-29s raided the home islands of Japan nearly every day, raining thousands of tons of bombs on the civilian population. There was little left of the Japanese Imperial Navy, nor the air force. For VPB-102's Lt. (jg) R. R. Lowman and crew, the eighth would end in tragedy for a devoted four-legged member of the crew.

While searching the southern coast of Honshu, Lowman spotted a five to 700-ton freighter and went in for an attack. The bomb bay doors were opened as the bow gunner began strafing the ship and three 100-pound bombs and one of the crew were dropped on the ship. The bombs were direct hits, destroying the vessel, but "Queenie," the crew's dog, which had run toward the open bomb bay and fallen out, missed the ship. For Lt.Cdr. Pressler's squadron the death of "Queenie" would be the last combat casualty.

Two-plane missions continued, with small shipping—mostly weighing 100 tons or less—being attacked, the majority being fishing boats, although a few patrol boats were attacked. Enemy shipping was now hugging close to shore near land-based anti-aircraft positions during the day and only leaving the sight of shore during the evening hours. Due to forthcoming work of Fleet Air Wing 18 with the Third Fleet off Japan by mid-July, patrol squadrons 102, 108, 109, 116, and 121 joined VPB-108 on Iwo Jima to provide fleet barrier protection.

VPB-116's Lt. David Bronson's crew standing beside *Sea Ducer* during an awards ceremony. *Courtesy of David Smith*

VPB-116's mascot "Chubby." *Courtesy of David Smith*

Fleet Barrier Patrol

It was a fast-paced time, with a plane taking off every thirty minutes with the role of fleet barrier between the fleet and any outgoing Japanese force. Navy Liberators and Privateers flew special weather flights, air-sea rescue, anti-submarine patrols, and daily search and reconnaissance of the Honshu coast. Squadron aircraft were used extensively for fleet barrier duty in conjunction with the Third Fleet's strikes at Honshu on the eighteenth and twenty-first, and in the Inland Sea on the twenty-fourth and twenty-eighth.

The skies over Japan had become crowded with carrier-based fighters and B-29s pounding the country day and night, not to mention Navy patrol planes. Each squadron has stories of what it was like being in the air, in lousy weather, in the closing weeks

of the war. The sky was indeed crowded, and a crew had to be very watchful for friendly aircraft in their air space. On one such flight, Lt. Thomas W. Challis and his crew were ordered to escort a photo plane to Tokyo Bay, which turned out to be uneventful, and they were on their way back to Iwo when one of the engines had to be feathered.

After dumping all remaining bombs and ammunition to make the plane lighter, the crew settled back for their journey home. Wayne

Members of a VPB-116 crew receive medals on Iwo Jima with what appears to be a late production PB4Y-2, as it appears to have the overall dark blue coloring. *Courtesy of David Smith*

VPB-108's Lt.Cdr. Lefever encountered enemy merchant ships off Kozu Shima, a small island of the Izu group some 110 miles off Kyushu. Twelve runs were conducted against the vessels which took an hour (0630–0730), leaving three of them destroyed. The crew expended six 350 lb. bombs, 3,500 rounds of .50-caliber machine gun rounds, and 200 20 mm cannon rounds from a pair of field modified, fixed, forward-firing cannons installed in the bombardier station. *Courtesy of the NARA*

Turner, the primary radar operator, was tired from being on the radar and radio watch all day and decided to take a break. Herbert K. Ferguson, the 3rd radioman, was on radar when he called Turner on the intercom to come and look at the screen. He thought there was something wrong with the set because of so many blips. Turner looked and discovered that airplanes surrounded them. It was a flight of B-29s headed to Japan flying at 8,000 feet. He told the pilot, and he turned on the IFF and the landing lights. Turner got on radar and guided the pilot through the planes, sometimes so close that the crew could feel the B-29s' prop wash.[4]

In air-sea rescue PB4Y squadrons proved invaluable. Although squadron personnel had no formal training in this highly specialized field, some eighteen flights were performed, resulting in the rescue of three downed airmen. Lt. Chay and Lt. (jg) Braddock of VPB-109 conducted one such flight on 26 July.

The two pilots were briefed to be on the alert for possible survivors of a Dumbo B-17 thought to be down near the far northeast

corner of their search sector. Lt. Braddock, on Lt. Chay's wing at 1,500 feet, sighted an object in the water, and investigation by both planes at 400 feet showed it to be an overturned life boat of the type carried by B-17 Dumbo planes. Light blue in color, it was nearly awash with a boxed propeller with a parachute still attached and dragging in the water. A fifteen-minute search disclosed no survivors in the area, full information was given to four Air-Sea Rescue planes, and the search was turned over to them.

After spotting the empty lifeboat, the two planes approached the Japanese coast of Southern Honshu and began ferreting from Nakiri to Shingu. Five fifty foot fishing boats were spotted close together inshore in a cove at Shingu Harbor, with two others 200 yards away ashore. Seeing nothing else worthy of attacking, the two Privateers headed toward the fishing boats. In one circling strafing run accurate hits caused the boats to smoke.

In hopes of better targets the planes continued to comb the shore to Kusimoto, but heavy rain near Koza and around O-Shima reduced visibility to a minimum, so the planes turned back to Shingu for a second run on the fishing boats. As Lt. Chay's gunners were heavily strafing the boats, Braddock dropped one 250-pound bomb in the center of the group. Cascades of explosions covered the boats and tossed them around violently. Then both planes went in on two strafing runs on Shingu Town as Braddock dropped a bomb from 200 feet in the village near some central docks, causing one dock and two buildings to disintegrate.

Braddock (leading) headed up a railroad track toward Udona and dropped his final bomb directly on the track short of a railroad tunnel between Shingu and Udano. Chay (following) dropped three more bombs. Two landed short of the tunnel on the tracks, while the third bomb went in the tunnel's mouth as the plane zoomed sharply up to avoid a steep cliff. The explosions caved in the tunnel mouth and tore up the tracks for an eighth of a mile. As the planes pulled up, belated intense light and medium anti-aircraft fire was received from Shingu town and the planes made a final deck-level run through the town, strafing gun positions before heading out to continue patrol.

Homeward bound, at 800 feet Lt. Chay sighted a yellow one-man life raft. Almost immediately the raft's occupant attracted the pilot's attention by firing off three tracers from his pistol in the air and waving a yellow poncho. Both planes dropped to 300 feet, circling and dropping float lights to mark the spot, for the rough sea made constant sight contact a near impossibility. Lt. Chay climbed to 2,000 feet and succeeded in contacting a lifeguard submarine. He estimated his gas was sufficient to remain on station for another two hours and the submarine revised its estimated time of arrival. A Dumbo B-17 code-named "JukeBox 37" intercepted the conversation and estimated he could reach the position in an hour.

While Lt. Chay handled communication, Braddock circled to the left at 300 feet while maintaining visual contact with the small life raft. Having exhausted the float lights and dye marker carried in the plane, Braddock's crew stripped dye markers from their individual Mae West life jackets and dropped them upwind from the raft for the downed aviator to float into. Twenty-three miles away the submarine picked up Lt. Chay's plane on his radar.

Chay varied his altitude between 300 and 800 feet to home in the B-17 and the submarine. The B-17 arrived, with the submarine arriving fifteen minutes later, having averaged better than twenty knots. All dye marker and float lights were gone and Braddock was dropping parachute flares when the B-17 arrived. The rescue was made by the submarine at 1630, and the pilot, Sub-Lt. D. W. Banks, RAF, off HMS *Indefatigable* and in the water for three and a half days, radioed his thanks. Course was set for base and the PB4Ys made a successful landing at Iwo Jima.

By the end of the month VPB-109 returned to Okinawa, leaving the other four squadrons to continue staging from the island. By August there were little worthwhile targets to engage, and the patrol planes ventured deeper into Japan with little or no opposition. During the last few weeks of the war the Reluctant Dragons of VPB-102 engaged nearly two dozen enemy vessels, destroying nearly all they attacked, but these were small ships, most weighing less than 100 tons. The Japanese merchant fleet no longer existed, and supplies and men were now being ferried by these wooden craft; Japan's ocean going capability and commerce had been thrown back to the nineteenth century.

The last strike conducted by the Reluctant Dragons of VPB102 took place on 10 August, when R. M. Barnes strafed fishing boats in Tokyo Bay. At the end of hostilities the squadron moved back to Tinian. The squadron continued after WWII, with its designation and aircraft changing over the years. In 1946, it became VP-102 and flew Privateers out of Guam. Later it was renamed VP-HL-2, and then VP-22 before the squadron was decommissioned in 1994. During its existence it flew the PBY-5 Catalina, PB4Y-1 Liberator, PB4Y-2 Privateer, P2V5F Neptune, and P-3 Orion.[5]

Lt.Cdr. Lefever and Lt. J. R. Hubbard struck an enemy armed transport off Hachijo Shima and military installations (pictured) on Miyake Shima of the Izu group on 28 July 1945. *Courtesy of the NARA*

11

Okinawa
Battlefield and Airbase
April–May 1945

During the third week of April, an advanced echelon of the "Old Crows" of 118 left Tinian for Yontan Field, Okinawa. They left the warmth of Quonset huts and hot food for muddy tents and K rations. By May, the majority of the squadron was stationed there, leaving 102 and 108 to continue missions from Tinian. Harper's squadron had fought well in the Mariana Islands and would continue to do so from Okinawa.

Okinawa, only 350 miles southwest of Tokyo, was invaded under the code name Operation Iceberg on 1 April; the island would not be declared secured until 3 July. It became the bloodiest land battle of the Pacific War, with some 110,000 Japanese killed and another 10,755 taken prisoner during the eighty-three-day struggle for the island. The invasion would cost the United States Navy thirty-four vessels and craft and 368 damaged with the loss of 4,900 sailors killed, while the Army would lose 7,613.

The "Old Crows" of 118 were the first Privateer squadron, and in April became the first such squadron to base at Okinawa. Between 16–22 April, Privateers of VPB-118 began movement to Yontan Field, Okinawa, and reported for duty to Rear Admiral John D. Price, Commander of Fleet Air Wing 1, 5th Fleet. (As discussed earlier, some crews did stage raids from Tinian throughout April and May.) As the squadron was moving to Yontan, Cdr. Harper received orders back to the United States and Cdr. Art Farwell assumed command, with Lt. Cdr. Binning as executive officer.

The runways on the island, already five thousand feet in length, were being rapidly extended. Living facilities were strained, and the squadron flew in its own tents, cots, and equipment from Tinian. Foxholes were a necessity at Yontan. Nightly at sunset came the first alert, followed frequently by actual enemy air raids. The Japanese were largely accurate in their bombing, even from altitude, and bombs invariably struck the airfield. Loss of sleep occasioned by the foxhole life and the loss of evening hours for work or personal pursuits were major irritations.

Operationally, the nightly alerts forced all patrol flights into daylight hours because the planes could not be serviced, gassed, or take off during an alert. Similarly, all flights returned before dark to avoid mix-ups with the numerous bogeys and the 5th Fleet's propensity to fire at anything with wings after dark.

Patrols consisted of two to six plane patrols to ferret the southern and eastern coasts of Korea, the west coast of Kyushu, Shimono and Kamino Shima, Goto Retto, and Saishu To of Japan. Such flights were largely anti-shipping, and special anti-shipping strikes were permitted wherever hunting seemed best. With Privateers skirting the enemy coasts, encounters with enemy planes became more frequent and deadly for both sides.

The new hunting grounds were rich in shipping, and two days after arriving two VPB-118 Privateers flown by Lts. DeGolia and Dodson were the first to strike. Flying a patrol oft southern Korea, they attacked a 325-foot long cargo vessel, leaving it seriously damaged after fourteen bombing and strafing runs. The following day two more 118 crews heavily damaged a 6,000-ton merchantman off Kyushu. On the last day of the month Cdr. Farwell and Lt. Dodson took their planes to the Korean coast.

A Privateer takes off while in the foreground sits VPB-121 's "Aboard for Action." *Courtesy of Bob Baird*

Bureau Number 59755 *Peace Feeler* with overall mottled blue-gray coloring appeared in the Central Pacific late in the war with VPB-116. *Courtesy of Bob Baird*

The weather was lousy, with almost zero visibility. Compounding the poor weather was false returns from the on board radar. Hundreds of small islands dotting the coast made it virtually impossible to tell land from ship. Soon the planes lost contact with each other and both crews were now alone. Farwell headed west, and soon the weather began clearing. His radar operator picked up a blip thirty-six miles to the south so the skipper of 118 headed for it. It was a large ship, some 5,000 tons, and was heading for Korea at less than ten knots. It was beginning to get dark and he was at the end of his search sector, so Farwell had to attack now and not wait for Dodson.

Pressing in alone at less than one hundred feet off the water, Farwell pickled off a 500-pound bomb as his gunners strafed. The bomb sailed over the ship, missing it by fifty feet. Farwell turned the Privateer around for another bombing run as a machine gun position on the ship sent back a steady stream of fire, with all rounds missing the advancing plane. The second bomb was pickled off and hit the side of the ship between the bridge and the stern. The ship buckled from the explosion as the Privateer circled to inspect the damage. Burning oil flowed from the decks and lights from the fires cast a glow across the water, with the ship sagging in the middle. The following day Adm. Price sent a dispatch commending Farwell and his crew for the successful attack.

The attacks in late April were only a precursor to what was to follow within a week. The "Old Crows" were about to embark on the most successful anti-shipping campaigns in patrol bombing history. In May, the Japanese merchant fleet would lose approximately 67,000 tons of shipping to Navy land-based aircraft, most of it to Privateer squadrons; the most successful was VPB-118.

Japanese merchant shipping losses began on 1 May, when two of 118's Privateers flown by Lt. Earl A. Luehman and Lt. (jg) Allan Lasater took off from Yontan at 0653 hours, heading for the west coast of Korea and the Yellow Sea. At 1100 hours they spotted four Japanese destroyers in a small harbor. A few minutes later a heavy cruiser, three destroyers, and four merchant ships were sighted in

two adjacent coves. All were at anchor, except for the largest merchant ship, the 6,800-ton *Kyogyoku Maru*, which was moving to the northwest out of the harbor. The Privateers circled, made a contact report, then went in for an attack.

The warships in the adjoining cove immediately opened fire but the shooting was inaccurate. Luehman provided protective fire with his bow, top, and port waist guns as Lasater began his bombing run. Lasater pickled off two 500-pound bombs as he crossed over the ship at 200 feet. Both bombs missed, with the closest falling twenty feet short. Luehman's gunners continued strafing as Lasater made another unsuccessful run. The ship turned toward land, her crew busy uncovering three-inch deck guns on the stern as the warships got underway and continued firing when the Privateers came into view.

The *Kyogyoku Maru* was approaching the shore, her three-inch guns now firing at the Privateers. Lasater had one bomb left and decided to let his enlisted bombardier, Robert E. Miller Jr., try to hit the ship. Miller had been the top student at bombardier school, yet this would be his first time dropping a bomb in combat. Lasater went in and Miller dropped the bomb ten feet short of the ship. The tail gunner saw the ship lift as the bomb exploded, fall back, and break in two. On the stern of the broken ship the gunners kept firing as it slid under the waves.

The Old Crows Strike Kanoya Airfield
About mid-morning on 3 May, Cdr. Farwell received orders for 118 to send all available aircraft on a strike against Kanoya Airfield on Kyushu. Intelligence reports indicated the Japanese were preparing a Kamikaze attack using Betty and Baka bombs on the fleet anchored off Okinawa. The only squadron available to head off such a potential threat to American shipping was VPB-118.[1]

This VPB-118 squadron member with helmet and no shirt in front of the Quonset huts is Robert E. Miller, Jr., AOM2c, and Bombardier. Picture was shot either on Tinian, where they were based from 16 January 1945-22 April 1945, or in Okinawa from 22 April 1945, until his plane, *Torchy Tess*, disappeared on 6 May 1945. *Courtesy of Davis McAlister*

Late in the afternoon Cdr. Farwell took off with six Privateers and headed for the target. A few minutes later an engine failure forced Farwell back to base. The squadron commander landed, climbed in another PB4Y-2, and was in the air again. As luck would have it, the number two engine failed on this aircraft after forty minutes, and he returned to Yontan a second time. Another aircraft flown by Lt. Finley had to return after radar and IFF failed.

Lt. Montgomery was now in command of the remaining four Privateers as they headed onward one hundred feet off the water, trying to reach the target before dusk. A hundred miles from Kenoya Airfield the planes went down until they were barely above the water before reaching the coast at dusk. As the Privateers raced northwest along the coast Lasater's number two engine began shooting out jets of flame. He feathered the engine and turned around for home, the third plane to suffer similar mechanical problems. Montgomery was now faced with the difficult decision whether to continue with the mission. He decided to hit the airfield.

It was early evening as the Privateers swept over land, barely missing the tops of houses and trees. Montgomery called the other planes to ask if they saw the field, and "No" was the reply. He climbed to 200 feet and announced over the intercom, "I got it."

The field lights were burning, lights glowed from the radio towers and roof tops, and ahead a plane was taking off, its running lights clearly visible. Lt. (jg) Thompson's port waist and tail gunners were first to break the eerie silence with their twin .50-caliber guns (they had sighted a locomotive pulling some cars just short of the field). Then all hell broke loose.

Lt. Robert M. Finley's Crew Six of VPB-118 consisted of (back row, L to R) Lt. Robert M. Finley; Harold W. Childs, ARM2c; Eugene T. Johnston, AMM2c; J. B. Pryor, AMM2c; Jack H. Lindell Jr., ARM1c; and Lt. (jg) Charles Fernandez. Front row (L to R): Carl Seimers Jr., AOMB2c; Alex Trahan, AMM3c; Fred Grochmal, AMM2c; and C. C. Keith, AOM2c. Not shown are Ens. John B. Abeln and possibly replacements with the names D. K. Hatch, L. R. Mayernik, Gibson (?), and L. H. Weber. *Courtesy of Richard Peterson*

All three Privateers went in bombing and strafing aircraft in revetments, and then barracks and hangars were hit. Lt. Pette's forward top turret gunner picked out the plane that was taking off, while Thompson's top turret gunner aimed for a plane coming in for a landing.

The Privateers swept over the entire length of the field, leaving behind them three aircraft destroyed and a dozen fires burning. Four hours later the planes were back on Okinawa. Montgomery was recommended for the Navy Cross, his wing men Thompson and Pette the Silver Star, and the rest were awarded the DFC.

Raids intensified, with continued anti-shipping strikes around Japan and Korea and with stunning attacks carried out on the fifth and sixth of May. Less than a day after the raid on Kenoya Lt. Finley, along with Lt. Duba, pointed their Privateers toward Fusan, Korea, to look for the enemy.

Anti-Shipping Strikes off Korea

A number of merchant ships were seen just outside the harbor. Finley directed his attack on a 2,500-ton tanker. With his gunners firing, he came in at masthead height and prepared to drop a 500-pound bomb. Just before he released the ship exploded, blowing the stern off, and Finley had to take evasive action to avoid flying pieces of the ship. The ship settled by the stern as the Privateer came around again to make sure the ship sank. From 200 feet another bomb was dropped that exploded along the starboard side of the vessel. It rolled over and sank without putting up any type of opposition.

Three minutes later Finley went after a 2,000-ton cargo ship and dropped a 500-pound bomb on her. Debris from the ship and her cargo flew into the air from a direct hit on the starboard side.

The crew of VPB-118's *Navy's Torchy Tess*. Top Row (L to R): Ewell W. Smith, AMM; Ens. Kenneth W. Gibson; Lt J. A. "Tex" Lasater; Lt. (jg) Clarence J. Mimer; Charles W. Jacobs, AMM3c; and Sterlin C. Bryant Jr., AMMF3c. Bottom Row (L to R): Harry F. Brockhorst, ARM3c; Robert E. Miller Jr., AOM2c; Arden M. Ardaiz, AOM3c; Robed A. Carr, AMMF3c; Davis McAlister, ARM2c; and William J. Hawkins, ARM3c. The crew was lost on 6 May 1945, returning from a mission. Arden Ardaiz was not on the flight that day. *Courtesy of Davis McAlister, nephew of VPB-118's Davis McAlister*

VPB-118's Crew 8 in front of Bureau Number 59380 *Summer Storm*. *Summer Storm* nose art, based on Linda Darnell pinup art, was painted just before a B-29 lost power and crashed into her, destroying the Privateer. When Lt. Paris' Crew 3 went MIA they were flying Crew 8's replacement plane, 59449. The crew consisted of (back row, L to R) Robert L. Hinson, AMM3c; David S. Nevelstein, ARM3c; Ens. John E. Hayes; Lt. Julian D. Serrill; and Ens. Harold R. Jones. Front row (L to R): Johnnie D. Butts, ARM1c; Philip J. Hirrel, AOM2c; John F. Leonard, AMM1c; Robert E. Korn, AOM3c; Jerome P. Malin, S1c (ARM); and Donald W. First, AMM3c. *Courtesy of Richard Peterson via Guy Jones, son of Harold Jones, and crew notes courtesy of Jack Leonard*

The ship went down by the stern and sank. The two Privateers parted ways and went on their own, with Duba attacking and damaging a fishing vessel with bombs and strafing. Meanwhile, Finley found another large merchantman three miles off shore and damaged it with a near miss from a bomb and with machine gun fire. As the Privateer pulled away from the run the number four engine went out and Finley had to feather it. Both planes joined up and headed for home, leaving some 6,000 tons of Japanese shipping either sunk or damaged.

May 5 was a costly day for the Japanese merchant fleet, as four of the squadron's Privateers took off and headed for the coast of Korea. Just after 11 a.m., Lt. Serrill and Lt. (jg) Lodato spotted a convoy of three freighters and two destroyer escorts moving east toward Sasebo. The two Privateers passed the convoy, leading the escorts into the belief the two patrol planes had not seen them. The ruse worked, as the ships sailed on as Serrill turned sharply around for an attack on a freighter transport. Coming in at 150 feet, the plane crossed over the entire length of the ship as 20 mm cannon fire opened up. Serrill pickled off 500-pound bombs which hit the stern, causing a flash of fire and smoke that obscured the vessel.

The vessel was done for, as smoke and flame poured out of the freighter, and her crew began abandoning ship by lowering themselves into the water with ropes and ladders. The two planes resumed patrol and within a few minutes sighted another convoy of three freighters

and a small oil tanker. It was Lodato's turn to attack while Serrill circled as protective cover. The Privateer's pilot picked out the largest freighter and began a bombing run. As the plane approached, the ship opened fire with a three-inch cannon on the bow. Lodato's bow and top turrets answered by pouring machine gun fire toward the gun position while the port waist gunner hit the tanker from his position. Two 500-pound bombs were dropped from 200 feet, with the first hitting the side of the ship and the other a direct hit on the ship's deck.

Pulling out from his run, Lodato spotted an enemy aircraft carrying a depth charge under its fuselage six miles away. The Privateer approached the unsuspecting plane from behind and opened fire with its top and bow turrets. The other aircraft immediately dropped the depth charge and banked sharply to the left, with the Privateer following. It was too late to outmaneuver the four-engine bomber, as fire from the bow and port waist turrets went into the plane, starting a fire on its starboard wing. Out of control, the Japanese plane rolled over and plunged into the sea. Lodato turned back and rejoined Serrill. The freighter that Lodato had attacked was now gone, but debris floating across the water marked where she had gone down. The oil tanker his port waist gunner had fired at was now burning.

The planes still had bombs and ammunition left so another freighter was targeted. Serrill's bombs missed, but strafing by both planes caused the ship's cargo to catch fire, with flames quickly spreading across the vessel's deck. Forty-five minutes later another merchant ship fell victim to the Privateers off Korea; the victim of the deadly accuracy of the patrol planes' gunners.

As Serrill and Lodato were making their runs on the second convoy, Cdr. Farwell and Lt. (jg) Keiser were off the southern tip of Korea when a large freighter was seen between two small islands. As Keiser began his run three-inch anti-aircraft guns from the two islands opened fire, making him have to take evasive action at 150 feet. Both the top and bow turrets were firing, with bullets going into the ship's superstructure as Keiser dropped two bombs. Both missed, and seeing the shore guns firing at him, Keiser decided to look elsewhere for shipping.

Fifteen minutes later he found a tanker about five miles off shore. Flying over the length of the ship, Keiser pickled off a bomb that hit the water some ten feet from the vessel. The bomb exploded under water and lifted the stern out of the water. Coming back around, the Privateer's gunners strafed the ship unmercifully as the ship's crew vainly fired back with light machine guns. After four runs the tanker was blazing, as was the water around it.

Cdr. Farwell contacted the other Privateer pilot to join him on an attack against a freighter transport. Keiser obliged, and soon his gunners were strafing the vessel as Farwell made a bombing run. The first bomb hit the stern, starting a fire which soon spread over the entire rear portion of the ship. Swinging back around, he dropped another bomb which sailed right through the superstructure, exited out the other side, hit the water seventy-five feet beyond and exploded.

Crewmen AOM1c Troy A. McClure and AFC2c Harry I. Horton of VPB-109's Crew 10 loading bombs into a PB4Y-2 Privateer's bomb bay. *A Pictorial Record of the Combat Duty of Patrol Bombing Squadron 109*

Lt.Cdr. Arthur F. Farwell was Executive Officer and VPB-118's patrol plane commander of Crew Seven, consisting of (back row, L to R): Vincent S. Episcopia, ARM1c; Lt. (jg) William B. Bowers; Lt. Cdr. Arthur F. Farwell; Lt. (jg) William P. Whitmore; and Clifford Bell, AOM2c. Front row (L to R): Paul L. Camerzell, ARM2c; John J. Rider, AMM3c; Conrad Burback Jr., AOM3c; Jack A. Cusey, ARM2c; Victor Siivonen, AMM2c; and Howard E. Riggins Jr., AMM3c. *Courtesy of James Pettit via Richard Peterson*

The transport continued on its way with no attempt to shoot back. Keiser made a run, but his bomb missed the target by thirty feet. He circled back and his gunners strafed as Farwell made a third run. This time the bomb hit the ship squarely, bounced, and went in the water. He had one bomb left, and by God, he was going to sink this ship. Same as before, the Privateer flew across the ship from 150 feet and Farwell pickled off a bomb, but this time the bomb did not bounce—it hit dead center. The explosion caused the ship to finally stop, fires reaching across its entire length, and it began to slowly sink.

Leaving the sinking ship, both Privateers headed down the coast and found another tanker. They had no bombs, so Farwell contacted a couple of PBMs flying nearby. "This one is for you," he told them. The two seaplanes acknowledged the transmission, and soon they were credited with sinking one Japanese tanker.

Farwell and Keiser had guts and nerves of steel as they headed for Fusan Ku Airfield, flying their PB4Y-2s as though they were four-engine fighters. Together they formed up and moved into the traffic circle around the field. A Tess came in for a landing from the opposite direction; the pilot more than likely saw the two planes in front of him but probably believed they were friendly, thus making a fateful mistake. The Privateers were slightly below the Tess as Farwell's bow and top turrets opened fire, immediately starting a fire on the enemy plane.

Seeing four Nicks taking off, Farwell abandoned the attack to thwart an attack by the fighters. Keiser took up where his commanding officer left off, flying next to the Tess as his gunners poured more machine gun fire into it. Now over the field some 200 feet below,

the Tess' engines were afire, with flames spreading to the fuselage. Out of control and burning like a Roman candle, it plunged to the ground.

Farwell made a run on one of the fighters just taking off, diving until his airspeed reached 250 knots while trying to stop the Nick before it could harm the bombers. It was too late, as the fighter banked sharply one hundred feet off the ground and came in head on. The Nick's pilot fired his machine guns, two rounds hitting one of the Privateer's propellers, then passed within a few feet of the bomber. Instantly the Privateer's gunners hit the plane as it passed the bow, top, and tail turrets. The fighter went into a long glide to the ground where it exploded a half mile from the airfield.

The Loss of Lt. (jg) Lasater's Crew

May 6, 1945, was the day VPB-118 lost its first combat air crew during an anti-shipping strike off the southern Korean coast in conjunction with Lt. Montgomery. After strafing a fishing boat, Montgomery found a tanker at the mouth of a harbor. Coming in at 200 feet, he planted a 500-pound bomb against the side of the ship. The explosion hurled water into the air and the ship began to sink. Enemy warships in the harbor sent up anti-aircraft fire in vain as the Privateer headed away.

While Montgomery finished off the tanker Lasater went after a large transport, the ship's 20 mm deck guns firing at the attacking plane as he dropped two bombs that missed the vessel. Montgomery came to his assistance from the opposite direction. The Privateer's bow and top turrets blazed away at the ship as the pilot prepared to drop a bomb. Before the release point, when the plane was some 400 feet from the ship, the transport exploded in a mass of flame. There was no chance for Montgomery to turn away from the blast, and the plane flew directly over the explosion. The Privateer was hit in a dozen places by flying debris, resulting in the wounding of the copilot and an engine being knocked out. Only after landing back on Okinawa did the crew realize the extent of the damage. Upon inspection, an eight-foot piece of the ship's rigging was found

Lt. Henry J. "Horse" Thompson's Crew 17 of VPB-118 consisted of (back row, L to R): Robert E. Roper, AOM1c; Wlliam R. Knudsen Jr., AMM1c; Lt. (jg) Paul W. Prior; Lt. Henry J. Thompson; Lt. (jg) Gaylord H. Lloyd; and James A. Halley, ACRM. Front row (L to R): William R. Brown, ARM2c; Bernard M. Haughsby, AMM3c; Edward A. Kwiatkowski, AOM1; Kellis C. Bostick, ARM2c; William E. Morgan, AMM2c; and Lloyd J. Jones AMM2c. *Courtesy of James Pettit via Richard Peterson*

embedded in the wing, hanging down like the cord on a curtain, and the rest of the wing was perforated as if it had been blasted by a shotgun.

Meanwhile, Lasater and his crew remained behind to continue the attack. Later, the base received a transmission that he had spotted several enemy destroyers, but there was no indication that he attacked them. Five hours after the attack on the transport, Okinawa received one last transmission from Lasater, and he was never seen again. It was a mystery never solved, nor were the remains of the crew found. The Pacific had claimed another twelve men.

Strikes Continue

Three hours after Montgomery and Lasater had struck the shipping, and still two hours before the latter was presumed missing, two other Privateers from the squadron began searching the Korean coast.

Lts. Finley and Thompson were patrolling the same waters in which Finley had attacked shipping two days before. A few minutes after 1 p.m. a tanker became the first victim of the duo, as both planes began a series of figure eight runs on the ship. Finley started with an unsuccessful bombing attack with a 500-pound bomb which skimmed along the deck before exploding some thirty feet beyond the target. Both crews then began two strafing runs which failed to start any fires. After seeing that machine gun fire alone was ineffective Finely came in to drop a bomb. The explosive hit right above the waterline just behind the superstructure. The force of the 500-pound bomb blew the ship completely apart and it sank within seconds. As the ship slipped beneath the water the Privateers headed for their

next target, a freighter five miles away. What were the thoughts racing through the minds of the ships' crew as they watched the American planes sink one of their own and were now heading toward them?

Thompson made the first run with a strafing attack, the bow, top, and port waist turrets blasting away at the unfortunate vessel; behind him Finely followed, both planes making a traffic circle around the target, which was receiving a deadly hail of machine gun fire.

Smoke was pouring from the ship as Thompson delivered a 500-pound bomb which landed ten feet from the stern. The ship reeled from the violent explosion and it began settling in the water; a thick black cloud of smoke, thicker than the one caused by the strafing, exited the forward hatch and superstructure. The ship lay dead in the water, seriously damaged, as the ship-busting Privateers of 118 headed onward, their crews alert for additional targets to hit.

Fifteen minutes later they found a large tanker lying at anchor in the mouth of a harbor with cliffs on two sides rising several hundred feet high from the water's surface. Both planes circled over the land to the south of the harbor to start the attack. The tanker posed a perfect target as Finley's Privateer dived down with its turrets firing at the ship 150 feet below. The concentrated fire started several fires and black smoke poured from the vessel. There was no return fire as the pilot released a 500-pound bomb that struck the ship just below the waterline. The tanker shuddered as the bomb exploded and flames raced along the deck before shooting up into the sky, reaching a thousand feet.

The smoke was intense, so much so that it blocked Thompson's view as he followed Finley for his bombing run. At 200 feet he was below the crests of the cliffs that were straight ahead of the plane. Thompson turned the bomber, shore guns firing at him, tracers flying past the Privateer's wings, and passed alongside the cliff.

As they headed home a small cargo ship was seen twenty miles distant. The vessel's crew saw the approaching American planes and manned a three-inch gun on the stern. It opened fire as Thompson closed in for a strafing run, but the fire was inaccurate and none hit the Privateer. Meanwhile, Finley came down and released a bomb that failed to explode. Low on gas and ammunition, they headed home as the tough little ship defiantly kept firing at the departing planes.

Later that afternoon, it was Lts. Lloyd's and Pettes' turn to hit shipping off Korea. After a fruitless search that took the Privateers across the western coast of Kyushu, shipping was observed near Fusan Harbor. The first target was a heavily laden cargo vessel, its deck covered with cargo. Lloyd banked his plane and circled, eight of his .50-caliber guns spitting out a hail of gunfire toward the target. The bullets found their mark and the ship shuddered from a violent explosion. Flames spewed from the deck and a few moments later the vessel was gone. A sister ship a mile away saw the attack and tried in vain to reach safety within the harbor. Both planes swooped down and this one fell victim to machine gun fire.

Lt. Phil E. Pettes' Crew Five of VPB-118 consisted of (back row, L to R) John A. Bodde, ARM2c; Lt. (jg) Robert G. Gorman; Lt. Phil E. Pettes (PPC); Lt. (jg) D. T. Francis; Elmor B. Jones, AMM2c; and John Queen Jr., ARM2c. Front row (L to R): Robert D. Mason, AMM2c; John E. Waddell, AMM3c; Frank Young Jr., AMM3c; Albert S. Tankersley, AOM2c; Robert L. Reeves, AOM1c; and Edward I. Bonsall, ARM2c. *Courtesy of James Pettit via Richard Peterson*

The PB4Y-2s now headed toward a freighter weighing several thousand tons. It was now time to use the 500-pound bombs hanging in the bomb bays, as a coordinated run was made from minimum altitude with Lloyd leading the way. While Pettes' gunners strafed the ship from bow to stern the other Privateer came in, releasing one bomb. The device exploded forty feet from the ship and the vessel staggered from the concussion; a trail of oil appeared, indicating some damage had been done.

After one more attack both planes broke off and headed toward the south, leaving the freighter behind slightly damaged. Fifteen minutes later a freighter larger than the one they had attacked was sighted four miles off the coast. Dropping a bomb by "seaman's eye" was not precision bombing, and invariably several runs would have to be made before a direct hit was scored. This attack was no different, as both pilots took turns bombing, with the closest one falling thirty feet short of the intended victim. After two unsuccessful runs both planes were now down to one bomb each.

Lloyd came in first and released a 500-pound bomb which sailed down and hit the ship's stern. The force of the explosion lifted one end of the ship high out of the water. Pettes came in with an attack that took his plane across the length of the ship. His bomb landed in the water alongside the bow as the ship passed over it. With the effectiveness of a mine the bomb exploded underneath the vessel,

tearing the bow off completely, and as the crews of the Privateers watched the ship slipped beneath the water.

The following day, a lone Privateer piloted by Lt. Keiser took off on a mission that stretched across the Japanese Empire and Korea. It was customary to fly in pairs for mutual support, however, this time Keiser flew alone. A few minutes after noon two enemy destroyers were spotted, and beyond them a large freighter. It was no use to attack the warships; their combined defensive power could easily bring down a solitary patrol bomber. Instead the merchant ship was targeted, which was far beyond the capability for the destroyers to intervene.

The ship was riding low in the water, her decks piled high with cargo as the Privateer came down to strafe. Men on board began scattering across the deck as the plane's machine gun fire quickly started the cargo to burn. The PB4Y-2 crossed over the ship and Keiser pickled off a 500-pound bomb which struck the ship, exploded, and tore out a tremendous hole in her side; a hole large enough for the Privateer's crew to see through one side of the ship to the other. There was no need for another attack, as the freighter was afire from bow to stern and her crew was quickly abandoning the sinking vessel. Seeing the destroyers approaching Keiser left the scene and continued on patrol.

Fifteen minutes later a tanker no more than half a mile off the coast became the second victim of Keiser's one-plane blitz. This time the Privateer was met by a slow but steady hail of gunfire from the ship's three-inch gun on its stern.

Keiser banked the plane, making a steady turn, altitude dropping as he approached until he was 190 feet off the water. He pickled off a bomb which hit squarely amidships several feet above the water line. There was a flash of fire and smoke which at first seemed to envelope the ship, but it went out as quickly as it started. As the four-engine bomber passed over two 20 mm guns opened up in an attempt to bring the attacker down. Keiser's gunners noticed the positions and opened fire on them as the bomber came back around. Another bomb was released and hit fifteen feet short, sending water crashing over the ship's deck.

There was no return fire, as the vessel's gunners decided to hide instead of fight the tenacious American Privateer. The third bomb hit just forward of the superstructure, sending up another brief intense sheet of flame. The tanker headed for the beach, her captain intent on grounding her as Keiser's gunners kept a steady stream of machine gun fire on it for another six runs. The ship, carrying much needed fuel for the Japanese war effort, never made it to port, as it was rocked by an internal explosion and slowly settled in the shallows.

12

The Old Crows and Hicks' Raiders
May 1945

The relentless strikes on Japanese shipping continued undaunted, as four VPB-118 PB4Y-2s went out in pairs and hit targets around Japan and Korea. For one Privateer it would be her last mission. Lts. Lodato and Serrill were the first to take their planes out for the primary mission of looking for a missing American plane; instead, they too joined in attacking merchant ships and helped in rescuing a fellow crew that had been shot down.

After a fruitless search for the missing plane the Privateers began searching for shipping on their return home. Just after noon a small freighter was attacked, and after two bombing and six strafing runs the little ship was left listing to starboard, smoke drifting from it as a result of well-placed bombs. Soon after the attack Lt. Duba called on the radio to say that Lt.Cdr. Farwell and crew had been shot down by anti-aircraft fire while attacking a Japanese airfield at Kusan Fu. PBMs were called as Lodato and Serrill headed toward the crash site.

Around the same time the freighter was being demolished by Lodato and Serrill, Cdr. Farwell and Lt. Duba were closing in on a

dark blue painted Val. Although the Japanese plane had distance and speed advantage over the Privateers, the American planes quickly overtook the single-engine plane, and in an aerial battle which took hunter and hunted down to fifty feet, Farwell's gunners shot the Val out of the sky.

Crossing the northern limit of their search sector, the PB4Y-2s found a medium size freighter weighing some 1,500 tons. Lt. Duba flew protective cover, with his gunners laying down suppressing fire as Farwell came in for a bombing run. The first 500-pound bomb hit the superstructure on the stern, passed through the ship, and exploded in the engine room, sending up a cloud of steam and white smoke. The explosion caused the ship to stop dead in the water as Farwell crossed over the ship and came back around for another run. The Privateer approached at a slow 145 knots and another bomb was pickled off—another direct hit near the forward hatch. The ship's entire center section was blown away and it began sinking.[1] As the freighter slipped beneath the water another target was located and both planes headed toward it. It was a small tanker heading

A VPB-109 Privateer warming up on Iwo Jima (left) and a flight line of PB4Y-2s staging from the volcanic island circa mid-1945. *Left image courtesy of Roy Balke, right image courtesy of Bob Baird*

toward a small island. Mounted on the stern was an unmanned 20 mm gun, and two miles ahead of her was a destroyer escort.

Farwell went down for the attack as Duba's gunners raked the target with their machine guns. There had been no return fire as Duba came in to strafe, but as Farwell advanced the 20 mm gun position came to life and opened fire on the plane. The gunners were highly accurate, with the first bursts hitting the number three engine and setting it on fire; the number four engine took hits and began losing oil pressure; the hydraulic system was shot away; and in the bow turret Clifford R. Bell (AOM2c) was wounded by shell fragments.

Farwell headed the wounded bomber out to sea as the destroyer escort began firing her three-inch guns toward him. The situation got worse, as the electrical system failed and Farwell was unable to jettison the remaining bombs. A ray of hope was gained when he managed to feather the number three engine and put out the fire. Five minutes after being hit luck began running out for the crew, as the number four engine failed. The Privateer was dying and the men knew it as they headed toward their ditching stations, carrying the wounded Bell with them.

Two of the engines were out, the bomb bays were stuck in the open position, and bombs remained on board as Farwell headed the plane into the wind one hundred feet above the water. Five feet above the waves the bomber stalled, causing the port wing to drop. The plane hit the water and immediately the cockpit began to fill with water. Twelve of the crew quickly escaped the sinking aircraft, but one, pinned inside by an inflating life raft, was trapped.

Seeing one of their own struggling, the men slashed the raft with survival knives and shot holes into it with their revolvers to free the man. Seconds before the plane sank the man was freed, and all thirteen members of the crew were floating in the choppy water. There were only three one-man rafts left and injured members of the crew took them. The remaining ten clung to the sides in the cold water, waiting for rescue. Within twenty minutes Privateers flown

Enlisted members of VPB-109's Bureau Number 59522 *Miss Lotta Tail* with Roy Balke on the far left. *Courtesy of Roy Balke*

by Duba, Lodato, and Serrill arrived on the scene, followed by two PBMs. As the three Privateers circled Farwell and his men were picked up and flown home.

VPB-109 Arrives

While Farwell and his men recovered from their narrow escape, Navy land-based bomber operations on Okinawa doubled in size when the first three planes of VPB-109 reached Yontan on 10 May, after flying across the Pacific from Palawan.

Besides daily missions that taxed men and machine, the nerves of personnel on and around Okinawa were stretched even thinner by Japanese air attacks throughout the month. Yontan Field was hit during the nights of 10–12 May, but the attacks failed to cause any major damage. Men often wondered whether it was safer flying than spending time on the ground; at least it was a more comfortable feeling manning twin .50-caliber machine guns in a plane than lying defenseless in a canvas tent or a hastily dug foxhole.

Attacks on enemy shipping continued with strikes conducted by both squadrons 10–16 May. The Old Crows and the Raiders teamed up for the first time on 12 May, with 109's Lt. Don Chay and Lt. Lloyd of 118 teaming up. Off Shimono Shima they came across a 3,000-ton freighter. Turning in to attack, Chay's gunners began strafing the ship as Lloyd began a bombing run.

Chay's gunners concentrated their fire on a 20 mm gun on the bow and a 40 mm gun on the stern. Coming in at one hundred feet from stern to bow, Lloyd dropped two 500-pound bombs which fell short near the stern. The whole aft section of the ship lifted out of the water, sending up debris and oily water as the ship went dead in the water.

While Chay made a curving strafing run along the ship Lloyd made another run from port to starboard. Anti-aircraft fire became intense, with a 40 mm firing a steady stream at the attacking plane. As Lloyd approached the plane took several hits to the wings and fuselage. Under the intensifying fire Lloyd's second run resulted in two near misses with two 500-pound bombs. The ship got underway and began moving slowly in a circle as if the steering gear had been damaged. Once more Lloyd and Chay coordinated a run.

The ship's gunners concentrated on the bombing plane and their fire became more intense and accurate. Lloyd continued on his run, although the defensive fire was bracketing the plane, with the Privateer taking hits to the bow, wings, fuselage, and waist turrets. Lloyd dropped four 100-pound bombs in a string from stern to bow and the ship disappeared as a cascade of water came crashing down on the decks. The Privateer's number two engine failed as he pulled out of the bombing run, but the pilot feathered the prop and turned for home on three engines with Chay flying close to him.

Minutes after leaving the freighter the Privateers were intercepted by three enemy fighters. The fighters proved to be unassertive, as the patrol planes' gunners' fire drove them away after firing a few short bursts. After forty-five minutes the fighters broke off and left. Lloyd landed at Yontan, and upon inspecting his ship counted eighty holes in his plane caused by the freighter's gunfire.

Unidentified crewmen beside PB4Y-2 *Shanghai LiL* (Bureau Number 59475), reportedly lost in action with VPB-109. *Courtesy of Roy Balke*

Problems with the SWOD Mk-9 Bat Guided Bomb

The squadron still retained the Bat guided bomb, but now realized they were not worth a damn, and by summer kept only two aircraft armed with the weapon. The missile's failure was blamed on the heat, humidity, and mildew that wreaked havoc on the plywood shell and the internal electronics. It was amazing they worked at all. Still, they had to be used, and when they were, the desired results were not achieved. From the viewpoint of squadron members, the Raiders wanted to get down to minimum altitude and attack with machine guns and bombs, not stand miles away and launch a missile that in all probability would spiral into the ocean.

On the thirteenth both squadrons teamed up again, with Cdr. Hicks joining Lt. Cdr. Binning of VPB-118 on a search northward from Yontan to the Southern coast of Korea. Hicks' Privateer carried a Bat under each wing.

Four large merchant ships were sighted off the Korean coast. While Binning conducted bombing and strafing runs on three smaller ships Hicks made a Bat attack against a 2,000-ton freighter. The first missile was launched from eight miles out and 4,000 feet. The missile traveled true, but hit the water twenty feet ahead of the ship's bow. The bow was raised out of the water by the explosion but it failed to sink her. Hicks' gunners started strafing the vessel, and shortly the other plane joined him. Steam began pouring out around the superstructure, followed by fire and smoke, and the ship was left burning briskly and dead in the water as the two planes headed home.

Personnel who worked on the Bat struggled with overwhelming difficulties. The Bats had been flown through two typhoons, with subsequent warping and deterioration. They were assembled and disassembled numerous times, stacked in the hot sun and dust of the Philippines, and left unprotected in the mud and mold of Okinawa. No test equipment was available, and it is a tribute to the perseverance

and untiring energy of the men that the weapon managed even negative results.

On the sixteenth, Cdr. Hicks took off from Yontan Field with a mixed armament of one Bat and three 100-pound bombs on anti-shipping patrol in the Yellow Sea. Off Southwestern Korea he sighted a destroyer moving at twenty knots. The Bat locked on to the warship and was released at 4,000 feet from a range of three miles. The missile passed over and beyond the target and hit the water 500 yards beyond the ship's stern. Knowing the potential hazard of attacking a destroyer on the high seas Hicks sought out other game and soon found a 100-ton oil tanker.

The pilot had not made a low-level drop in several weeks and made a bombing run at one hundred feet, dropping one bomb largely for practice and then planning to destroy the ship by strafing. However, the bomb struck the ship at the water line thirty feet from the stern and the ship went down rapidly. The successful attack on the tanker was the squadron's first confirmed kill from Okinawa. The sixteenth also brought rain, and by the end of May, Okinawa would receive some twenty-one inches of precipitation. The water mixed with the soil made a thick, muddy "goo" that clung to both men and machines and made life miserable on the island.

Jacks and Georges Jump Privateers

A week after narrowly escaping death, Cdr. Farwell was back in the air, this time teaming up with Lt. Cdr. Finley on a search across Tsushima Strait for survivors of a PBM shot down the day before. Reaching an area near Tsushima Strait just before 9 a.m., Jack fighters intercepted the two Privateers. Both patrol planes closed together for mutual protection, reduced altitude to 300 feet, and for the next several minutes fought off eight attacks by the nimble single-engine fighters. As soon as the fighters came in both bombers took evasive action, consisting of shallow turns into the attack. Such tactics enabled both bombers to always keep at least three of their gun positions trained on the incoming Jacks.

An elaborate painting of a nude appearing on VPB-109's Bureau Number 59501 *Punkie. Courtesy of Roy Balke*

The Jacks began their attacks singly and in pairs, with the first beginning with unsuccessful phosphorous bomb drops. Two more Jacks came in separately, firing at the bombers from 1,600 feet before breaking off at 400 feet. The Privateers' gunners fired back, scoring numerous hits on both fighters. A piece flew off one near the engine cowling, and it was last seen trailing a thin trail of black smoke. The Privateers did not escape unscathed, as several 20 mm rounds hit both planes, causing slight damage.

The remaining three fighters pressed on, dropping phosphorous bombs and opening up with their wing guns. The gunners opened fire and hit one from nose to tail with .50-caliber machine gun rounds. The fighter went straight for half a mile, stalled, then plummeted into the water. Another Jack became a victim of the concentrated gunfire and went out of control before crashing into the sea. In the first documented case of PB4Y-2 Privateers going up against Jacks Japan lost two of its best fighters and another one was severely damaged.

This was the last combat patrol for 118 for a while, as they were sent to Tinian for rest and relaxation on the seventeenth. VPB-109 carried the burden of being the lone Privateer squadron for the next two weeks as they continued to ferret out enemy shipping.

As the men of 118 flew toward Tinian, on 17 May, 109's Lts. Warren and G. D. Fairbanks were searching an island group off southeastern Korea when they sighted a 100-ton oceangoing tug. Light, intense, accurate anti-aircraft fire was received from the tug and from nearby shore batteries. The planes circled it twice, silencing the boat's anti-aircraft fire before Lt. Warren made a bombing run at 300 feet.

Crossing the tug amidships from starboard to port, he dropped two 500-pound bombs. One of the bombs was a dud, but the other hit the water forty feet from the tug's stern and detonated. The explosion knocked the boat ninety degrees to starboard and it began to settle stern first. With the tug afire forward of the stack, a large fire in the after hatch, and the ship obviously sinking, the planes continued on patrol.

Crew Seven of VPB-109, led by Lt. George D. Fairbanks. Standing (L to R): Alfred V. Sandquist, AMM3c; Dean R. Johnson, ARM2C; Ens. Robert J. Groce; Lt. George D. Fairbanks; Ens. Abraham Shore; Evans R. Lally Jr., AMM2c; and Richard Jenkins, AMM3c. Kneeling (L to R): Donald J. Hamilton, AOM3c; Kasper E. Weigant, AOM3c; Marion E. Kinser, ARM2c; Robert L. Berry, ARM2c; and (not present for photo) Franklin Shlyk, AMM2c. *Courtesy of Roy Balke*

On the homeward leg of their sector three hours later, eleven Georges from the 343 Ku jumped the planes. This Air Group was an elite unit formed by Capt. Genda to protect the home islands. As Val M. Higgins, a member of Lt. Warren's crew, remembers, "If we had known what we were up against it would have scared the dickens out of us."[2]

The Japanese had picked the American planes on radar and intercepted them at 1448 hours. A running battle continued for the next half hour. Fairbanks' port waist turret gunner spotted the fighters as the Privateers were at 1,200 feet. The fighters were composed of

Two additional nudes that appeared on VPB-109 Privateers were *Blind Bomber* (Bureau Number 59514) and *Bachelor's Delight* (Bureau Number 59521). *Bachelor's Delight* was lost in action with its crew on 5 August 1945. *Courtesy of Roy Balke*

Lt. William A. Warren's Crew 12 of VPB-109. Standing (L to R): Richard T. Coleman, ARM2c; William R. Smith, AOM3c, Ens. Leo F. Haas; Lt. William A. Warren; Ens. Paul E. Geyer; Chester E. Rosell, AMM1c; and Richard P. Edson, ARM3c. Kneeling (L to R): Floyd D. King, AOM2c; Earl W. Newton, ARM2c; Val M. Higgins, AMM3C; Lowell E. Tiller, AMM3c; and Harold J. Carter, AMM2c. *Courtesy of Roy Balke*

three four-plane sections flying at 6,000 feet. The Privateers nosed over and reduced altitude to 400 feet, and throughout the action remained between 400 and 700 feet, constantly altering altitude slightly and making gentle turns toward the fighters.

Fairbanks flew close to Warren's starboard wing and remained in position throughout the action. Almost immediately the fighters began attacking by dropping phosphorous bombs. In all, ten phosphorous bombs were dropped: three being duds, but the other seven were accurate, with streamers striking the wing surfaces of the search planes with each burst. The fighters then broke up into individual runs, pulling up in front of the Privateers within 3,000 feet before making runs and then breaking to the rear.

Aggressive runs were made by single fighters, but were readily discouraged by a few bursts from the gunners. Then fighters attacking in pairs broke off under the search planes, which were at 600 feet, and both Privateers were damaged. Fairbanks' plane took hits in the fuselage fore and aft of the number one top turret when a 20 mm shell burst inside the plane, wounding the gunner and knocking the turret out of commission. Faulty installation of the side plate slides sheared off two ammunition belts and put his number two top turret out of commission early in the battle. After fifteen minutes the ejectors on the starboard waist turret broke, further diminishing the plane's firepower. Radio communication was destroyed and the throttle control to the number two engine was destroyed, necessitating feathering the engine. Within minutes Lt. Fairbanks had three wounded crewmembers.

The two Privateers managed to fight back, with Lt. Warren's bow, number one top turret, and tail turret gunners scoring hits at 1,000 feet on one George flown by Chief Petty Officer Shiro Hirotome.

The fighter took hits in the engine, fuselage, starboard wing, and wing root, and the plane crashed in flames. A second fighter flown by Petty Officer Second Class Ei Hoshino was hit simultaneously by the bow and number one top turrets of both planes.

Lt. Warren's gunners struck at the engine, belly, and starboard wing root as the fighter broke off below, and Lt. Fairbanks' gunners hit the port wing root and fuselage. Smoking, it crashed into the sea afire. After thirty minutes the fighters broke off the attack and left individually and in pairs. Five minutes after the last enemy plane cleared the area two PBM search planes of Fleet Air Wing One arrived at the scene and the Mariners stayed with the Privateers until certain that Lt. Fairbanks could make it back to base safely. Upon landing it was found Warren's Privateer had sustained considerable damage, with its main spar blown out of the vertical stabilizer. It was amazing it had made it back to base.[3]

Japanese Fighter Interception Continues

On 18 May, Lts. Hewitt and Serbin sighted a 2,000-ton attack transport three hours into their mission off southern Korea. Following the two-plane tactics used successfully against shipping in this area by pilots of VPB-118, both planes circled the target several times, with maximum machine gun fire directed at deck gun positions before a bombing run was initiated. One plane continued the heavy strafing until the second had begun a bombing run, ceasing fire as the bombing plane came in.

At one hundred feet Hewitt made a run and released three bombs: one fell eighty feet short and one was a direct hit amidships, while the third was considerably over. Circling, Hewitt came in but his bombs hung up. Trying again, the Privateer flew down the ship

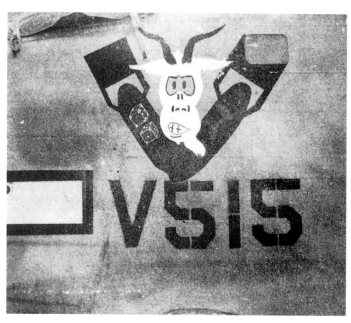

The crew of VPB-109's Bureau Number 59515 applied a different nose art motif from the often-seen female nude and named it *Hogan's Goat*. *Courtesy of Roy Balke*

from stern to bow, dropping a string of five bombs. One was a direct hit on the deck twenty-five feet from the stern, while another was a near miss twenty-five feet off the starboard side.

While Hewitt circled the ship, providing suppressing fire, Lt. Serbin initiated his bomb run and dropped two 250-pound bombs. Both bombs straddled the ship, with the first falling fifty feet short and the second fifty feet over. Serbin swung the Privateer around, made a second bombing run, and released a 500-pound bomb that hit the water fifty feet beyond the target. The ship was stopped dead in the water with a sharp starboard list and was blazing furiously aft and amidships by Hewitt's direct hit. The freighter was settling by the stern as the two Privateers left.

The same day Lts. Turner and Braddock were patrolling along the Southeastern Korean coast, fruitlessly investigating the many small harbors of the islands off the coast. Rounding the coast, they entered a harbor and spotted a 1,000-ton oil tanker at anchor and other smaller shipping. The ship began sending up meager anti-aircraft fire as the planes began their attack. Circling the oiler, the ship's fire was silenced by repeated strafing by both planes. The strafing caused the oiler to catch fire on its forward deck near the superstructure. Both planes then took turns making bombing runs on the burning ship.

Turner came in at 150 feet and dropped four 250-pound bombs which fell short. The bomb detonations caused a cascade of water to envelop the ship, but apparently caused little damage. Lt. Braddock had better luck on his run. Crossing over the length of the tanker—stern to bow—at 150 feet, Braddock dropped two 500-pound bombs. The first fell twenty feet short near the stern, but the second entered the water fifteen feet off the bow and detonated twenty-five feet beyond. The ship was tossed violently by the explosions and began to settle down by the bow, listing twelve degrees to port. Leaving the tanker sinking, the two Privateers headed toward the other merchant shipping in the harbor.

Moderate fire from heavy gun batteries on shore and light anti-aircraft fire from ships became increasingly accurate as the planes began their attacks. Lt. Turner selected a small coastal freighter as a target, but the bombs hung up in their racks. Unable to bomb the ship, his gunners selected three coastal ships and began strafing.

As Turner's crew was raking the vessels with .50-caliber machine gun fire, Braddock made a run on another freighter at anchor in the outer harbor. Before making a bombing run he circled the target so his gunners could suppress the light anti-aircraft fire coming from the ship. Crossing the freighter from bow to stern at 150 feet, Turner pickled off four 250-pound bombs. The first fell short, but the second was a direct hit on the forward deck and the third a direct hit on the stern, blowing it off. The freighter, in flames with a large hole torn in its deck and starboard bow, sank rapidly.

As Turner began a second bombing run on a small coastal his copilot sighted larger shipping in the distance in an inner harbor. The attack was broken off and both planes turned to investigate. The investigation was short, for seven destroyer escorts, three large

merchant ships in the 3,500–7,500 ton range, a larger ship of 7,000 tons, and several other ships of medium size were at anchor and began to put up a heavy curtain of anti-aircraft fire. As the planes turned to port out of range, Lt. Turner's number one top turret gunner sighted two enemy fighters and alerted both search planes.

The patrol planes were at 300 feet and immediately dropped down to the deck thirty feet off the water, turning south away from the harbor. The enemy fighters, identified as a Zeke and a Tojo, passed ahead and turned in for head-on runs. The search planes took no evasive action as the fighters broke off all runs before coming into range. After five minutes the fighters retired and the search planes extended their formation. Ten minutes later a single Tojo appeared and made a head-on run.

The run was directed at Turner's plane in the lead but came in between the two planes. Turner's gunners scored hits on the engine, cockpit, and along the starboard fuselage, while Lt. Braddock's bow and number one top turret gunners struck the engine, fuselage, and port wing root. The Tojo, smoking and losing altitude, disappeared to the north. Amazingly neither search plane was hit during the attack.

For two successive days VPB-109 search planes had been attacked by enemy fighters on the return leg of their search sectors, and two search PBM Mariners of Fleet Air Wing One were shot down in the same area a day earlier. Enemy radar stations along Kyushu and on the islands just off the coast were continuously tracking search planes as they moved north past Kyushu. This had given the enemy sufficient information of search planes' courses and times to vector out intercepting fighters on the return leg. To provide variety for the enemy interceptors it was planned that two regular patrol planes would fly routine patrol as scheduled at habitual latitudes and with no great time variation, consciously remaining on enemy radar screens.

Cdr. Hicks led eight Army P-47s south to Kyushu in an effort to decoy and intercept enemy fighters. Over Ie Shima he rendezvoused

VPB-108 Privateer Bureau Number 59460 was named *Els Notcho*.
Author's Collection

VPB-123 and 124 apparently operated Bureau Number 59504, the suggestive *Pastime*. *Author's Collection*

with fighters from the 318th Fighter Group. After reaching a point fifty miles due west of the returning patrol planes they entered the area of probable enemy interception. No enemy air activity materialized and the mission turned to destroying targets of opportunity.

Hicks sighted a 150-ton picket boat and the search plane and P-47s circled it twice to port, strafing and silencing the boat's anti-aircraft fire. Diving from 1,000 feet to 300 feet on the initial strafing run, the ship's deck gunners were killed and their 20 mm gun spun around like a pinwheel. The patrol boat, ablaze after Hicks' first run, exploded and sank. The pilots of the P-47s were pleased that this was not another routine patrol. With permission from Cdr. Hicks they flew over to attack Tonis Field at Gotto Retto, strafing and discharging their rockets and destroying a hangar and setting fire to an oil dump before returning to the PB4Y for the return trip back to base.

By mid-1945, the Japanese were reduced to shipping supplies and personnel by small coastal vessels weighing less than 100 tons. Working together singly or in small convoys, these vessels sailed back and forth along the Korean, Chinese, and Japanese coasts. These vessels rapidly diminished as the Raiders went after them day after day.

On 24 May, Lts. Jobe and Serbin sighted a large amount of shipping in the Korean Strait. Both planes carried only one Bat plus a bomb load, for the continued trouble with the guided missile allowed targets to escape which might have otherwise been attacked and destroyed by low altitude bombing runs. Three small coastal freighters in line sailing at eight knots were targeted and Lt. Jobe attacked the first ship in line. One of the two bombs dropped entered the water fifteen feet short, passed under the ship, and exploded on the port side. Jobe then turned his attention to the second ship. Releasing a 500-pound bomb, it fell short amidships and detonated beneath the hull. The ship was literally blown to pieces by the explosion, leaving only scattered debris on the water. Returning to

strafe the first ship, he made another three strafing runs and the ship was left sinking.

Attacking the third ship, Lt. Serbin made a bombing run from bow to stern and dropped three bombs which fell within twenty feet of the target. Explosions stopped it dead in the water, and four heavy strafing runs by Serbin and one by Jobe completed the ship's destruction. A larger 800-ton freighter sailing at ten knots was the next victim of Lt. Jobe. In several strafing runs to port at altitudes ranging 100–400 feet the ship was set afire, causing a large internal explosion that blew the stern off.

Less than two hours after sinking the four freighters a 7,000-ton troop transport was spotted. It was time to try the SWOD Mark 9 Bat again. Lt. Serbin launched his Bat from ten miles out at 4,000 feet. The missile traveled nose high and dove vertically into the sea three miles short of the target. Lt. Jobe sighted the ship visually on very rough seas and released his Bat from eight miles out at 5,000 feet. The missile functioned normally until it neared the transport, then struck the water a quarter mile short.

Lts. Chay and Hewitt, thirty minutes into their search, were off the southern coast of Korea, seeking enemy shipping, when an enemy destroyer was sighted which immediately opened fire at the planes. The planes started to gain altitude from their search altitude of 200 feet to 10,000 feet to prepare for an attack when Lt. Chay sighted three Rufe fighters coming up. The Privateers immediately joined up to present their gun power for whatever aggressiveness the enemy cared to show. While at 4,000 feet the enemy planes bracketed the planes, with one coming to port at 5,000 feet, one to starboard at 4,000 feet, and the remaining astern at 2,000 feet, outside the range of the bomber's gunners.

Evidently awaiting more fighters, the Rufes continued to follow the bombers. Suddenly a Nick, Zeke, and Tony came into sight to present their attacks. These aircraft possibly belonged to the 951 Ku based at Chinkai, Korea. A Rufe made a head on run on Lt. Chay's plane in an attempt to pull off to the starboard. Chay's bow

Lady Luck II* (Bureau Number 59446) of VPB-108 ran out of luck on 10 June 1945, and was replaced by *Lady Luck III*. *Courtesy of Bob Baird

gunner scored several hits that caused the Rufe to pull up, presenting a perfect target for the forward top turret. The top turret gunner opened fire and the fighter began a steep, wobbly glide before crashing into the water.[4]

The fighters used an altitude advantage of 1,000 feet, but simple evasive action of changing course and altitude rendered the attacks ineffective. The Tony made a head on run on Lt. Hewitt's plane, pulling away to the starboard and slightly under. His bow turret and forward top turret scored hits that caused the fighter to start on a downward journey to the water.

The Zeke attempted a side run on Lt. Chay, who was covering Hewitt's wing, and attempted to pull away to port. The starboard waist and tail guns of Chay's plane opened up, scoring hits and causing the Zeke to leave a trail of black smoke as it disappeared out of sight. While the Zeke was trailing smoke, the fight was broken off just as the number two engine of Lt. Chay's plane started a gas leak and two of his turrets became inoperative.

Japanese dead lie in the mud after a failed suicide attack on Yontan Field, Okinawa. *Courtesy of Roy Balke*

VPB-109 Un-phased

Throughout May, the Japanese tried to hamper an American build-up on Okinawa by sending in airborne raiding parties. Under a full moon and clear sky, the night of 24 May was full of Japanese air activity directed against Yontan Field, climaxed by the successful crash-landing of a Sally with its load of *Giretsu* (a special airborne attack unit) on the airstrip. Six Sallys carrying suicide squads attempted to land. Five were shot down by anti-aircraft fire, but one landed wheels up on the airfield and fifteen Japanese from the plane scrambled out. Before they were all killed they succeeded in destroying seven planes (including two of VPB-109), damaged another twenty-five, destroyed a 70,000-gallon fuel dump, and made two runways inoperable until the next morning. John O. Oates, a member of VPB109, standing as plane guard on the field, was seriously wounded when caught in the crossfire between the Japanese and the defending Marines. One of the planes shot down in flames crashed just short of squadron enlisted personnel tents and two more men were injured seeking foxhole protection.[5]

The Japanese suicide attack did not impede Hicks's Raiders from combat operations, as Lts. Keeling and Challis managed to take off the following morning to attack a 3,000-ton transport off Korea. Heavily and repeatedly strafed by both planes during eight runs, Keeling crossed over the transport at one hundred feet and dropped three bombs, scoring direct hits on the superstructure and bow. Challis, following in, dropped three bombs and scored one hit, causing the ship to list severely. Keeling came back at sixty feet and dropped a string of three bombs that straddled the target. Out of bombs and low on fuel, the planes left the area with the ship smoking and afire afloat. The ship was the *Amoy Maru*, and it later sank with a loss of forty-two crewmembers.

Successful anti-shipping strikes continued, including the first and only successful Bat attack conducted by VPB-109 against an enemy warship. Lts. Jadin and Moyer, on routine search and reconnaissance along the Southern Korean coast, were told to pay

Another of the Japanese commandos killed on Okinawa during the evening of 24 May 1945, who attempted to destroy American aircraft at Yontan Field. *Courtesy of Dr. M. F. Ebersol*

particular attention to Japanese shipping along reported shipping lanes. A 2,300-ton stack-aft freighter was sighted and both planes commenced strafing attacks. Meager anti-aircraft fire from 20 mm and 7.7 mm guns was encountered but the Privateers' gunners soon silenced them. Both planes then started bombing runs. One 250-pound bomb hit below the superstructure, causing major damage. On the second and third runs the ship took a hit on the stern from 500-pound bombs, causing the ship to emit a heavy flow of oil. The ship was left afire and the Privateers returned home. On the return leg Lt. Moyer headed to Gaja Shima and spotted an operating radio and radar station. Encountering meager anti-aircraft fire, both installations were hit by strafing and two 250-pound bombs.

Commander Hicks and wingman Lt. Kennedy conducted a special strike against enemy civilian and military shipping along

Lt. Leo Kennedy at the controls of a PB4Y-2 was on his second tour of duty with VPB-109 when he was killed in action at the end of May 1945. *Courtesy of the Joe Jobe Family*

the Korean coast between China and the Inland Sea, systematically ferreting the maze and myriad of coastal islands. Both Privateers carried a bomb load and a Bat suspended beneath their wings. The first target of the day was a 100-ton freighter moving slowly at four knots. Strafing caused the ship to beach itself. Five minutes later a large, 120-ton four-masted schooner was sighted at anchor. Hicks went in at one hundred feet and released two bombs. Both dropped just short of the schooner and detonated with a mining effect beneath the keel. The whole stern was blown off and the target sank by the stern. Less than ten minutes later two 100-ton freighters were discovered at anchor.

Hicks, at one hundred feet, dropped one 500-pound bomb, and one ship literally disintegrated in the explosion, leaving only floating debris. Lt. Kennedy, attacking the other ship, released three bombs. One fell short, but two hit the deck near the stack and the ship was blown out of the water. Seven minutes later two 150-ton freighters were discovered at anchor in a small harbor. Hicks sunk the first when one 500-pound bomb broke the ship into two parts. The two sections keeled over and sank. Attacking the other freighter, Kennedy's gunners began strafing and suddenly the ship exploded internally near the stern. It blazed brightly, then turned over to port and sank. As the planes skimmed over the countryside two small freighters were discovered at anchor in an adjacent small harbor. Again, Lt. Kennedy's gunners set one rapidly afire, which sank after several small internal explosions. The second ship was strafed heavily and began to burn brightly as the planes withdrew.

Almost an hour passed before a coastal freighter moving slowly was spotted and was strafed by Lt. Kennedy in passing, drawing some smoke. Minutes later they encountered a large 3,000 ton stack-aft freighter. Cdr. Hicks went in first and dropped a bomb which fell fifty feet short, causing no apparent damage. At one hundred feet Lt. Kennedy dropped one 500-pound bomb for a direct hit above the water line near stern. The explosion blew the stern off, causing the ship to rapidly heal over to port and sink.

On their homeward path two large single-stack destroyer escorts of 2,300 tons were sighted by radar from twenty miles on the high

seas cruising at fifteen knots, and identified visually at fifteen miles from 2,000 feet. The ships were the *Kuga* and *Aguni*, classified as *Kaibōkan* (ocean defense ships) of 940 tons with a complement of 150 men. Range was closed to six miles as the planes began their Bat attack, with both warships sending up heavy moderate inaccurate anti-aircraft fire. The planes made a 180-degree turn, with Lt. Kennedy climbing to 8,500 feet. Cdr. Hicks, at 6,000 feet, followed two miles behind. The anti-aircraft fire, which was intense and increasingly accurate as the planes neared, ceased as Lt. Kennedy began his run. Three miles from the target the missile was released from 6,000 feet. This time the weapon traveled true, hitting the warship directly on the bow above the water line and blowing off the bow back to the first turret. The bomb destroyed the *Aguni's* foredeck and killed thirty-three men, but the *Kuga* was able to tow her to the Korean port Chinhae, where repairs were made. She sailed under her own power to Pusan, Korea, where she remained until the end of the war.[6]

Both planes circled at 5,000 feet to assess the damage before anti-aircraft fire from the undamaged warship was received, forcing withdrawal. As soon as the Bat detonated the undamaged escort, originally a mile away, proceeded to a position one hundred yards from her damaged sister ship. She then turned broadside and started throwing heavy moderate accurate anti-aircraft fire. The planes headed for base, leaving behind eleven ships sunk or damaged.

A USAAF evaluation study of the Bat bomb stated thirty-three were expended in combat situations April–July 1945, with four hits and four near misses. VPB-109 is credited with destroying two small merchant ships in Balikpapan Harbor during April, and damaged another while the squadron was based on Okinawa. Neither VPB-123 nor VPB-124 scored using the Bat. The weapon was highly inaccurate, with a success rate of only twelve percent, primarily due to its early tracking and radar system, which at times could not track an individual target if the vessel was part of a convoy; and damage to some of the weapons while being flown to the forward area and maintenance issues caused by heat, humidity, and dust.

Lady Luck III, **stripped of usable parts, lies abandoned in the boneyard of Iwo Jima.** *Courtesy of Bob Baird*

13

VPB-123 and the Return of 118
May–June 1945

On 27 May, VPB-123 joined the Raiders of 109 on Okinawa. Under the leadership of Lt.Cdr. Samuel G. Shilling, VPB-123 was back in the Pacific after being away for thirteen months. Earlier in the war they had earned a reputation in the Solomon Islands as VB-140, flying the twin-engine Lockheed PV1 Ventura. Under Lt.Cdr. Vernon Williams, VB140 was the first PV-1 squadron to operate in the South Pacific, and before their tour of duty was over flew 664 missions.

On 30 May 1945, the reestablished squadron began new combat missions; it would be the first of 230 missions. One of the first crews to arrive was Lt. Ken Sanford, a veteran of VPB140. He and his crew were immediately baptized by the primitive living conditions and the ruthlessness of war. The evening of the twenty-sixth, Japanese suicide squads attempted another attack by crash landing a Sally on to the airfield. The Marines guarding the base quickly dispatched the twelve commandos on board. A Privateer commanded by Kenneth Sanford landed amid the debris and taxied to a halt. Climbing out of the aircraft, he walked past a destroyed Corsair fighter and behind it he could see the body of one of the Japanese commandos.

Looking down, he saw an example of what men can do to each other in war. "He laid there, twisted, eyes opened, with his severed penis jammed in his mouth." Sanford thought he was glad the Marines were on his side as he walked away and headed for his quarters. For Sanford and many others life on Okinawa continued amid rain, mud, broken equipment, and destroyed planes.[1]

On 29 May, VPB-109's Lt. Vadnais and Lt. (jg) Albert Vidal, on an anti-shipping campaign against Japanese shipping off the southeastern Korean coast, attacked a 2,300-ton freighter. Strafing by both planes killed personnel on the ship's deck as they were preparing to man the deck guns. Lt. Vadnais came around again from port to starboard amidships but missed with his two 500-pound bombs. Lt. Vidal scored a direct hit amidships, throwing bodies and debris 200 feet in the air, and the ship sank to the bottom in thirty-four seconds.

Bureau Number 59480 was a VPB-108 Privateer with the name *Hippin Kitten II. Courtesy of Bob Baird*

Privateers based on Iwo Jima waiting to be called into action circa mid-1945. *Courtesy of Bob Baird*

Lt. N. Michael Keiser's Crew 12 of VPB-118. Back row (l to r): George P. Schwartz, ARM2c; Hubert A. Colclasure, AMM1c (plane captain); Lt. N. Michael Keiser; Ensign Samuel I. Heublein; Lt. (jg) John O. Hanan; and R. J. McKay, AOM2c. Front row (l to r): Stanley J. Labieniec, AMM2c; Glenn A. Barnes, ARM2c; Donald V. Gray, AMM2c; Robert E. Clark, AOM3c; and Winston D. Jones Jr., AMM2c. *Courtesy of Al Marks and names courtesy of Richard Peterson*

A group of PB4Y-2 Privateers from VPB-109 heading toward Shanghai, China, to attack Japanese shipping at the end of May 1945. *Courtesy of Roy Balke*

VPB-109 Yangtze River Adventure

Continued reports of worthwhile shipping targets off the coast of China and the diminishing number of large merchant ships encountered along the Korean coast in regular patrol areas prompted the decision by Cdr. Hicks to ferret the China coast. With reports of large shipping near Shanghai, Lts. Turner and Warren were sent to cover the Yangtze River mouth, where they conducted unsuccessful Bat attacks against a 6,000-ton attack transport and a 4,000-ton freighter.

Approaching the coast, they sighted the two ships and Lt. Turner released his Bat at 8,000 feet two miles from target. The missile fell off on its own starboard wing and exploded on impact with the

surface. Lt. Warren's Bat, released from 8,000 feet and ten miles from the target, made a wide turn to starboard before straightening out. However, it hit the water three miles from the ship.

They encountered so much shipping that four planes were dispatched the following day to the mouth of the Yangtze. The flight consisted of two sections consisting of Lts. Davis, Jobe, Kennedy, and Serbin. The first to arrive on the scene were Davis and Serbin, and for the next hour the four planes would be engaged in continuous action.

Ten minutes past noon Davis and Serbin spotted a 3,000-ton attack transport and two small picket boats slowly moving off the coast. Lt. Davis began his run strafing at low level as Serbin prepared for a Bat attack. Davis' plane immediately took hits and was seriously damaged. Four bursts from 20 mm and 40 mm guns near the

VPB-123's Kenneth Sanford at the controls. *Courtesy of Ken Sanford*

Kenneth Sanford's copilot Wally Howison. *Courtesy of Ken Sanford*

"Jumping" Joe Weller's Crew 16 of VPB-118 consisted of Lt. Nolan W. Weller; Lt. (jg) J. D. Brewis; Lt. (jg) Walter E. Meier Jr.; Earl R. Mann Jr., AMM2c; Paul F. O'Neil, AMM2c; John F. Healey, AMM2c; Edwin R. Palzynski, AMM2c; Harold P. Bower, ARM2c; Joseph E. Travascio, ARM2c; Richard C. Burns, AOM2c; and Donald F. Berger, AOM2c. *Courtesy of Steve Hawley, names courtesy of Richard Peterson*

transport's bridge section damaged the number one and three engines, rudder controls, radio, and the starboard fuselage. Davis' copilot, Ensign Chester F. Szewczyk, and plane captain William Y. Toellen were severely wounded. Because his radio was knocked out Davis could not warn the following planes of the intense defensive fire being put up by the ships. Davis immediately set course for base, where he made a safe landing in near zero visibility. For the next hour the three Privateers were in constant contact with enemy shipping. Their first target was an anchored 2,300-ton freighter. After one strafing run at 200 feet to silence the ship's anti-aircraft fire the planes commenced two bombing runs from one hundred feet. Two near misses by 500-pound bombs started fires, and the ship listed sharply to port and began to settle when last observed.

The next targets for Jobe and Kennedy were a 4,000-ton merchantman and a picket boat. Heavily strafed by both planes, Kennedy flew along the ship from stern to bow and dropped two bombs for near misses. He began circling for a second run when Serbin told them of the two large attack transports. Preferring to save his bombs Kennedy broke off the attack. It proved to be a costly mistake.

Fifteen minutes later the Privateers made strafing runs on a 200-ton lightship, four picket boats, and a 300-ton oil tanker. Light, moderate, inaccurate anti-aircraft fire was received during three circular strafing runs. The picket boats were heavily strafed by the three planes and were left ablaze as the planes withdrew. One of the ships burst into a tower of flames as it split in two, with the bow sinking rapidly, while the stern remained afloat when last observed. The attack on the tanker proved to be the last successful one conducted by Jobe and Kennedy. They withdrew and headed for the two transports moving in line a half mile apart at fifteen knots.

The pilots planned only a strafing run on the transports until certain anti-aircraft fire was eliminated before making bomb runs. Jobe cut across the bow of the lead ship with his gunners strafing. He circled again and flew up the ship from stern to bow of the trailing ship and crossing to port of the lead ship. Kennedy, a quarter mile behind, bracketed the transport by strafing the length of the starboard side and then falling in behind Jobe as he crossed over. Suddenly the lead transport turned hard to port, and as the planes came around broadside on the starboard side opened fire with heavy accurate anti-aircraft fire.

The first burst from the lead transport caught both planes. Jobe's plane was severely damaged, with his horizontal stabilizer and vertical stabilizer shot out and a bomb bay door blown off. With loss of rudder control he was forced to retire and return to base. Then a 20 mm shell exploded in Lt. Kennedy's cockpit, killing him almost instantly and wounding copilot Ensign William E. Wassner. Although wounded and with most of his instruments shot away, Wassner made a successful crash landing at Okinawa three hours later. Leo Kennedy, the bushy blond-haired veteran of the squadron's first tour, was gone—he would not be the last combat veteran to die. The last day of the month Hicks' squadron received verbal orders from Cdr. Fleet Air Wing 1 to retire to Tinian for rest and repair. They would not be back on Okinawa for nearly two months. In their place, after a relaxing time on Tinian, the Old Crows of 118 arrived back on Okinawa on 1 June.

The Old Crows moved back to Okinawa and found that 109 was gone, with VPB-123 in its place. Camp life still consisted of living in tents and eating K rations, but life was improving, with showers being installed and hard flooring in the tents replacing dirt. The hard flooring had been stolen from the Army by scavengers of VPB-123.

One of the large Japanese transports attacked in the Yangtze River by VPB-109 on 30 May 1945. The ships were heavily armed, resulting in the death of Lt. Kennedy and the wounding of four other men. *A Pictorial Record of the Combat Duty of Patrol Bombing Squadron 109*

The Troublemakers of VPB-123

On 4 June, 123's Lts. Sanford and Al G. McCuaig teamed up for an anti-shipping sweep around Tsushima Island. Flight crews awoke at 0200 for an 0400 take-off. The weather was terrible, with gusting winds and heavy rain. After the pre-flight briefing the now rain-soaked crews climbed into their aircraft, the preflight check was completed, and both planes moved down the runway and into the air.

Two hours after take-off Sanford's radar operator picked up surface targets at a distance of fifty miles. Sanford called McCuaig to confirm the targets, which he did. Through the haze two enemy destroyers were seen moving at flank speed as the Privateers approached just feet off the water. The warships had spotted the planes and began sending a thick curtain of anti-aircraft fire so intense the attack was aborted. Both plane commanders knew their aircraft were no match for the destroyers so they decided to look for easier game.

Along the southern coast of Korea, near small islands that dot the area, a 1,500-ton freighter was attacked. During two bombing and strafing runs by both Privateers the ship sank after being hit by one 500-pound bomb dropped by McCuaig. A few minutes later several smaller cargo ships were hit, leaving all severely damaged or sunk. The day was not over for them, as they headed for Kyushu, where a large tanker was spotted.

Sanford saw small boats around the tanker and thought they were fishing boats, but he was wrong; they were well-armed picket boats protecting the valuable cargo in the ship. McCuaig went in first and his plane immediately took a hit to its number four engine. Sanford came in behind, fifty feet off the water, all guns trained and firing at the tanker. Puffs of anti-aircraft fire peppered the sky around the attacking plane. Sanford crossed over the ship and released two 500-pound bombs. The first hit in front of the vessel at the waterline and the second hit the superstructure; the ship started to burn. Suddenly his Privateer lurched, shuddered, and started going down. The picket boats had hit the Privateer with three 40 mm rounds and the aileron controls would not respond; the plane began heading back toward the picket boats. Sanford called the other plane commander and told him he was going to ditch. The other Privateer was in a similar predicament, with its number four engine out and the bomb bay doors hanging down in shreds.

Sanford's copilot, Lt. Wally Howison, managed to manually set the aileron trim tab and the aircraft gradually straightened out just out of range of the picket boats. The crew began jettisoning everything except for survival gear to lighten the plane and gain altitude. Sanford looked out the window and at the wing; it had been perforated with 40 mm rounds and it was now flapping in the wind. The possibility of ditching kept entering Sanford's mind as the aircraft shook violently. He was worried the wing would shear off. The plane continued and communication was later

VPB-118's *Modest O' Miss* (Bureau Number 59402) crashed while landing on Iwo Jima on 6 March 1945. *Courtesy of Steve Hawley*

established with friendly warships and Yontan. Even in the most stressful of circumstances the human body continues its normal routine, and for Sanford, the need to urinate took over his mind. He had to keep control of the aircraft and did the only thing he could do—he relieved himself. Miraculously, four hours after the planes had been hit both Privateers reached Yontan and landed safely. For their work in getting the plane back and sinking a large oil tanker both pilots received the Silver Star Medal and their crew, the DFC.[2]

The aggressiveness exhibited by McCuaig in the attack, and for others that followed, earned him the nickname, "Troublemaker." Even the commanding officer was leery of flying wing with him, as "Troublemaker" had a tendency to break away for an attack, leaving his wingman behind. After a brief stint with the skipper McCuaig teamed up again with Kenneth Sanford. The team set new ground rules for attacking targets to keep McCuaig from killing himself. Sanford recalls "Mac" let him decide which targets to attack. As "Troublemaker" put it, "since you have a wife and a kid on the way, you can decide the odds." Sanford responded, "I'm looking for the Victory Medal and don't plan to be posthumously heroic. I'll at least offer an opinion." With the ground rules established the McCuaig-Sanford team remained intact for the duration, with both men and their crews surviving the war. As a team the two Privateer crews sunk thirteen ships, damaged seven, and shot down two enemy aircraft. Sanford was also credited with destroying four trains, two factories, and a bridge.[3]

Mining Campaign

The arrival of VPB-118 coincided with a mining campaign in Korean waters that took place between 9 and 30 June. The Old Crows were picked for the assignment. At the peak of this campaign 118 sent out six planes carrying twelve mines with a total weight of 24,000 pounds. However, mining did not interfere with the squadron's quest for enemy shipping, as they succeeded in sinking or damaging an estimated twenty-six ships for a total tonnage of some 16,000 tons. This effort was not without cost to man or material. On the twenty-fourth, five Privateers, each carrying two 1,000-pound mines, took off from Okinawa and headed toward southwestern Korea.[4]

Lt. Montgomery led the flight across the width of Korea and on the way managed to damage a passenger train, with the gunners being warned not to hit the passenger cars to limit civilian casualties. As the flight headed toward the coast two airfields were strafed in passing, causing serious damage to gun emplacements, barracks, and possibly damaging two Tony fighters on the ground. Now over a channel across from the airfields, two small freighters and a tugboat towing four barges became targets of the Privateer's gunners. The next targets came into view and this time the Japanese gunners were ready.

Some four miles separated two ships, one grossing 5,000-tons and the other 1,000-tons as the five patrol bombers swung into action. Immediately both ships, as well as a shore battery on a nearby island, began sending up anti-aircraft fire. The Privateers broke off into two sections, with three of them concentrating on the larger ship, while the remaining two went after the smaller one.

Aboard Lt. Keiser's plane, Ensign S. L. Heublein began taking pictures of the attack with his K-20 camera. After his third run Keiser turned away as a 25 mm round found the Privateer just aft of the radar operator's seat. Heublein and AMM1c Hubert Colcasure took shrapnel hits to the legs. The ensign was in bad shape, with a wound to his right leg so serious it was doubtful it could be saved. Seeing his men injured Keiser informed the other planes he was returning home. To keep protective cover Lt. Lloyd flew alongside Keiser all the way back to Okinawa. The other planes then started silencing the 25 mm gun positions on the ship and left it burning.

Photographic developing lab of VD-5 taken on Guam. *Courtesy of the NARA*

PB4Y-2 Privateer *Red Wing* **(Bureau Number 59505) was one of two such aircraft that bore similar names. This one belonged to VPB-123.** *Author's Collection*

14

Sons, Fathers, and Friends
The Saga of VPB-124
June–September 1945

On 16 June, VPB-124 arrived at Yontan after a brief two-week stay on Tinian under FAW-18. The squadron's leader, Cdr. Charles E. Houston, was the former executive officer of VPB-140 and a 1936 graduate of Annapolis. His executive officer, Lt. (later Lt.Cdr.) John M. Miller, was a 1940 Academy man. Like her sister squadron VPB-123, VPB-124 had its roots as a PV-1 squadron when it was known as VB-138. Indeed, quite a few men of VPB-124 had belonged to VB-138. Now both of the ex-Ventura squadrons had traded in their twin-engine bombers for the Privateer.

Before their arrival, squadron personnel had created quite a few stories that lived on in their memories of a war that sometimes had a lighter side to it. The following stories are the recollections of Ted Rowcliffe:

"One of 124's pilots was Dave Davis, who was a lieutenant (jg) stationed in the Navy Personnel Department in Washington, DC, when he applied for naval aviation training. After subjecting himself to all the mental and physical tests and examinations he passed with

flying colors (having been a distinguished scholar at Princeton and the number two hammer throw athlete in the United States), except he was turned down for flight training. In his disappointment he told his personal friend, who picked up the torch and charged into the boss' office to find out why.

"When his friend was told the reason was malocclusion (an irregular contact of opposing teeth in the upper and lower jaws) he retorted, 'What the hell! Dave's not going out there to bite the yellow bastards!' He was able to get Dave a waiver to resign his commission and start over as a naval cadet, which is somewhat lower than a coffeepot. Anyhow, he was eventually commissioned again as an ensign and naval aviator. Later he was flying with Bob Brower when they were shot down and ditched off Goto Retto, Japan. With the four other survivors of the ditching he was taken to Ofuna prison camp and remained there for the rest of the war."

"Another story concerns 'Little Joe' Rolleri when he was in primary flight training. He was awed by all the wonders of flight,

The formal squadron photograph of VPB-124 taken before departing to the Central Pacific circa late May–early June 1945. Seventy-two of the men pictured would either become prisoners of war or be killed 6 June–21 July 1945. *Courtesy of F. T. Pierce*

Cdr. Charles E. Houston, Commanding Officer of VPB-124. *Courtesy of F. T. Pierce*

Lt. Cdr. John M. Miller, the Executive Officer of VPB124 who took command after Cdr. Houston was shot down. *Courtesy of F. T. Pierce*

particularly aerobatics. After he was finally able to get the N2S (a Navy primary training plane) off the ground and back again without losing the landing gear, his instructor took him up to teach him the basics of aerobatic flying. Joe looked forward to the first lesson with great anticipation. After 'Little Joe' took off and climbed to the specified altitude his instructor said 'Ok, I've got it,' and proceeded to do a slow roll. The only problem was 'Little Joe' Rolleri had forgotten to hook his seat belt and fell out of the plane when it rolled upside down.

"The chute opened as it was supposed to do when the ripcord is pulled. Moreover, the glide down toward Mother Earth was delightful after you get over the stark terror of the free fall. However, as Joe got closer to the ground, he recognized he was going to land on a big red barn in the middle of green fields. Well, he didn't quite land on the barn, but he was close enough that his chute caught on

Lts. (jg) Ellis and Rowcliffe in Hutchinson, Kansas, were patrol plane commanders with VPB-124. *Courtesy of F. T. Pierce*

the end of the ridge beam of the roof and slammed him into the end of the barn. At least that was the last he remembered for a while. Nevertheless, it wasn't all bad, because when he came to, he was being cradled in the ample bosom of the farmer's wife, who thought he was dying or dead. Joe never told any of his friends about the incident because he thought they might give him a bad time about it. And you know, he was right!

"In Kaneohe, Hawaii, before 124's departure to the forward area, some of the men found themselves in strange predicaments. There are times when lieutenant (jg) should not be turned loose on a base. This is particularly true at night when the bar is open. Dan Donovan and his partner were like that. After playing Acey Deucey all afternoon and noting the sun had dissected the yardarm they put on their hats and headed up the cliff stairs to the O-Club. It did not take long to consume enough of the medicine to produce the euphoric effect relatively common on those nights before the TransPac to Johnson, Kwajalein, Guam, and Tinian.

"As the melodious evening progressed in the sterling company of others of VPB-124, nature's demanding call preempted the good times and there was a forced march downstairs to the head. Everything was under control and proceeding in good shape with great relief when another officer pulled into the urinal stall next to Donovan.

"Turning his fogged over, bleary eyes toward the newcomer, Dan acknowledged his presence by saying, 'Hi, mate, my name's Donovan. What's yours?' In that instant Donovan's partner took in the gold braids on that sleeve, shut off the flow, and tried to disappear when he heard a rather soft voice reply, 'Mitscher [Vice Admiral Marc Mitscher, Commander of Task Force 58]. . . .' Fortunately, it was foggy everywhere that night!

"In each of our crews, we had one or two gunners who had seen action in the previous squadron [VB-138] or in P-boats. But that still left us with about four or five crewmembers that were a little green and overeager to burn up some real live ammunition. The

Four photographs show the wreckage of a PB4Y-2 Privateer from which Lt. (jg) F.T. Pierce and his crew escaped uninjured. *Courtesy of F. T. Pierce*

VPB-124 living quarters on Okinawa. *Courtesy of F. T. Pierce*

Lt. G.E. Miller and Lt. (jg) D.E. Ellis spotted merchant vessels in a harbor on the south coast of Korea. *Courtesy of Ted Rowcliffe*

One of four Japanese merchant vessels attacked by Lieutenants Jack F. Griffin and James R. Preis on 24 June 1945. *Courtesy of Ted Rowcliffe*

twin .50-caliber guns in the turrets could really chew up the ammo when the six turrets were busy. However, there was one major drawback to the scene. When you clamp down on the trigger in the excitement of pulverizing the target, there is a real tendency to hold on too long, overheating and warping the gun barrels; this isn't good because the bullets do not go where you are aiming.

"Well, Jim Preis and I were shocked to find out that we had to replace about a dozen gun barrels after two days of firing practice, and in my exasperation I told Dusty Rhodes and Jack Patterson, 'I reckoned that even I could do better than that.' Now, if you say something like that to a couple good, competent gunners who know what it is all about you better be ready for whatever comes next.

"The next day I was cornered by Dusty and Pat, directed to the forward top deck turret, and told, 'OK, now show us!' This was a pure case of stuffing your foot into your mouth up to your ankle and wishing you were back at the club having a beer. I did not find any escape mechanism except a parachute, and I was a little hesitant about climbing out of the plane at 6,000 feet, so I figured I'd better try the guns.

"In the first place the turret was built for a midget, and my six two, one-hundred-eighty pounds almost fit into it, leaving just about room enough to turn my head and barely maneuver the controls. On the way out to the range I was trying to remember how to operate the turret and all the aiming wisdom I had learned on the gunnery trainers.

"Suddenly, coming down at us from two o'clock high was a Wildcat, stringing his cable and target behind. I was so surprised I almost forgot to fire, but Dusty didn't forget. He tracked that target and gave it a good clean burst. Fortunately we went into a cloud bank about then and the exercise was called off. Unfortunately for me, when I took my finger off the trigger the gun stopped firing, but the ammunition feeders continued to feed the .50-caliber cartridges

Japanese trawlers under attack by Lieutenants Griffin and Preis on 29 June 1945. *Courtesy of Ted Rowcliffe*

The Japanese subchaser that shot down Lt. Brower under attack on 7 July 1945. Note the ejected .50-caliber shell casings from the Privateer just above the ship. *Courtesy of Ted Rowcliffe*

into the now inoperative guns and began to fill the remaining space in the turret around my head while I was trying—not too successfully—to get out of the turret. After what seemed to be a long time Pat cut the power off and got me out of his turret. I have not been able to prove it, but I'm positive that there was some chicanery involved by the crew involving the malfunctioning ammo feeders.

"I sure learned my lesson there, but they didn't have to rub it in that twenty of the twenty-eight slugs from Dusty's guns hit the target and my eight rounds were still headed toward Guam! Fortunately the point was made, the crew settled right down after that, and turned out to be top hands with the guns for the rest of the cruise."[1]

VPB-124 Begin Combat Operations

Before their arrival at Okinawa, VPB-124 got its feet wet when a couple crews flew harassing raids on Truk. On Okinawa, the three Privateer squadrons continued their special strike and anti-shipping operations along the China coast, Tsushima Straits, and coastal areas of Korea and Kyushu. In the weeks to come Houston's squadron

Lt. F. T. Pierce's crew. Front row (L to R): R. R. Zanotelli, G. A. Cyrus, L. W. Stuckey, J. F. Coles, C. B. Smith, and J. A. Monheiser. Back row (L to R): G. E. Zard, C. E. Vermillion, T. F. Pierce, B. J. Scott, and A. J. Conte. *Courtesy of F. T. Pierce*

Lt. Cdr. Miller's crew. Back row (L to R): J.E. Fruits, J. Rolleri, J.M. Miller, R.C. Utter, F.L. Acosta. Front row (L to R): R.A. Smith, J.L. Holcomb, G.L. Molloy, J.V. Maliszewski, M.E. Ford, J.L. Mullen. *Courtesy of David Mullen*

would be chewed to pieces, losing six aircraft and some seventy men, with the commanding officer being one of the unlucky ones.

Lts. J. E. Vincent and R. D. Johnston conducted the first search for the new squadron in the Sea of Japan during the morning hours of 18 June. The victims of their search were six fishing boats and a small cargo ship. The following day an 800-ton cargo ship went to the bottom of the Sea of Japan after a successful bombing conducted by Lt. R. J. Brower and Lt. (jg) Osborn.

VPB-124's first encounters with enemy fighters occurred the following day while on a joint operation with 118 involving the mining of Korean waters. Lts. Gil Miller and J. E. Sanders ran into two small ships and a large coastal passenger steamer in Rakuti harbor, on the southeast tip of Korea. Miller scored two direct hits on the steamer while Sanders strafed the smaller ships. Just before Miller made his third run his gunners spotted eight Tojos coming down toward them. Seeing the trouble he was about to get into the Privateer pilot headed the bomber out to sea and away from the pursuers.

The slower patrol bomber was no match for the speed of the Japanese fighters, and for the next fifteen minutes Miller and his

Lt. Cdr. Miller and Lt. (jg) G.P. Arnold hit a factory on Kyushu, Japan. *Courtesy of Ted Rowcliffe*

Railroad facilities under attack on Kyushu. *Courtesy of Ted Rowcliffe*

Lt. Ramsey attacking a 1,000-ton freighter off Korea on 14 July 1945. *Courtesy of Ted Rowcliffe*

Smoke billows from a direct bomb hit on the freighter identified as a Sugar Able Sugar. *Courtesy of Ted Rowcliffe*

Lt. J.E. Ramsey and crew. Back row (L to R): H.H. Hamlett, M.H. Williams, J.E. Ramsey, R.F. Stengelin, A.E. Kallstrom. Front row (L to R): R.L. Rummel, R.S. Nicholes, H. Hobbs, W.A. Yankow, J.H. Anson, H.C. Wilson. *Courtesy of Trudy Jones*

Hugh Crae Wilson, a member of Ramsey's crew, left behind a young wife and a two-week-old daughter when he was killed in July 1945. *Courtesy of Trudy Jones*

Gear Down and Locked **(Bureau Number 59519) was one of two VPB-124 Privateers lost in action on 21 July 1945.** *Courtesy of Ted Rowcliffe*

crew fought off eight attacks, as both attacker and attacked dove down to within fifty feet of the water. The Tojos tried the unsuccessful tactic of dropping phosphorous bombs on the Privateer to no avail before deciding to peel off and attack. Two came in at eleven and one o'clock and were hit repeatedly by the Privateer's bow, top, and waist guns. The rounds found their mark, as one fighter broke off from the attack, smoking heavily as it retired. Another one came in and was hit by the aft upper turret and tail turret. The rounds hit the fighter's cockpit area and it flipped on its back and plunged into the water.

The remaining Tojos broke off the attack and Miller rejoined Sanders. Gil Miller would go on to become one of the squadron's most aggressive patrol plane commanders, and he, along with Lt. Ramsey, would wage war against all types of enemy shipping, from single vessels to entire convoys. In doing so some called them too eager and foolhardy.

For the next several days VPB-124 aircraft found small shipping in the Sea of Japan and Korea. Lt.Cdr. Miller and Lt. (jg) G. P. Arnold netted two small merchant ships and five more damaged on the twenty-first, while Lts. R. D. Johnston and J. E. Vincent damaged six similar vessels a day later. On the twenty-fifth, Miller and Arnold went out again. On a search between Gotto Retto and Kyushu, Japan, they sighted a convoy of merchant ships being escorted by a destroyer escort. A 1,000-ton freighter had fallen behind the main convoy and became the target of the two Privateers. After several bombing and strafing attacks that expended fifteen 250-pound bombs and 3,100 rounds of ammunition the ship was left a burning wreck, slowly slipping under the sea.

June 23 and 25 were days VPB-124 tried to use their SWOD MK-9 Bats, with both attempts failing. Not only were the Bat attacks

Bureau Number 59536 was an unadorned Privateer belonging to VPB-124 and reportedly flown by LtCdr. Miller. *Courtesy of David Mullen*

Lt. Pierce attacking a barracks area in Korea. *Courtesy of F. T. Pierce*

The torn belly of Lt. Miller's plane hangs down after the plane hit the mast of a Japanese ship. *Courtesy of Ted Rowcliffe*

A small cargo ship under attack by VPB-124. *Courtesy of Ted Rowcliffe*

failures for the new Okinawa squadron, but they ended the squadron's use of the weapon.

Patrolling above the Tsushima Straits between Korea and Japan, Lts. Preis and Griffin spotted three patrol boats in line. First contact was made by radar from ten miles away and at 2,000 feet. Preis contacted Griffin, "We will climb up and drop Bat." Griffin replied, "Roger, we'll stay down here." Preis made a climbing turn to 8,000 feet while Griffin stayed down.

From 8,000 feet and eight miles out the Bat locked on to the lead ship and was released as the ships sent up anti-aircraft fire that burst close to the Privateer's wings. The weapon traveled true, but exploded between two of the patrol boats. Preis turned away and headed home with Griffin, thus ending the squadron's use of the SWOD Mk-9 Bat.[2]

June 26 started out routinely, with VPB-124's Lt. W. J. "Porky" Yund's tail gunner spotting a passenger train moving along the

Smoke rises where Lt. Vincent's Privateer went down on 27 June 1945. *Courtesy of Ted Rowcliffe*

The patrol boat that shot down Lt. Vincent under attack by Lt. Robert D. Johnson. *Courtesy of Ted Rowcliffe*

western shore of Kyushu. Yund called his wingman, Lt. (jg) W. P. Howland Jr., on his intent to attack the train. Howland responded, "You and me all the way, Porky." As the two PB4Y-2s headed in every gun that could be brought to bear opened fire on the train. Yund came in at 500 feet and dropped two 250-pound bombs.

Howland came down and delivered his deadly cargo. The strafing and bombing brought the train to a stop with most of the wooden cars on fire. Several shots from small arms fire were seen in the brush near the train, but none hit the attacking Privateers. Leaving the burning train, the Privateers headed seaward and caught a couple small cargo ships, which were thoroughly worked over and left damaged as the two crews headed back to Okinawa. That same day two other squadron aircraft headed for the China coast.

The Loss of Houston and Crist Crews

Take off was 0715 hours as Cdr. Houston and his wingman, Lt. (jg) J. R. Crist, headed for China with the intention of making a sweep to the north of Shanghai. All was routine until a little before noon, when Houston dropped through a cloud layer and spotted a convoy of five ships in line, consisting of freighters in the 7–10,000-ton range; they were being escorted by two destroyers. There was no indication the Privateers had been picked up visually or by radar as Houston came in at 150 feet with a 10,000-ton freighter as his target. Two miles from the target every ship opened fire as he pressed home at one hundred feet and dropped seven 250-pound bombs as the bomber crossed over the ship's stern. Ensign G. W. Eves, standing in the bomb bay, watched as the bombs were released and sailed down toward the ship. One hit the deck, while a second exploded along the water line.

Meanwhile Jack Crist followed, crossed over her bow, and scored a direct hit. What happened afterward is not clearly known. Members of Houston's crew saw Crist's number three engine smoking as the Privateer turned away from the ship, headed for the China coast, and was never seen again. As for Houston, time also ran out.

The Privateer's path took him over a second ship and the plane took hits to the port wing and bow turret. In the radio compartment T. P. Metz (ARM2c) was killed as he sent out an attack report, his body slumped over his table. The bow turret took a direct hit, killing gunner R. J. Skulyna (AOM1c). With his number two engine out and his number one on fire Houston still managed to pickle off two bombs alongside a 7,000-ton ship.

The bomber was in serious trouble, losing power and altitude as Houston called his men to prepare for ditching. The stricken bomber flew on for another eight miles before it ditched, breaking apart into three pieces. From the fractured aircraft eight of her crew managed to get out before it sank. Navigator Ensign G. W. Eves and radar operator J. C. Cameron never joined the survivors struggling in the water. Most of the men were injured, the more seriously being copilot Lt. (jg) C. L. Prestien, bleeding profusely from a deep cut on his head, and W. Pallack (AMM1c) having a deep gash down to the bone of his calf.

The survivors managed to break out two life rafts and climbed aboard. Over the horizon one of the Japanese destroyers appeared and headed toward the wreckage. Houston and his men had managed to drift away and watched as a boat was lowered from the warship to search the wreckage. Knowing their chances of survival among men they had just tried to kill was doubtful at best, Houston and his men decided to turn their life rafts over and hide underneath, since the bottoms of the rafts were supposed to be painted sea blue as a means of concealment. Unfortunately somebody had forgotten to paint them and the bright yellow color floating on the water quickly caught the attention of the Japanese. Firing a machine gun over their heads, the Japanese sailors in the boat approached and soon the survivors were aboard.

Coming aboard the destroyer, the enlisted men and officers were separated and were subjected to interrogation and severe beatings. For some they were locked inside lockers, only to be beaten by passers-by with baseball bats. Most of the beatings came from survivors of the transport Houston and his men had sunk. In one instance Prestien was beaten and fell to the floor unconscious, only to be revived by a bucket of water and beaten again. Below deck,

the ship's doctor and several others took turns interrogating VPB-124's commanding officer, trying to obtain information on tactics, Allied shipping at Okinawa, and radar equipment.

A day after being captured the men were taken off the ship at Shanghai, taken to naval headquarters, and placed in solitary confinement, with meals consisting of three warm cups of water a day. For the next several days they were subjected to further interrogation, but the beatings were less frequent. After a week Houston, Prestien, and their radar man, Francis W. Wellmen, were blindfolded, taken aboard a transport plane, and flown to Korea. The Japanese were unaware that Wellman was only one of two American airborne radar technicians in that area of operations trained to operate and maintain the Privateer's radar and RCM equipment. The other was Donald H. Van Steenwyk, ART2c, Crew 19 of VPB-109. Both knew the capabilities and were tagged to obtain specific data on the characteristics of Japanese radar, such as PRF (pulse repetition frequency), pulse width, and signal strength. Two days later they were off again to Japan. Only after arriving at Ofuna prison camp outside Yokahara were the blindfolds finally removed.[3]

Two photographs show a Japanese cargo ship identified as a Tare Baker of seven to eight thousand tons. *Courtesy of Ted Rowcliffe*

Japanese shipping spotted along the Korean coast by VPB-124. *Courtesy of Ted Rowcliffe*

VPB-124 coming in low towards enemy shipping. *Courtesy of Ted Rowcliffe*

Two weeks of solitary confinement were followed by typical daily life at a Japanese prisoner of war camp, i.e., beatings and a bowl of rice and soup for food. Lt.Cdr. John M. Miller immediately assumed command upon Houston's disappearance, as the squadron lost a third combat air crew the following day. While Houston and his men endured the beatings aboard the Japanese ship, two Privateers from VPB-124 belonging to Lts. Jack Vincent and Bob Johnston took off in their planes and headed for their search sector that would bring them near Korea.

As they neared the southeast coast of Korea a heavy fog hid the sea below. Through it Lt. Johnston briefly made out a ship a quarter mile ahead. He called Vincent about the ship and then changed course to intercept. Closing in, he identified it as a destroyer escort. Vincent was already approaching the warship and Johnston could see puffs of anti-aircraft fire following the incoming Privateer. Johnston and his crew saw Vincent's plane take hits to the bomb bay area and the port wing near the engines. The damaged Privateer climbed for an instant, smoke pouring from the port engines, then glided into the water with a horrendous explosion. Smoke billowed some 1,500 feet into the air, flames spread across the water, and a few pieces of wreckage floated; there were no survivors.

Miller Takes Command

Lt.Cdr. Miller was determined to carry on his predecessor's accomplishments, and on 11 July, he and Arnold went on an early morning search. Crossing the Tsushima Strait, they flew through heavy fog with low visibility. There they found four merchant ships, and for the next fifteen minutes they attacked, leaving three 100-ton vessels burning and a 1,000-ton ship afire, listing, and trailing oil.

The Privateer's ability to withstand major battle damage and still bring her crew home was exemplified on 2 July. Lt. Gil Miller and Lt. (jg) D. E. Ellis spotted a small merchant ship in the Tsushima Straits. Strafing caused the ship to explode and black smoke enveloped

Miller's plane (Bureau Number 59534). Unable to pull up in time, the Privateer hit the ship's main mast, ripping out the belly. It took Miller and his copilot to regain control of the aircraft and prevent it crashing into the sea. A couple of the crew went aft to inspect the damage and found a hole forty-five feet long and five to seven feet wide had been ripped away from the bottom of the plane, carrying away all bomb bay doors, the hydraulic system, and radar and radio equipment.

For an hour and a half, standing in the oily catwalk, the plane captain cut away bomb bay tanks, bomb racks, and other loose equipment that had been smashed inside the bomb bay. A Marine aerologist who was observing from behind the bow turret was severely injured. He was carried along the side of the plane—as there was now no bottom remaining—by Ensign Littman, who also gave emergency medical treatment which saved the Marine's life. After a four-hour trip in which the only communication between Ellis and Miller was by flashlight and Morse code, the pilot made a wheels-up belly landing at Yontan. Inspection later revealed a piece of the ship's mast inside the plane's wreckage.

Miller, Pierce, and Ramsey

In between multi-squadron strikes, the Okinawa squadrons continued the job of neutralizing enemy merchant shipping, but such strikes cost VPB-124 additional aircraft and crews. The first loss occurred on 7 July, when VPB-124's Lt. Robert Brower and Lt. (jg) Everett Osborn teamed up for a sweep of the Tsushima Straits between Kyushu and Korea.

The first visual contact was made on two enemy warships that opened fire with their five-inch guns but failed to hit the patrol bombers. Shortly thereafter, a pair of Rex reconnaissance fighters attacked the patrol bombers, and in a five-minute battle the twelve .50-caliber guns of each Privateer proved to be too deadly for the attacking enemy planes. Lt. (jg) Osborn's gunners shot down one

The waist turret trains on a cargo ship. *Courtesy of Ted Rowcliffe*

that spiraled into the sea, while the other turned tail and headed for home with smoke pouring from its fuselage.

Heading for base, the crews made visual contact with a small enemy ship identified after the attack as a sub-chaser. Lt. Brower, leading the section in Bureau Number 59538, started in for the attack, followed closely by Lt. Osborn. As Brower's plane flew into range the sub-chaser opened fire and caught the incoming Privateer. Just before reaching the ship Brower's copilot, Lt. (jg) Dave Davis, called via radio to Osborne, "Get out of the way, Ossie; we're going in!"

Brower's plane, badly crippled and on fire, crashed into the water almost immediately about one and one-half miles from the sub-chaser and about six miles off shore from Uki Shima, the northernmost island in the Goto Retto group. Five of the crew escaped from the plane: Lt. (jg) Davis, Jack Lewis, George Dacier, Theodore Kalmuk, and Frank Gardner. Osborne circled over the five men in the water, receiving intense fire from the sub-chaser and from shore batteries. He dropped a life raft, advised base of the situation, and set a course for home, as his fuel supply was running low. Five men escaped from Brower's plane after it crashed, while the others were apparently killed when the big bomber hit the water. The survivors were picked up by a Japanese boat and joined Cdr. Houston's crew as prisoners of war.[4]

Four days later Lts. J. E. Ramsey and F. T. Pierce took their planes to Korea. Pierce was no stranger to combat, as he was a veteran of VB-138, a Ventura squadron in the South Pacific. Born in the small town of Bartlett, Texas, he was the only son of a wealthy cotton baron. He went on to graduate from the University of Texas before joining the Navy, earning his wings in 1942 and serving with VB-138. In January 1945, he had a narrow escape while attempting to take off in a Privateer at Camp Kearny. One of the waist turrets rotated downward with the turret door open. The door pressed against the plane structure and pinched the control cables until they would

not function properly. The plane crashed and broke up into several pieces, but none of the crew was injured.[5]

On 14 July, Ramsey and Pierce teamed up and were joined by two planes from VPB-123 for a strike on a shipping port along the western coast of Korea. As they approached their target weather closed in and they were forced to climb above the overcast. Suddenly, through a hole in the clouds, Ramsey observed the bay literally filled with merchant ships. Advising the others of his intentions, he and Pierce nosed their planes down and went through the overcast at 270 knots.

Pierce came in on the deck and suddenly saw a mountain in front of him. Pulling up on the yoke he barely missed it. He then turned the Privateer around and went back in for the attack. Ramsey sank an 840-ton vessel within thirty seconds in four runs. He then went after another ship trying to get protection in a cove, blew its stern up into the air, turned the ship around, and left it listing at twenty degrees. During the strikes the four planes dropped twenty 500 and 250-pound bombs and fired 25,000 rounds of ammunition. Pierce successfully kept Ramsey from going in and attacking targets he deemed too dangerous to tangle with. He thought he was an eager pilot, but he paled in comparison to Miller and Ramsey. It succeeded quite well until Pierce went on a mail flight and Ramsey teamed up with Gil Miller a few weeks later.

VPB-124 continued to lose men through the end of July, when Lt. Ramsey, piloting Bureau Number 59519 (*Gear Locked and Down*) and Lt. Gil Miller aboard Bureau Number 59747 were lost on the twenty-fourth while on an anti-shipping sweep along the western coast of Korea. Three hours after take off a morning contact report from Ramsey stated enemy aircraft were attacking him. Later in the morning a radioman from another VPB-124 aircraft intercepted a transmission from Ramsey telling Miller that he had made a successful attack on a ship and telling him they had sufficient gas to continue searching. A short time later Ramsey's radioman started an enemy contact report, but was told by home base to wait because of other radio traffic. After that there was nothing. They were never

Lt. Pierce attacking shipping among small islands off Korea. *Courtesy of Ted Rowcliffe*

heard from again. The following day two planes from another unit sighted two beached and partially submerged ships approximately where Ramsey and Miller were last reported.

According to Japanese sources, it is known that JAAF fighters of the 25th *Hiko Sentai* intercepted two Privateers two kilometers north of Saishu-To Island (known as Cheju Do today, off the south coast of Korea). Several Japanese Army fighters intercepted them, and one, flown by Sgt. Yamaguchi, was lost with the pilot. However, the record is unclear on this point, as the Japanese claimed to have downed both PB4Ys. Like most of the men that flew on Ramsey's and Miller's planes, they left behind families.[6]

A crewmember of Ramsey's plane was Hugh Crae Wilson, ARM3c. Two weeks before his final flight he received news that he was the father of a baby girl, Trudy, born on 8 July. Hearing that her husband was MIA, Wilson's wife never remarried—she was devastated. She refused to believe he was not coming back. This was how Trudy was raised, waiting for word about a husband and a father. Years went by and Trudy, now a young woman, sent her own husband off to Vietnam as a second lieutenant in the US Marine Corps. They had a three-month-old baby girl at the time. Her father-in-law was a pilot in the United States Air Force at the same time and was seriously injured and several of his crew were killed when his plane crashed into the jungles of Thailand after completing a mission over North Vietnam.

Trudy was deathly afraid that her husband would either be killed or, like her father-in-law, seriously injured. The latter came true, but he returned to her and his daughter; however, she still ponders the ultimate fate of her father.[7]

Operations Terminated

Before temporary rest and relaxation on Tinian, VPB-124 delivered one last punch against the enemy. On 27 July, Lt. Johnston teamed up with Lt. Cdr. W. D. Bliss, the new executive officer of VPB-124, for a patrol along the eastern coast of Korea. It would be the squadron's last operation against the Japanese. An estimated 4,000-ton merchant ship was spotted, and Johnson came in at 200 feet, but his bombs failed to release. Bliss came in and two bombs straddled the target. Johnston came back around, and this time the bombs fell from the Privateer. A direct hit with a 500-pound bomb caused the ship to disintegrate in a mass of flames, debris, and smoke. They continued with the hunt and spotted an 850-ton ship steaming into a harbor. The harbor was narrow and surrounded by high hills, so Johnston circled and came in from over a hill toward the ship, releasing three 500-pound bombs; two hit, blowing off parts of the bridge and superstructure 300 feet in the air. The ship then burned and sank. VPB-124's active combat duty came to a hasty end on 28 July, as they were temporarily sent to Tinian.

Squadron air crews flew 124 combat missions in two months, sinking twenty-nine enemy ships at the cost of eighteen officers and fifty-four enlisted men—thirteen of those becoming POWs—and nine aircraft—a loss rate of nearly forty percent. Other squadrons suffered similar losses as seen with VPB-117 and -119, but not in such a short time span. Replacement crews had not become available and remaining PB4Y-2s were in dire need of overhaul. The squadron had lost more men and aircraft than any other sister squadron in such a short period; they had achieved a record that no one else envied—a record of death. F. T. Pierce recalls his feelings:

"I had three other officers living with me. Within a week I was the only one left. I felt lonely. I thought, 'Well goddamn, what's going to happen to me?' That was the most forlorn feeling I ever had. I felt like a protector, because I was Ramsey's wingman but didn't go out that day. Therefore, it made me feel pretty bad. However, unlike Ramsey and Miller, I had survived."[8]

Kenneth Sanford from VPB-123 remembers walking past the empty tents that once housed the lost men of VPB-124: "Walking past their lifeless tents, the silence was gut wrenching, knowing there were no occupants." He wondered if he would be next and his tent would also stand empty. Empty canvas dwellings that once housed young men with dreams of a future life they would never experience.[9]

On Tinian, the remaining personnel of VPB-124 took the time for rest and relax. They were short of crews and aircraft, and would not be going back to combat until replacements were received. Less than two weeks later a naval aviator on patrol was overheard on the radio by some of the men saying, "The war is over." It was a sudden and shocking announcement. Ted Rowcliffe remembers that every man and woman on the island spontaneously reveled in his or her own way, mostly by getting drunk. He remembers, "There was a strange feeling, but it wasn't happiness." Rather, it was a feeling of

Lt. Pierce being awarded a medal for his service with VPB124. *Courtesy of F. T. Pierce*

disappointment. "We wouldn't be able to get back at the enemy for what they did to our squadron shipmates."[10]

About the same time, on a routine patrol Lt. F. T. Pierce heard the news from a peculiar radio transmission. Radio silence was broken and a southern voice came on, "God damn, y'all hear! They dropped a bomb on Nagasaki and killed 100,000 people. The war is over, let's go home!"[11]

They had lost many friends, men they had grown close to in some eighteen months of training and combat. So close that they knew each other's wives and children. Now they would have to go home and tell the widows and children who no longer had a father.

A few days after the war ended VPB-124 sent Privateers to fly cover for the surrender ceremony at Truk. Below the passing patrol bombers they saw something very few westerners had ever seen—a ritualistic suicide by members of a Japanese garrison. They chose death before dishonor and would not surrender to the victorious American forces.

VPB-124 returned to Okinawa from Tinian and flew many missions looking for stray Japanese shipping to alert them that the war was over and plot their location. Additionally, long-range weather hops were flown by the squadron to track typhoons. Four days later they tracked a very strong storm headed toward Okinawa. On 9 October, the storm slammed into the island. Living quarters, mess halls, storage warehouses, and airplanes were all damaged. Lt. Pierce's copilot Ensign C. E. Vermillion recalls: "He was never

The Bureau Number for *Supreme Zu Zu* remains unknown, but reportedly it was flown by VPB-124's Lt. Ramsey and his crew were called "Zu Zu's Men." *Author's Collection*

scared on combat flights like he was flying a typhoon hop in which the engines were missing and drowned by the torrential rain, in the practically zero visibility, and severe buffeting winds of the storms."[12]

By November, Lt.Cdr. Delbert M. Minner had relieved Lt. Cdr. John Miller as commanding officer, and most of the original squadron personnel had returned to the United States. In mid-December 1945, the squadron was relieved by VPB-108.

Three officers of VPB-124 standing near one of the squadron's Privateers *Little Joe* (Bureau Number 59545, L to R): C. E. Vermillon of Crew 11, "Eb" Ebersol of Crew Six, and O. H. Denhart of Crew 4. *Courtesy of Dr. M. F. Ebersol*

15

Final Missions
July–August 1945

Land-based squadrons on Okinawa stepped up their attacks on enemy shipping in the Yellow, East China, and Japan Seas, along the coast of Japan, and into the Inland Sea. Mounting strikes and anti-shipping missions had caused a noticeable decrease in enemy shipping, and it was steadily cutting down Japan's surface communications with the continent. The Chinese ports Shanghai and Hangchow were in the process of being neutralized, as was Hong Kong and the Formosa ports in the south. The Korea-Japan shipping lanes across the Tsushima Straits were obliged to rely on heavier escort, move in smaller convoys, and proceed more and more at night. However, attacking mainland China and Japan would prove costly to some of the Okinawa squadrons during the next few days and weeks.

Crew 11, led by Lt. Leland P. McCutcheon of VPB-118, was ambushed by heavy anti-aircraft guns aboard a gunboat disguised as a ferry during an anti-shipping sweep near Shanghai on 21 July with "Horse" Thompson's Crew 17 of VPB-109. A hail of heavy fire hit the Privateer, killing or seriously wounding copilot Ensign William E. Bucklew, while a fire erupted inside the cockpit, engulfing lower extremities. The plane broke apart as it hit the water, but somehow seven of the crew survived the crash and managed to climb into life rafts. Thompson stayed on station, keeping the "ferry" from approaching the survivors until a PB2Y-2 Coronado flying boat arrived two hours later and picked them up. The survivors were plane captain and bow gunner G. L. White, aft (rear) top turret gunner J. F. Proctor, tail turret gunner M. L. Miller, and forward top turret gunner R. C. Dodl. Passengers or replacements named D. Feldman and N. A. Marquis also survived the ditching.

July brought changes to the Privateer squadrons of Fleet Air Wing 1. On 26 May 1941, Rinehart flew as copilot and US Navy

A navy photographer taking the official photo of VPB-118's original Crew 11 next to Bureau Number 59378. The crew consisted of Lt. Leland P. McCutcheon (kneeling third from left); Lt. (jg) Frank Reeve; Ens. William E. Bucklew; Glen W. White, AMM1c; Malden L. Miller, AMM2c; Allen D. Nelson, AMM2c; James N. Welch, AMM3c; Ben L. Slack, ARM2c; R. Conrad Dodl, ARM3c; Otto A. Bunkers, AFC1c (standing far right); and James F. Proctor, AOM2c. Six of the crew were killed in action on 21 July 1945: Patrol Plane Commander McCutcheon, copilot Reeve, copilot Bucklew, bombardier Bunkers, port waist gunner Nelson, and starboard waist gunner Welch. Slack was not on the mission, and two men named D. Feldman and N. A. Marquis (either passengers or replacements) survived the crash. *Courtesy of Darrel White via Richard Peterson*

Lt.Cdr. C. W. Rinehart assumed command of VPB-118 on 21 July 1945. The crew consisted of Lt.Cdr. C. W. Rinehart (back center); Ens. Joseph B. Ambler; Ens. Edward M. Brodhead; Leobard A. Verbeck, AMM1c; Cecil R. Gillespie, AMM2c; Rogers A. Fiedler, AMM3c; Harold G. Coker, ARM2c; Edgar M. Mattson, ARM1c; Joseph A. Ryner, ARM3c; James R. Harvill Jr., AOM1c; Walter J. Kentner, AOM2c; and Milton R. Cooper, S1c. *Courtesy of Rogers Fielder Richard Peterson*

special observer aboard a British PBY Catalina during the hunt for the German battleship *Bismarck*. On the twenty-fifth, VPB-118's Lt.Cdr. Farwell was relieved of command by Lt.Cdr. C. W. Rinehart. The last week of July brought forth the reappearance of the Raiders after two weeks on Iwo Jima. The men of 109 were amazed at the alterations that had taken place at Yontan Field. Navy Sea-Bees and Army Construction Engineers had built a surfaced airstrip. Parking areas and a taxiway now ran across VPB-109's old living area. Living conditions improved considerably, with tents having wooden or coral floors that protected against the

mud caused by frequent rain showers. Oil drum showers were available to all personnel, electricity had been installed, and Lister bags of drinking water were stationed throughout the camp. Moreover, less frequent air raid alerts made recreational activities such as motion pictures possible.

Anti-shipping sweeps for VPB-109 began on 30 July, with Lts. Jobe and Turner on patrol in southeast Korea. They sighted a large number of enemy shipping, including a 1,900-ton freighter that was selected as the primary target in the Tsushima Straits sector. This attack would be the beginning of a series of engagements that would last an hour.

As Lt. Turner circled the ship his gunners laid down suppressing fire against the ship's gun crew as Lt. Jobe initiated a bombing run across the target's starboard bow. Jobe released two 500 and one 250-pound bomb that entered the water but missed the ship by twenty-five feet. Swinging around for another run, he dropped another 500 and 250-pound bomb. The ship took a direct hit on the midsection and it blew up and sank rapidly.

Thirty minutes later, two 70-ton luggars were spotted abreast of each other cruising at five knots. Not wanting to waste their remaining bombs on the small ships, both Privateers made a strafing run that caused both targets to burn and sink. Fifteen minutes later two similar vessels were spotted and strafed by the planes, causing one of the luggars to blow up. Looking for bigger game, an 850-ton freighter was spotted twenty minutes later cruising at ten knots. While Lt. Turner initiated a bombing run Jobe's gunners kept the ship's gun crew busy with strafing. Turner pickled off one 250-pound bomb, only to have it explode in the air. Fragments of the bomb damaged parts of the wings and tail sections of both planes. Another bomb was a direct hit amidships, and the ship began to blaze before it started sinking. Having expended all of their bombs and most of their ammunition, the Privateers headed home. In all, three ships were either badly damaged or sunk. The ships were the *Hakushin Maru*, *Kamokawa Maru*, and the *Sumiyoshi Maru No. 18*.

An unidentified PB4Y-1 Liberator casts its shadow above an unknown Japanese coastal village during the closing weeks of the Pacific War. *Courtesy of Bob Baird*

Pirate Princess. Courtesy of Bob Baird

Two images of bridgeworks in northwestern Korea targeted by Privateers of VPB-109 and 118 on 31 July 1945. *Courtesy of the NARA*

Combined Effort

The following day, in a daring strike, Cdr. Hicks led six Privateers belonging to 109, 118, and 123 on a special strike against rail transportation and railroad facilities in Northwestern Korea.[1] The primary target, as selected by Cdr. Fleet Air Wing 1, was a steel 2,700 foot long, multiple span, single track bridge on the Seisin K River, just two miles north of the town of Shinanshu. The bridge works consisted of three parallel sections: a highway bridge to the east, a partially completed railroad bridge in the center, and a completed railroad bridge on the west. The primary target was the completed railroad bridge. The bridge was vital to the supply of war materials flowing south through Korea to the ports of Fusan and Kunsan and other important shipping areas. To render this important artery useless it was necessary to cut it off by destroying the bridge.

Taking off at 6 a.m., Hicks led the six planes low and outside of radar detection; he planned to strike the target so that retirement

Crew Six of VPB-109 was lost on 5 August 1945, one year exactly since the squadron lost its last crew during the unit's first combat tour. Standing (L to R): James E. Krieger, AMM3C; Frank R. Kramer, AOM1C; Ens. Henry Baier Jr.; Lt. John D. Keeling; Ens. Keith W. Radcliffe; James R. T. Carswell, AFC2C; and Lawrence R. Conroy, AOM3C. Kneeling (L to R): Peter G. Ilacqua, ARM2C; William L. Willocks, AMM1C; William F. Krier, ARM1C; Alexander J. Boyd, ARM1C; and Melvin M. Rager, AMM2C. *Courtesy of Roy Balke*

A pair of unidentified PB4Y-1 Liberators possibly belonging to VD-5, with the left possibly being Bureau Number 65292, while the right, named *Tourist*, displays camera mission markings above and to the left of the woman. *Courtesy of Bob Baird*

would be made away from the direction of the towns Shinanshu and Anshu. The planes hit the bridge at noon, with Hicks' first 1,000-pound bomb entering the water on the starboard center of the pier for a perfect hit. The steel span lifted, covered by a geyser of water, and immediately the northern end of the southernmost span dropped twenty feet below the level of the tracks. A second bomb was a near miss on the second span pier. As they retired an enemy gun position vainly fired at them from between the two towns.

After hitting a locomotive, the planes from 118 arrived at the bridge area just after Hicks' attack. Lt.Cdr. Rinehart scored a near miss with his 1,000-pound bombs and strafed the area while Shortlidge saved his bombs for his secondary target, a bridge across the Kei-no Sen; both bombs missed this bridge and all six Privateers headed across country on a southerly course.

Return to base was started over land, looking for targets of opportunity along the railroad bed. A locomotive and twelve cars were spotted and attacked by Hicks and Rinehart and were seriously damaged by bombing and strafing. Bombing and strafing by Hewitt, Shortlidge, and Rinehart damaged a rail junction yard containing several small buildings. Additionally six buildings, a hopper elevator, and a mine were strafed by Hicks' plane and were left blazing. Just as they were leaving the coast four small power trawlers tied up together at a landing at the mouth of the Gaisan Ho River were strafed and bombed in passing, with bombs scoring direct hits when they landed among the moored craft, sending debris into the air.

August 1945 began like previous months for the PB4Y squadrons, with anti-shipping strikes off Korea and Japan. Allied air and naval blockades of the home islands continued as preparations for the

The crew of the last PB4Y-2 Privateer shot down in World War II. Back row (L to R): K.C. Gaber, C.A. Bremer, R.E. Guth, J. Frashure, R.W. Cox, and A.R. Dugger. Front row (L to R): D.W. Mott, H.H. Whitted, J.B. Rainey, E.J. Heeb, and W.R. Long. *Courtesy of Richard Jeffreys Jr.*

A Privateer from VPB-124 photographed Japanese military personnel standing in formation, possibly during the surrender ceremony. *Courtesy of F. T. Pierce*

These are emaciated Japanese sailors on one of the bypassed Marshall Islands. *Courtesy of the NARA*

invasion of the Japanese home islands proceeded under the codename Operation Olympic. The first of a two-stage operation was scheduled for 1 November, with landings on Kyushu, followed by the invasion of Honshu set for 1 March 1946. Combat air crews continued operations with most, if not all, under the impression the war was far from over. Only a few select individuals in Washington and on Tinian knew the war could be over within a few weeks.

A new B-29 squadron had arrived on Tinian (509th Composite) and had flown a few bombing missions to Japan. Many on the island wondered who in the hell these guys were because of the security and special treatment they received. Two weeks later most would know why the 509th was so special. Until then the war continued unabated, except for weather. For the Privateer squadrons, August would bring the deaths of additional combat air crewmen before final victory was achieved.

Regular flight operations were canceled for nearly a week as a typhoon approached the Japanese coast. Instead, squadrons were ordered to conduct special weather flights to track the storm on 30 July and 1 and 3 August. Favorable weather the following week had planes from Okinawa going up in strength against shipping around Kyushu, Southern Honshu, Korea, and over the Inland Sea, Sea of Japan, and the Yellow and East China Seas.

For the Old Crows of 118, Lts. Scheck and Terrell went hunting for ships in the Tsushima Straits, where they caught a small cargo ship and sank it with strafing. Onward they flew, and twenty miles from the first attack they spotted a 1,000-ton merchant ship. Bob Armstrong, Schmuck's bombardier, dropped one 500-pound bomb that hit the vessel squarely. The ship seemed to break in two and sink, although records suggest otherwise. The two Privateers continued with their search, only to find an old four-masted sailing ship. For fifteen minutes the two bomber crews poured .50-cailiber fire and 500-pound bombs at the ship, but it refused to sink. Not wanting to

spend the rest of their ammunition trying to sink the damaged vessel they turned toward home.

On the homeward leg Terrell decided to attack a radio-radar station. During a strafing run that seriously damaged the station the Privateer took hits to a wing and a top turret from 20 mm and 7.7 mm gunfire. Donald Slator was hit and mortally wounded by fragments from a 20 mm round. The attack was broken off and Terrell headed home. As Terrell's crew tried vainly to save their fellow crewmember, 109's Lts. Keeling and Vidal were on anti-shipping patrol off Korea when they spotted a 2,500-ton tanker.

Dropping from 1,000 feet to 200 feet, the planes circled the ship to port and began strafing. Light and medium inaccurate anti-aircraft fire was received during the strafing run. The search planes pulled up to 1,000 feet, still circling to port as Lt. Keeling initiated a bombing run. Lt. Vidal planned to follow with a bombing run and remained a mile and a half behind Keeling. By now the planes were being subjected to intense medium and light defensive fire from the ships. Completing his run, Lt. Keeling pulled up to 500 feet with his number three engine smoking. His plane gradually nosed over in a slight turn to starboard and crashed into the water two miles west of the ship.

Following behind, Lt. Vidal broke off his bombing run when he observed Lt. Keeling in trouble and headed directly to the scene of the crash. Smoke and flames reached a height of 200 feet after the plane hit the water and only a few pieces of debris and heavy oily smoke were visible when Vidal's plane reached the scene. An uninflated life raft, wheel, and a large amount of dye marker was floating on the surface. Lt. Vidal had one of his crew members throw out an inflated life raft and a survival kit adjacent to the crash, but no survivors were sighted. He then left the area and returned to Okinawa. Lt. Keeling and his entire crew were listed as missing in action one year to the day since the loss of VB-109's Lt. Kasperson's crew on 5 August 1944.

Squadron doctrine was that coordinated attacks against heavily armed ships were considered most effective in reducing anti-aircraft

The Presidential Unit Citation being awarded to three former commanding officers of VPB-117 in 1947. *Courtesy of the VPB-117 Association*

VPB-118 relief crew of Lt. (jg) James R. Park, which joined the squadron on 7 July 1945. They were lost in action on 8 August 1945. Front row (L to R): Joseph S. Piquette, AMM2c; Ens. Glen W. Lewton; Lt. (jg) James R. Park; Ens. Loris H. Lowe; and Mike R. Marich, ACOM. Back row (L to R): Herbert J. Wartzack, ARM3c; Carroll A. "Tex" McKinney Jr., S1c; Michael E. Hedrick, S1c; Paul Preitz, S1c; John M. "Jim" James, AMM3c; Robert Koontz, AOM3c; and Raymond R. Reinhart, ARM3c. Not in the photo is Ernest K. Hall, ARM3c. *Courtesy of Park nephew John Park and Marich niece Diane Mcleod via Richard Peterson*

fire. Squadron policy was for one plane to strafe the target ship using a circular attack, thus bringing maximum guns to bear on the target, while the second plane was closing on a straight in bombing attack. Therefore, it was believed anti-aircraft fire would have been materially reduced on the bombing run had this type of attack been employed during this action. However, Vidal was more than a mile away and could not provide the other Privateer with the needed suppressing fire.

Final Missions

On the morning of the sixth, Col. Paul W. Tibbets of the 509th Composite Group took off from North Field, Tinian, in the B-29 *Enola Gay* and headed for the Japanese city Hiroshima. On board was a U-235 bomb *Little Boy*. Coming over the city at 31,600 feet, bombardier Maj. Thomas Ferebee released the bomb and at 2,000 feet, the bomb detonated over Hiroshima with a force equal to 20,000 tons of TNT.

On the seventh, VPB-109's Lts. Wilkinson and Braddock spotted a power oil barge of 300 tons in the Tsushima Strait. Both planes attacked at low altitude. Lt. Wilkinson continued to strafe while Braddock made two low-level bombing runs. Braddock's first run was ineffective, but on his second bombing run a 500-pound bomb hit twenty feet short and traveled underwater directly beneath the target. The explosion completely covered the ship, causing it to list to port. While both planes continued to strafe the target rolled over and sank. Forty minutes later a 100-ton coastal was attacked. Both planes coordinated strafing runs before Lt. Braddock dropped a 250-pound bomb. The bomb went through the ship's superstructure and detonated in the water fifteen feet beyond. Continued strafing by both planes set fire to the freighter, which soon sank.

Thirty minutes later a heavily laden two-masted schooner approximately 125–150 feet long was attacked and sunk. The schooner was strafed until completely riddled by the withering fire of all bearable turrets, causing it to sink in a few minutes and leaving nothing but its cargo floating on the surface. While planes from 109 were busy, two Privateers from 123 were conducting a similar mission off the northwest coast of Honshu. Sighting a convoy of small ships, the planes flown by Lt. (jg) E. L. Klein and Lt. H. M. Sanderson attacked at masthead level. Sanderson's bombs would not release, so Klein went in on the run while his wingman kept a steady stream of machine gun fire on the ships. Anti-aircraft fire was intense as Klein came in, pickling off the bombs, and Joseph H. Farmer, the tail gunner, was killed. Farmer was the only squadron member killed in action during four months of combat.

A day after the dropping of the atomic bomb on Hiroshima Lt.Cdr. Rinehart and Lt. (jg) J. R. Park from 118 went on patrol along the western edge of Kyushu, through the Tsushima Straits, and along the western coast of Honshu. This time the strategy of attacking at minimum altitude would cost the lives of an entire Privateer crew. After successfully sinking a small 100-ton cargo ship in the Sea of Japan a merchant ship in the 2,000-ton range was spotted heading east, toward Honshu. Lt. Park went in first with his gunners laying down fire on the ship's superstructure and with the vessel's crew firing back with light machine gun fire. The ship began to burn from the strafing as Rinehart lined up his aircraft for a bombing run. He pickled off three 500-pound bombs, with one detonating under the ship's stern. Rinehart pulled away and turned back around as Park went in again. The fire that Park's gunners had started was blazing furiously as the Privateer neared.

Before the bomb drop the ship suddenly exploded, just as Park's bomber passed over. Apparently carrying ammunition, both the Japanese ship and the American bomber disintegrated in a flash of

Park's Privateer and the Japanese freighter are engulfed in a huge explosion in this photograph taken from Rinehart's plane. The blast hurled debris 1,000 feet in the air and threw Rinehart's plane 150–200 feet sideways, despite being a mile away. *Courtesy of Park nephew John Park and Marich niece Diane Mcleod via Richard Peterson*

A smaller burning mass on the right is where Park's plane crashed after being caught in the ship's massive explosion. The only identifiable remains from the Privateer were an empty life raft, a sleeping bag, and a nose wheel. The crew may have been killed or rendered unconscious from the blast and were hopefully unaware of their situation, as the main section of the aircraft struck the water within a few seconds of the explosion. *Courtesy of Park nephew John Park and Marich niece Diane Mcleod via Richard Peterson*

fire and smoke. The concussion shook Rinehart's plane, which was a mile away. Debris from the ship and possibly from Park's Privateer was hurled 1,000 feet into the sky, with a fiery plume of smoke rising another 2,000 feet. Rinehart approached the scene, only to find wreckage floating on the water. A fire in the shape of a wing burned where the port side of the ship had been. Nearby an inflated life raft and a sleeping bag floated on the water—the only remains of a PB4Y-2 and her crew.

On the ninth, Maj. Charles W. Sweeney in B-29 *Bockscar* dropped a plutonium bomb *Fat Boy* on the city of Nagasaki. During the following day 109, 118, and 123 completed their last missions of the war with ant-shipping strikes off Japan. For 109, Lts. Chay and Moyer set out with Bats under their Privateers. They spotted a tanker of 2,400 tons escorted by one picket boat. Both planes immediately went to 6,000 feet to launch their Bats. Lt. Chay launched his, but Lt. Moyer's had mechanical problems and was not released. Lt. Chay's went over the target and exploded harmlessly. Further attack at low level was decided against due to the presence of the picket boat and the planes continued on patrol.

An hour later five freighters were sighted by both planes. The ships were closely disbursed over an area of two miles, making it feasible to attack all targets in consecutive runs. Fires were started on all ships by strafing, and in passing over one ship Lt. Moyer scored a direct hit from 150 feet, causing the already flaming target to sink. A second freighter was sunk and the remaining three targets were left burning.

During the morning of 10 August 1945, two 118 Privateers commanded by Lts. G. H. Shortlidge and George King conducted the last attacks of the war when they encountered small shipping off southern Korea. While King's gunners strafed the other Privateer came in at 150 feet and dropped his bomb load on an 80-ton vessel;

all missed, but the strafing caused the ship to burn and list. Flying around small islands that dot the coast, the Privateers came upon a larger vessel of 175 tons, which they damaged through strafing. The Old Crows continued offensive patrols until the fifteenth, when word was received of the Japanese surrender. The story of 123 was the same as her sister squadron, with two Privateers flown by Lts. Carroll E. Koontz and James M. Reusswig engaging and sinking a small freighter, bringing the squadron's total score to sixty-seven ships sunk.

The war was over and there was no longer fear of being shot down in flames. VPB-123 and 118 continued to be based on Okinawa at Yonabaru, flying searches and weather flights. New crews and aircraft came and replaced the battle-hardened warriors—fresh faces mostly unscarred by war. The war was over, and would be placed in the backs of their memories as they headed home to start new lives.

For VPB-121, their war would end tragically on 11 August, marking the last WWII combat loss of a PB4Y-2 Privateer. At 0841 hours, Lts. J. B. Rainey and T. Allen took off from Iwo Jima to search the Honshu coast south of Tokyo. Allen was flying the lead plane at approximately 400 feet with Rainey behind. After making landfall at 1300 hours, they intended to make a reconnaissance of O Shima Island and then head for home. Allen's top aft gunner called "Fighters high at 12 o'clock." Rainey then called Allen, "Fighters at 8 o'clock." Allen immediately chopped his throttles and started to weave to allow Rainey to pull up close for mutual support. The Privateers were boxed in, with one group coming in head on toward Allen while another group dove down toward Rainey.

On the first run two fighters went after Allen, knocking out his number one engine and wounding the tail gunner. Meanwhile, his top turret gunners hit one of the incoming fighters, drawing smoke. When the engine was knocked out the Privateer was thrown into a flipper turn, stalled, and fell toward the sea. Miraculously Allen managed to gain control of the four-engine patrol bomber only seventy-five feet above the water.

The veterans of VB/VPB-117. *Courtesy of Norman B. Sellman*

As Allen tried to gain control three of his men saw Rainey's port wing on fire. The plane took a turn to the right and the starboard wing suddenly dropped and hit the water. Bouncing once, the Privateer cartwheeled in, leaving a patch of flame and smoke. Incredibly, Rainey and seven of the crew survived the crash and briefly became prisoners of war. The pilot responsible for bringing down the Privateer was Lt. (jg) Teizo Ota of the 302 Zu flying a Zero.[2]

After being hit on the first run Allen began a mad dash home, with the fighters pressing in their attacks for another thirty minutes before losing one of their own to the Privateer before departing. Six hours later Allen landed at Iwo Jima. Upon inspection of the plane it was found to have sustained two 20 mm and numerous 12.7 mm hits.

On V-J Day ten VPB-108 Privateers, six VPB-124 Privateers, and eight VPB-117 Liberators staged a demonstration of power over Truk concerning surrender ceremonies on board the USS *Portland*. The twenty-four PB4Ys flew in formation at low altitude over the once great island fortress. A year before some of the pilots and crew who participated in this aerial display had been among the first American aviators to fly reconnaissance and strike missions against the Gibraltar of the Pacific.

The veterans of VB/VPB-109 stand in front of an F-16 "Thunderbird" at Nellis AFB.

16
Patrols in the Aleutians

The story of United States Navy B-24 Liberator and PB4Y-2 Privateer squadrons would not be complete without mention of two squadrons that served in Alaska during the final days of the war with Japan. While Allied forces were advancing toward final victory in the Pacific, in the cold and mist-shrouded islands of the Aleutians to the north, American and Canadian aviators continued to fight a war of boredom and isolation, interrupted only by an occasional foray into enemy territory. Since the recapture of Attu and Kiska in the Aleutians during summer 1943, the campaign in the northern Pacific had consisted of harassing raids on the Kurile Islands, primarily Paramushiro.

Being in the "backwater" of the war, there was not an urgent need for long-range reconnaissance. Sending Privateers and trained crews would be a waste of time when they were still needed in the main area of operations for the final push on Japan. Therefore, no Navy Liberator squadrons appeared in Alaska, and only two Privateer squadrons made it before the end of the war, with VPB-120 having the distinct honor of being the first.

Commissioned as VP-12 in 1941, the squadron was redesignated VPB-120 in October 1944. Under the command of Lt.Cdr. Frank

G. Reynolds, the squadron was given six Liberators for training; however, unavailability of air crews prevented any extensive training for the next three months. Trading in their Liberators for Privateers, Reynolds and his crews began intensive training at Whidbey Island NAS in Washington. On 19 July, 120 departed for Shemya Island, in the Aleutians, for duty with Fleet Air Wing 4.

Shemya is a cold and mist-shrouded island lying between Attu and Kiska. It is the only island with flat terrain in the Aleutians and was only 800 miles from the Japanese base at Paramushiro, in the Northern Kurlies. After two weeks of indoctrination the squadron conducted anti-shipping sweeps in the Northern Kurlies during the last two weeks of the war.

The squadron conducted six combat missions between 3 and 14 August, with an anti-shipping sweep of Onekotan and Paramushir islands of the Northern Kurils by four Privateers flown by Lt.Cdr. Reynolds (promoted to commander), Lt. J. P. Doyle, Lt.Cdr. Richard J. Davis, and Eugene C. Marlin. The flight claimed the damage or destruction of one small coastal vessel, a pair of fishing boats, and ten landing craft. There were no significant enemy military assets on the Kurils, thus the squadron was regulated to strafing and bombing

A photograph of a VPB-122 Privateer taken in Alaska. *Courtesy of Steve Hawley*

A formation of VPB-122 Privateers. *Courtesy of Eddie Harding, USN(Ret) VPB-122*

targets with little if any military value.

A similar sweep was conducted two days later by four Privateers, with Lts. Noyer and Hofheimer targeting the Paramushir area, while Lt. Marlin and Ensign Chandler—the latter becoming separated due to limited visibility—hit Onekotan and Araido. The crews claimed damage of a fish cannery and a fishing barge. Lts. Doyle, R. E. Edwards, J. K. MacLean, and Lt. (jg) P. T. Kissling conducted a repeat on the seventh, with heavy fog halting operations until the twelfth, when Lt. R. J. Davis (squadron executive officer), Lt. McElnea, and Lt. (jg) Courtney bombed an airfield on Paramushir as a diversion for a fleet bombardment conducted by Task Force 92. VPB-120's last combat flight of the war was flown on 13 August by Lt. Marlin and Lt. (jg) Trust, who struck an airstrip, installations, fishing boats, and other structures at Torishima Retto and Kakumabetsu airstrip.

As the war with Japan ended the second Privateer squadron arrived at Shemya. VPB-122, under the command of Lt.Cdr. A. L. Burgess, should have arrived sooner to the Aleutians, except for some unforeseen circumstances. Commissioned as VP-72, the squadron was redesignated VPB-122 in October 1944. The following month, while training at Camp Kearney, California, the squadron had six of

its seven crews transferred to VPB-108, resulting in the squadron becoming inactive until March the following year. For the next four months it trained with PB4Y-1s around San Francisco and Seattle. Finally, in July, the squadron received Privateers. On 5 August, VPB-122 began their movement to Shemya, with the last plane arriving the very day the war ended.

A snow-covered mountain looms in the background as a member of VPB-122 inspects a PB4Y-2. *Courtesy of Eddie Harding, USN(Ret) VPB-122*

VPB-122 Privateers over the North Pacific. *Courtesy of Eddie Harding, USN(Ret) VPB-122*

A Crew standing next to their PB4Y-2. This photograph was probably taken after the war, since there are no machine guns installed in the bow turret. *Courtesy of Eddie Harding, USN(Ret) VPB-122*

Appendix A
Personnel Losses Including Killed in the Line of Duty
1 October 1944–11 August 1945

VPB-101

Killed in Action
19 October 1944
John A. Eckfield, ACOM
Dean W. Doering, AOM3c
Peter A. Villa, AMM1c
Francis M. Ford, ARM2c

23 October 1944
Harold H. Lewis Jr., Lieutenant
Frank L. Furbush, AMM2c
Tony D. Gonzales, AMM3c
Clifford E. McFarlane, AOM2c
Raymond R. Taylor, Ensign
Wilbur L. Williamson, AOM1c
Charles C. Boudreau, AMM1c
Frederick V. Cole, ARM3c
James W. Davis, AOM3c
Junius B. Duncan, ARM2c

25 October 1944
Albert O. Polston, Ensign
Robert W. Allen, Ensign
William H. Heide, AMM2c
Frank G. Meisner, ARM1c
John J. Reardon, ARM1c
Joe E. Ellsworth, ARM3c
Frank A. Albanello, AMM3c
Ralph G. Siley, AOM2F
Lewis E. Manning, AOM3c

26 October 1944
Joseph Downs, Ensign
Charles A. Newland, ACMMA
George S. Sloan, ARM3c
Russell E. Bowen, Lieutenant

31 October 1944
J.W. Shepard, Ensign

25 November 1944
Walter K. Rodgers, Lieutenant (jg)
Cyrus C. Coyle, AMMH2c
Basil R. Rosengrant, ARM3c
Edgar J. Cartwright, AMM3c
Coy F. Fielder, AOM2c

15 January 1945
Marvin T. Smith, Lt. Commander
William J. Fischer, AOM2c
Kenneth R. Platte, ARM2c
Melvin J. Roth, AMM3c
Talmadge C. Thurmond, ACMMA

Killed in the Line of Duty
25 November 1944
Walton K. Rodgers, Lieutenant
Edgar J. Cartwright, AMM3c
Coy F. Fielder, AOM2c
Basil R. Rosengrant
Sheridan L. Poston, AOM1c

VPB-102

Killed in Action
9 May 1945
E.E. Beard
R.B. Andrews
Y.R. McCluskey
A.A. Cooper
C.A. Brannen Jr.
Leslie A. Burril
R.C. Fowler
R.L. Holohan
A.J. Long

30 June 1945
R.L. Shiley, Ensign
Joseph R. Ricci

Killed in the Line of Duty
23 May 1945
Floyd E. Johnson
Frederick C. Keehn
D.E. Simmons

VPB-104

Killed in Action
11 November 1944
Maurice K. Hill, Lieutenant
James M. Wimberly, Ensign
James Diachin, AMM3c
Kenneth A. Waddle, AMM3c

Erwin J. Anderson, ARM1c
William R. Forrester, AOM2c
Thomas E. McKenzie, AOM1c

12 December 1944
William E. Abbott, AMM3c

11 January 1945
Joseph D. Shea, Lt. (jg)
Floyd M. Craven, Ensign
Walter J. Whelan, Ensign
Gordon D. Martin, AMM2c
James W. Clement, AMM3c
Otto A. Adams, AMM3c
Emmet J. McDonald, ARM2c
James D. Harrington, ARM3c
Walter E. Toice, ARM3c
Owen P. Dailey, AOM3c
Billy P. Casey, AOM3c

18 February 1945
Kenneth R. McHenry, Ensign (died 19 February)

18 February 1945
William E. Goodman, Lieutenant
John L. Keidel, Ensign
Richard S. Knight, Ensign
Elmer G. Krom, AMM3c
Alvie Y. Harris Jr., AMM3c
Lloyd M. Howard, AMM3c
John Bierman, AMM3c
Sidney M. Seifer, ARM3c
Cecil R. Colvin, ARM3c
Vernon L. McCoy, AOM3c
Samuel H. Newell, AOM3c
John J. Polesky Jr., ART3c

Killed in the Line of Duty
6 June 1944
Edward G. Woodward, ARM3c
Henry I. Ladowski, ARM3c
John D. Fuller, AMM3c

7 January 1945
Lasarus Der Vartanian, AMM3c
Raymond L. Kelsey, AOM1c

9 July 1945
Charles L. Crozier, Lt. (jg)
Albert A. Purola, Ensign
Paul D. Boyer, AMM2c
Robert F. Griffin, AMM3c
Earl E. Buck, ARM2c
Merrille Speake, ARM3c
George H. Anderson, AOM3c
Charles R. Harrison, AOM3c
Amato L. Bacchi, S1c
Lester J. Keene, S1c

VPB-106

Killed in Action 9 March 1945
Edward W. Ashley, Lieutenant (jg)
Robert M. Castiglia, Ensign
William G. Benes JR., Ensign
Frank B. Blake, AMM2c
Warren Kish, ARM1c
Beauford J. Grothe, AOM2c
Orin L Hackett, AOM2c
Bertram Brown, ARM3c
Gonzalo Mireles, S1c
Francis O. McLaughlin, Jr., AMM1c
Robert N. Williams Jr., 1st Lieutenant USMC
(passenger)
Jerome O. Campbell, AMM1c (passenger)
Joseph W. Schroeder, AMM1c (passenger)

Prisoner of War
Raymond W. Gray Jr., S1c
Charles W. Reddon, S1c

1 June 1945
H.F. Mears, Lt. Commander
R. Decker, Ensign
V. Carlson, Ensign
R.B. McCabe, AMM1c
J.J. Reiter, ARM1c
R.H. Blanton Jr, AFC1c
P. Davis Jr., ARM2c
A.J. George, AMM2c
E.L. Kitchen, AOM2c
H.E. Capen Jr., ARM3c
D.T. Morgan, AMM3c
B.R. O'Kane, S1c

14 June 1945
G.C. Goodloe, Lt. Commander
E.F. Conry, Ensign
N.S. Smith, Ensign
A.E. Krueger, AMM1c
R.B. O'Kon, AOM1c
A. Hernandez, ARM2c
D.J. Ashcroft, ARM2c
H.L Devasier, AMM2c
N.J. Kay Jr., AMM3c
G.G. Greenwood, AMM3c
G.F. Blakesley, ARM3c

30 July 1945
Joseph W. Swiencicki, Lieutenant
Jack Cranfill, Ensign
Robert K. Gunderson, Ensign
Leo E. Brown, AMM1c

William W. UbI, AOM2c
Leo J.E. Babineau, AMM2c
James J. Sherman, ARM2c
Raymond R. Menendez, AOM3c
Fredrick A. Gidel, AMM2c
Robert D. Buscher, S1c
John K. Jones Jr., AMM3c

Killed in the Line of Duty
12 December 1944
W.D. Dandy, AMM2c
L.E. LaVallee, AMM3c
G.J. Mandaville, AOM2c
A.R. Marett, AMM3c
M. Maslowsky, S1c
J.J. McManus, ARM3c
S. Perotta, S1c

VPB-108

Killed in Action
9 May 1945
John E. Muldrow, Lt. Commander
John C. O'Connell, Lt. (jg)
John J. Denton, AMM1c
James A. Brumley, ARM2c
Bill D. Martin, AOM3c
Daniel H. Webster, AFC3c
William P. Heaford, S1c (AOM)
Henry J. Struck, S1c (AOM)

VPB-109

Killed In Action
5 May 1945
Joe W. Kasperlik, AMM2c

30 May 1945
Leo E. Kennedy, Lieutenant

5 August 1945
John D. Keeling, Lieutenant
Henry Baier Jr., Ensign
Keith W. Radcliffe, Ensign
William L. Willocks Jr., AMM1c
Frank R. Kramer, AOM1c
William J. Krier, ARM1c
Alexander J. Boyd, ARM1c
Melvin M. Rager, AMM2c
James R.T. Carswell, AFC2c
Peter G. Ilacqua, ARM2c
James E. Krieger, AMM3c
Lawrence R. Conroy, AOM3c

VPB-111

Killed In Action
18 April 1945
W.E. Bartlett, Lieutenant
Henry Lee, Lieutenant (jg)
F.L. McLean, Ensign
R.W. Thomas, AOM2c
N.O. Phillips, AMMF2c
J.E. Rinkavage, AOM2c

Killed in the Line of Duty
16 June 1945
L.T. Bass, Lieutenant (jg)
W.L. Dernberger, Lieutenant (jg)
P.C. Stretcher, Ensign
A.P. Anders, ARM3c
R.H. Graham, ARM1c
R.P Kivitt, ARM3c
R.W. Mitchell, ARM3c
H.V. Philpott, AMM3c
G.W. Pringle, ACM3c
J. Regiac, ARM3c
W.A. Whitener, ARM3c
G.P. Oligschlager, AMM2c
W.F. Karls, AMM1c
J.L. Harney, ARM2c
J.R. Harvester Jr., ARM3c
J.J. Dillon, ARM3c

20 June 1945
D.J. Quinlan, Lieutenant
T. Gilmer, Lt. (jg)
J.L. Israel, Lt. (jg)
R.C. Affeldt, ARM3c
R.L. Kerr, AOM3c
H.D. Lang, AMM2c

VB/VPB-116

Killed in Action
11 October 1944
William H. Stimson, Lieutenant
Elmer H. Copeland, AMM2c
Herschel A. Daniel, S1c
Clarence H. Floersch Jr., ARM2c
Harry S. Groszyk, Lieutenant
Julius L. Maslack, AOM2c
Robert J. Nauman, ARM3c
Bernard J. Poeschl, Ensign
David D. Whitaker, AMM3c
Edward D. Wilson, AOM3c
James Q. Worley, S1c

2 January 1945
W.R. Robinson, Lt. (jg)

18 May 1945
Richard Goldner, Lieutenant
George H. Bowly, AMM2c
William H. Ferguson, ARM3c
Charles W. Fox, AMM2c
Clifford H. Helton, ARM3c
Earl L. Kirsch, AOM3c
Ernest Koepke, Ensign
Raymond G. Porter, S1c
Thomas C. Rowlands, S1c
David E. Sheehy, Ensign
Carlyle Willis, S1c

29 June 1945
J. Gerberding, Lt. Commander
S.S. Middleton, Lieutenant
T. Greer, Ensign
A.R. Chicirda, AMM3c

H.A. Gallagher, AMM1c
P.A. Goering, AOM3c
A.I. Levitt, ART2c
W.E. Mitchell, AMM3c
B.R. Odelberg, ARM2c
H.B. Pierson Jr., ARM2c
L.D. Simon, AMM3c
S.L. Vaughan Jr., ARM3c
F.G. Zutter, S1c

Killed in the Line of Duty
12 January 1945
Francisco Alesso, ARM3c

VPB-117

Killed in Action
12 November 1944
Wayne C. Kellogg, AMM1c
John L. Craig, AMM3c
Samuel M. Bagwell, ARM3c
Basil G. Martin, AOM2c
William R. Pierson, AOMB2c

10 December 1944
Bradford M. Brooks, Lieutenant
Gregory A. Robinson, Ensign
James L. Tedrowe, AOM3c
Melvin Long, AMM3c
Vergil T. Bolton Jr., ARM2c

15 December 1944
Rudolph Tonsick (died of wounds)

20 December 1944
Frank H. Wharton, S1c (died of wounds)
A.B. Crofford Jr., S1c (died of wounds)

28 January 1945
Robert E. White, Lt. (jg)
Harry P. Palritz, Ensign
J. C. Buchanan, AMM3c
(Executed while a POW on 19 June)
Edward A. Sieber, AMM2c
(Executed while a POW on 3 February)
Frank E. Collins Jr., ARM3c
Wayne W. Wilson, ARM3c
(Died while a POW on 19 June)
Delbert H. Carter, AOM3c
(Died while a POW on 19 June)
Donald K. Hathaway, AMM3c
(Died while a POW on 19 June)
Albert C. Kalishauskas, AMM3c
John R. Parker, AMM3c
(Died while a POW on 19 June)

17 February 1945
Harold W. McGaughey, Lt. Cdr. Nelson E.
McCaa, Lieutenant
William H. Handwerk, Ensign
Robert J. Brown, AMM3c
Frank C. Aiello, AMM2c
Robert J. Rudd, ARM3c
Neal L. Hamer, AOMB1c
Sidney S. Martin, ART1c

Will H. Eldridge Jr., AOM3c
George A. Womack, S1c
Ralph C. Haralson, AOM2c

25 April 1945
James G. Taylor, ARM3c

14 June 1945
J.P. Dougan, Lt. (jg)
L.G. Boutte, Lt. (jg)
V.C. Thomas, Ensign
V.P. Rider Jr., AOM2c
W.N. Sand, AOM3c
A.P. Riedel, AOM3c
W.H. Stewart, S1c
P.E. Curran, ARM2c
P.A. deMarrais, ACRM
G.C. French, AMM3c
K.J. Sullivan, AMM3c

22 June 1945
Stanley W. Sayre, Lieutenant (jg)
Marcellus P. Brownlee, Ensign
Joseph H. Taylor, Ensign
Leo J. Walkowisk, AMM2c
John J. Foley, AMM2c
Jordan M. Nicholas, ARM1c
Alfred V. Peterson, ARM1c
Harry W. Klotz, ARM2c
Peter L. Leydecker Jr., AOM2c
Homer B. Hansen, AOM3c
Ronald E. Ball, ARM2c
Thomas E. Thompson, ARM3c

1 July 1945
Robert E. Hepting, Lt. (jg)
Ralph B. Messick, Lt. (jg)
Donald L. Gross, Ensign
Charles R. Playne AMM1c
Peter A. Hourcade, AMM2c (Executed as a POW)
Leonard C. Fisher, ARM2c
William W. Core, ARM2c
John R. Palm, ARM3c
John F. Knauss, AOM3c

30 July 1945
Frederick F Thomas, AMM2c

Killed in the Line of Duty
31 December 1944
William T. Benn, Lt. (jg)

22 June 1945
S.W. Sayre, Lt. (jg)
M.F. Brownlee, Ensign
J.H. Taylor, Ensign
L.J. Walkowiak, AMM2c
J.J. Foley, AMM2c
J.M. Nichols, ARM1c
H.W. Klotz, ARM2c
P.L.J. Leydecker Jr., AOM2c
H.B. Hanson, AOM3c
R.E. Ball, ARM2c
T.R. Thompson, ARM3c

Prisoner of War
John F Bertrang, Ensign (28 January)
Lester L. Gottberg, AOM3c (1 July)
Joseph F Lowder, ARM3c (1 July)
Irving R. Stark, AMM3c (1 July)

VPB-118

Killed in Action
6 May 1945
J.A. Lasater, Lieutenant
M.L. Gibson, Ensign
C.J. Milner, Ensign
E.W. Smith, AMM2c
W.J. Hawkins, ARM2c
C.W. Jacobs, AMM3c
R.E. Miller, AOM2c
S.C. Bryant Jr., AMM2c
D. McAllister, ARM3c
H.F. Brockhorst, ARM3c
W.L. Thornton Jr., AOM3c
R.A. Carr, AMM3c

21 July 1945
L.P. McCutcheon, Lieutenant
F. Reeve, Lt. (jg)
W.E. Bucklwe, Ensign
O.A. Bunkers, AFC1c
A.D. Nelson, AMM2c
J.N. Welch, AMM3c

6 August 1945
D.C. Slator, AOM3c

8 August 1945
J.R. Park, Lt. (jg)
G. W. Lewton, Ensign
L.H. Lowe, Ensign
E.K. Hall Jr., ARM3c
M.E. Hedrick, S1c (ARM)
J.M. James, AMM3c
R.A. Koontz, AOM3c
C.A. McKinney, S1c (ARM)
M.M. Marich, ACOM
P. Preitz, S1c (ARM)
R.R. Reinhart, ARM3c
H.J. Wartzack, ARM3c

VPB-119

Killed In Action
22 March 1945
Francis W. Greene, Ensign
Robert J. Jenson, AMMF2c
Andrew J. Wilson, AMMF2c
Nicholas J. Meo, AOM3c
James L. Doss, AOM2c
Calvin C. Gipson, S1c

1 April 1945
Raymond C. Bales, Lt. Commander
Roscoe M. Obert, Lieutenant
Robert L. Fox Jr., Lt. (jg)
Robert I Suhl, AMMF1c
Everett F. Fees, ACOM

William J. Wagner, ACRM
Joseph A. Howard, ACOM
Walter R. Gainer, AOM1c
Barney D. Guthrie Jr., AMMF2c
Edward L. Atkin Jr., ARM3c
John P. McKeon, AOM3c
Jack O. Ballard, S1c

11 April 1945
Aubrey L. Althans, Lt. (jg)
William C. Mathews, Lt. (jg)
Donald C. Kirby, Ensign
James W. Adams, AMMF1c
Casimer J. Bogacz, AMMF1c
George H. Stein, ARM1c
Francis J. Christiano. AMMF2c
Edward A. Jakubiak, AOMB2c
Charles A. Bagley, AOM3c
Wilson W. Harner, AOM2c
Harold H. Elfreich, S1c
Bearl A. Lawrence, ARM3c

1 May 1945
John W. Holt, Lieutenant
Firmin J. Urban, Ensign
Marshall C. Baker, Ensign
John F. Moe, ACMM
Milton F. Smith, ACRM
Adolph H. Busse, AOMB1c
Henry B. Babb, AOM2c
Livio J. Banda, AMMF3c
Jesse L. Middleton, ARM3c
Paul D. Wilson, ARM3c
Fred Kautz, AOM3c
Leno G. Benuzzi, S1c

7 May 1945
Lloyd Allen Whitten, S1c

19 May 1945
Walter G. Vogelsang, Lt. (jg)
Robert E. Graner, Lt. (jg)
Alvin R. Martin, Ensign
Edward W. Brooks, AMMF1c
Louis J. Oronoz, AMMF2c
Carl H. Swift, ARM1c
Donald C. Hulick, ARM2c
Jackie E. Rigsby, AOM3c
Walter T. Long, AOMB2c
Robert C. Molter, S1c
Leonal L. Smith, S1c
Harold Raymond Davis, S1c
(passenger from CASU57)

17 June 1945
Thomas J. Robinson, Lt. (jg)
Robert M. Cahow, Ensign
William R. Stuard Jr., AOM1c
Harold C. Everett, ARM2c
Ralph J. Henderson, AFC2c
Harold Snider, AOM3c
Edward M. Loeser Jr., AMMF2c

24 June 1945
Williard P. Comstock, Lieutenant
George Chadick, Lt. (jg)
Kenneth E. Shaffer Jr., Lt. (jg)
Marvin R. Denzig, Lt. (jg)
John Francis Geraghty, Lt. (passenger)
Oriel A. Roadifer, ACMM
Robert E. Morin, AMMF2c
Garr L. Rose, ARM1c
Henry E. Reed, ARM3c
Lyle W. Wagner, AMMF3c
Leonard Pukita, AMMF3c
Louis D. Meyer, AOM3c
Norman E. Baters, S1c

Killed in the Line of Duty
2 March 1945
Leonard J. Reichert, Lieutenant

VPB-121

Killed in Action
7 March 1945
William McElwee Jr., Lieutenant
R.L. Vannice, Lt. (jg)
R.E. Artz, Ensign
C.C. Gibbany, AMM2c
A.H. Hill, AMM3c
D.N. Gibbons Jr., ARM3c
W.E. Roarty, ARM3c
H.P. Garrison, AOM3c
L. Siscoe, Jr., AOMB2c
C.L. Weiss, S1c
F.E. Marstiller, S1c
J.T. Houser, AOMT1c

11 July 1945
J.M. Cumbach, AOM2c

11 August 1945
E.J. Heeb, Ensign
D.W. Mott, AMM1c
R.E. Guth, AMM2c
C.A. Bremer, S1c

Prisoner of War
J.B. Rainey, Lt. Commander
H.H. Whitted, Lt. (jg)
J. Frashure, ARM2c
R.W. Cox, ARM2c
A.R. Dugger, AOM2c
W.R. Long, AFC1c
K.C. Gaber, AMM3c
P.E. Williams, ARM3c

VPB-123

Killed in Action
7 August 1945
Joseph H. Farmer, AOM3c

VD-5

Killed in the Line of Duty
24 February 1945
L.R. Gehlbach, Lt. Commander

VPB-124

Killed in Action
6 June 1945
William C. Lawson, AOM2c

26 June 1945
Jack "R" Crist, Lt. (jg)
Grant W. Smith, Lt. (jg)
Ralph M. W. Frailey, Ensign
John E. Cain, AMM2c
Charles Wilson, ARM2c
Donald L. Bott, AOM2c
Theodore Noonan, AMM3c
John B. Kaighn Jr., ARM3c
Norman F. Surface, AOM2c
Bernard J. Moriarty, S1c
Earnest E. Pike, S1c
Norman I. Sayre, ART1c
Gerald W. Eves, Ensign
Jack "C" Camerson, ARM
Raymond J. Skulina, AOM1c
Thomas P. Metz, ARM2c

27 June 1945
Jack E. Vincent, Lt. (jg)
Arnold R. Hardman, Lt. (jg)
Adolph U. Johnson, Ensign
Cleo E. Grapes, AMM1c
James J. Carrico, ARM1c
Max C. Leir, AOM3c
Philip S. Anderson, AMM3c
Stephen W. O'Brien, Jr., ARM2c
Victor R. Davis, AOM3c
William V. Morgan, S1c
Eugene J. Stellern, S1c

7 July 1945
Ned B. Brown, Ensign
John V. Brennan, Jr, AOM3c
Robert J. Brower, Lieutenant
Stanley Sunshine, ARM3c
Earl K. Elias, AOM3c
Robert B. Watson, S1c
William H. Cates, AMM3c

24 July 1945
Gilbert E. Miller, Lieutenant
Ralph H. Hepworth, Lt. (jg)
Robert A. Littmann, Ensign
Orvill M. Osborn, AMM1c
Albert A. Comminiello, ARM1c
Joseph F. Cholasta, AOM3c
Francis A. Spencer, Jr., AMM2c
Madison R. Stacy, ARM3c
Raymond E. Davis, AOM3c

James B. Ivie, S1c
John M. Gay, AMM3c
Wilborn P. Raney, ARM2c
John B. Ramsey, Lieutenant
Robert P. Stengelin, Lt. (jg)
Merlin H. Williams, Ensign
Howard Hobbs, AMM1c
Robert S. Nicholls, ARM1c
William A. Yankow, AOM1c
John H. Anson, AMM2c
Hugh C. Wilson, ARM3c
Hoyt H. Hamlett, AOM3c
Allen E. Kallstrom, S1c
Russell L. Rummel, S1c
Robert T. Dumas, ARM2c

Prisoner of War
Charles E. Houston
Clinton L. Prestien
Walter Pallack
Frank Maratea
Theodore A. Hauser
Jens M. Martinsen
Richard C. Warner
Francis C. Wellman
David G. Davis
Jack R. Lewis
Frank R. Gardner
Theodore Kalmuk
George A. Dacier

Appendix B
PB4Y Summary of Operations

Total Sorties	Tons of Bombs Dropped
3,640	1,413

Types of Land Targets Attacked

Airfields	Installations	Transportation	Harbor Areas	Other
411	482	181	102	104

Types of Shipping Attacked

Warships	Merchant	Unkown
137	1,547	91

492 were over 500 tons and 1,055 under 500 tons

PB4Y Aircraft Losses

To AA	To AC	Operational	Other Flights	On Ground
60	28	18	85	72

1943: 2 aircraft lost and another 31 damaged due to AA
1944: 15 lost and 101 damaged
1945: 43 lost and 269 damaged

Enemy Aircraft Destroyed

Year	Bombers	Fighters
1943	13	28
1944	59	72
1945	53	81
Total	125	181

Types of Japanese Aircraft encountered during aerial combat and results for 1 September 1944 to 15 August 1945.

Data for previous period was not available.

Type of Aircraft	Japanese Losses	PB4Y Losses
Zeke, Hamp	25	4
Oscar	15	2
Tony	5	2
Tojo	8	
Frank	1	
Jack	6	
Val	12	
Judy	1	
Kate	7	
Jill	3	
Sonia	2	
Jake	31	
Pete	8	
Rufe	2	
Rex	3	
Paul	2	
Dave	2	
Betty	14	
Dinah	3	
Frances	1	
Nick	3	
Sally	2	
Nell	7	
Flying Boats	8	
Transports	28	
Unknown	5	5

Appendix C
Estimated Individual Squadron Records

VPB-101
Ships Sunk: 41
Ships Damaged: 87
Aircraft Destroyed in Air and on Ground: 60
Damaged: 6

VPB-102 (The Reluctant Dragons)
Ships Sunk: 99
Ships Damaged: 151
Tonnage:105,520+
Aircraft Destroyed in Air: 14
Probable: 9
Damaged in Air: 15

VPB-104 to April 1945 (The Buccaneers)
Ships Sunk: 262
Ships Damaged: 269
Aircraft Destroyed in Air: 38
Probable: 12
Damaged in Air: 21
Destroyed on Ground: 11
Damaged on Ground: 15

VPB-106 (The Wolverators)
Ships Sunk: 30+
Ships Damaged: 78+
Aircraft Destroyed in Air: 2
Damaged in Air: 1
Destroyed on Ground: 2
Damaged on Ground: 2

VPB-108 (Hawaiian Warriors)
Ships Sunk: 118
Ships Damaged: 159
Aircraft Destroyed in Air: 3
Probable: 1
Damaged in Air: 3

VPB-109 (The Reluctant Raiders)
Ships Sunk: 118
Ships Damaged: 87
Tonnage: 87,200
Aircraft Destroyed in Air: 6
Probable: 1
Damaged in Air: 8
Damaged on Ground: 1

VPB-111
Ships Sunk: 260
Ships Damaged: 336
Aircraft Destroyed in Air: 17
Probable: 2
Damaged in Air: 15
Destroyed on Ground: 8
Damaged on Ground: 7
Attacks: 232

VPB-116 (The Blue Raiders)
Ships Sunk: 30
Ships Damaged: 40
Aircraft Destroyed in Air: 13
Probable: 1

VPB-117 (The Blue Raiders)
Ships Sunk: 210
Ships Damaged: 274
Aircraft Destroyed in Air: 58
Probable: 5
Destroyed on Ground: 16
Damaged on Ground: 4
Attacks: 300
Estimated Total Tonnage: 205,255

VPB-118 (The Old Crows)
Ships Sunk: 100
Ships Damaged: 105
Aircraft Destroyed in Air: 9
Damaged in Air: 6
Destroyed on Ground: 5

VPB-119
Ships Sunk: 114
Ships Damaged: 124
Aircraft Destroyed in Air: 8
Damaged in Air: 3
Destroyed on Ground: 2
Damaged on Ground: 3

VPB-121
Ships Sunk: 8
Ships Damaged: 10
Tonnage: Less than 5,000
Aircraft Destroyed in Air: 4
Probable: 1

VPB-123
Ships Sunk: 67
Ships Damaged: 38
Aircraft Destroyed in Air: 9
Probable: 3

VPB-124
Ships Sunk: 16
Ships Damaged: 21
Tonnage: 27,136
Aircraft Destroyed in Air: 3
Damaged in Air: 1

Appendix D
PB4Y Aerial Claims
October 1944–August 1945 (Confirmed Kills)

I would like to give special thanks to James C. Sawruk, who compiled the following data.

DATE	SQUADRON	PPC	TYPE
10/09/44	102	Lt/jg. Philip Knights	Betty
10/11/44	116	Lt. John Miller	Betty
10/11/44	116	Lt. William Beckham	Betty
10/11/44	101	Lt. Fred Morris	Pete
10/12/44	116	Lt. William Oliver	1/2Zeke
10/12/44	116	Lt. William Miller	1/2Zeke
10/12/44	116	Lt. William Oliver	1/2Zeke
10/12/44	116	Lt. William Miller	1/2Zeke
10/12/44	116	Lt. William Oliver	1/2Zeke
10/12/44	116	Lt. William Miller	1/2Zeke
10/12/44	116	Lt. William Oliver	1/2Zeke
10/12/44	116	Lt. William Miller	1/2Zeke
10/12/44	116	Lt. William Oliver	1/2Zeke
10/12/44	116	Lt. William Miller	1/2Zeke
10/13/44	102	Lt/jg. Edmond Elliot	Jake
10/14/44	117	LCDR. Thomas Mulvihill	Kate
10/20/44	101	Lt. Albert Bellsey	Betty
10/20/44	115	Lt. Hamilton Dawes Jr.	Topsy
10/22/44	101	Lt/jg. Kenneth Dunn	Tess
10/23/44	101	Ens. John Copeland	Betty
10/26/44	115	Lt. E.F. Kahle Jennings	Jake
10/31/44	117	Lt. Herbert Box	Emily
11/01/44	116	Lt. Guy Thompson Jr.	Emily
11/02/44	115	Ens. Paul Barker	Jake
11/07/44	VD-4	Lt. Earl Wright Jr.	Oscar
11/07/44	VD-4	LCDR. Charles Clark	Zeke
11/07/44	VD-4	Lt. Eugene O'Brien	Zeke
11/11/44	104	Lt. Maurice Hill	1/2Tony
11/11/44	104	Lt/jg. Gerald Didier	1/2Tony
11/21/44	101	Lt. Thad Williams	Oscar
11/22/44	101	Lt. Albert Bellsey	Mavis
11/24/44	104	Lt/jg. Jeff Hemphill	Pete
11/29/44	104	Lt. George Waldeck	Tess
12/02/44	117	Lt. Daniel Moore	Zeke
12/02/44	101	Lt. Albert Lubberts	Jack
12/02/44	101	Lt. Albert Lubberts	Zeke
12/02/44	101	Lt. Albert Lubberts	Zeke
12/02/44	101	Lt. Albert Lubberts	Zeke
12/03/44	117	Lt/jg. Warner Rhodes	Jake
12/04/44	101	Lt. Robert Hershberger	Betty
12/06/44	117	Lt. Daniel Moore	Jake
12/07/44	117	LCDR. Harold McGaughey	Jake
12/09/44	117	Lt. Robert Garlick	Jake
12/10/44	117	Lt. Bradford Brooks	Topsy
12/10/44	104	Lt. Henry Noon	Zeke
12/10/44	117	Lt. Bradford Brooks	Dinah
12/10/44	117	Lt/jg. Jan Carter	Judy
12/11/44	111	LCDR. Sylvan Bland	1/2Betty
12/11/44	111	Lt.William Bartlett	1/2Betty
12/11/44	117	Lt/jg. Homer Heard	Topsy
12/12/44	117	Lt/jg. Sheldon Sutton	Tony
12/12/44	117	LCDR. Harold McGaughey	Tess
12/15/44	104	Lt. John Burton	Sally
12/17/44	117	Lt. Daniel Moore	Tess
12/17/44	117	Lt. Daniel Moore	Tess
12/22/44	104	Lt. Walter Heider	Zeke
12/24/44	117	Lt/jg. Sheldon Sutton	Jake
12/24/44	104	Lt. William Goodman	Jake
12/24/44	117	Lt/jg. Sheldon Sutton	Pete
12/25/44	104	Lt. John Burton	Tabby
12/26/44	117	Lt. Ralph Castleton	Betty
12/27/44	102	Lt. Francis Burton	Betty
12/28/44	117	Lt/jg. Jan Carter	Topsy
12/28/44	104	Lt/jg. Edward Hagen	Mavis
12/30/44	117	Lt. Graham Squires	Emily
12/30/44	117	Lt/jg. Jan Carter	Jake
12/30/44	117	Lt/jg. Jan Carter	Val
12/31/44	117	Lt. William Quinn	Biplane
12/31/44	117	Lt. William Quinn	Jake
12/31/44	104	Lt. Paul Stevens	Nate
12/31/44	117	Lt. Robert Garlick	Tabby
01/03/45	117	LCDR. Harold McGaughey	Nell
01/04/45	104	Lt/jg. Edward Hagen	Biplane
01/05/45	117	Lt/jg. Sheldon Sutton	Jake
01/05/45	117	Lt/jg. Sheldon Sutton	Jake
01/07/45	117	Lt. Daniel Moore	Pete
01/08/45	117	Lt/jg. Sheldon Sutton	Jake
01/13/45	101	LCDR. Marvin Smith	Jack
01/21/45	117	Lt/jg. Sheldon Sutton	Kate
01/23/45	117	Ens. Harold Willyard	Nell
01/24/45	116	Lt. Donald Kirchberg	Zeke
01/26/45	104	Lt. William Goodman	Jake
01/28/45	111	Lt/jg. Wilbur Paris	Topsy
01/30/45	104	Lt/jg. Gerald Didier	Val
01/31/45	117	Lt. Robert Empey	Zeke
02/01/45	104	Lt/jg. Richard Jameson	Jake
02/03/45	104	Lt. William Goodman	Jake
02/05/45	104	Lt. Paul Stevens	Val
02/06/45	104	Lt. William Goodman	Betty
02/07/45	117	LCDR. Harold McGaughey	Paul

DATE	SQUADRON	PPC	TYPE
02/07/45	117	Lt. William Quinn	Jake
02/07/45	117	LCDR. Thomas Mulvihill	Zeke
02/07/45	117	LCDR. Thomas Mulvihill	Zeke
02/10/45	111	LCDR. Richard Field	Tony
02/10/45	117	LCDR. Harold McGaughey	Jake
02/11/45	117	Lt/jg. Jan Carter	Jake
02/12/45	111	LCDR. Albert Ellingson	Nell
02/13/45	104	Lt/jg. Edward Hagen	Nell
02/13/45	104	Lt/jg. Edward Hagen	Nell
02/15/45	117	Ens. John Bourchier	Kate
02/16/45	104	LCDR. Whitney Wright	Jake
02/18/45	104	Lt. Stanley Wood	Topsy
02/20/45	104	Lt. Raymond Ettinger	Kate
02/20/45	104	Lt. Raymond Ettinger	Zeke
02/20/45	117	Lt. Thomas Hyland	Jake
02/20/45	117	Lt. Thomas Hyland	Jake
02/21/45	111	LCDR. Albert Ellingson	Jill
02/22/45	111	Lt. Harold Ashton	Topsy
02/22/45	111	Lt/jg. Francis Kieper	Val
02/23/45	117	LCDR. Thomas Mulvihill	Jake
02/27/45	104	Lt/jg. Earl Bittenbender	Topsy
02/27/45	104	Lt/jg. Earl Bittenbender	Topsy
02/27/45	104	Lt/jg. Earl Bittenbender	Val
02/27/45	117	Lt. Thomas Hyland	Jake
03/03/45	104	Lt. Stanley Wood	Kate
03/03/45	117	Lt. William Quinn	Rex
03/04/45	104	Lt. Paul Stevens	Paul
03/04/45	117	Lt. Thomas Hyland	Nell
03/04/45	117	Lt. Thomas Hyland	Nell
03/05/45	104	Lt. George Waldeck	Topsy
03/05/45	104	Lt. George Waldeck	Topsy
03/07/45	104	Lt/jg. Richard Jameson	Frank
03/10/45	104	Lt. Paul Stevens	Val
03/10/45	119	Lt/jg. Virgil Evans	Oscar
03/10/45	111	Lt. Kenneth Johnson	Betty
03/11/45	118	Lt. Norman Keiser	Emily
03/12/45	119	Lt. Aubrey Althans	Jill
03/13/45	119	Lt. Frank Murphy	Oscar
03/15/45	104	Lt. Stanley Wood	Jill
03/17/45	117	Ens. John Bourchier	Oscar
03/17/45	104	Lt. Paul Stevens	Jake
03/17/45	104	Lt. Paul Stevens	Emily
03/22/45	117	Lt. Arthur Elder	Ann
03/23/45	119	Lt. William Lyle	Oscar
03/23/45	119	Lt. William Lyle	Oscar
03/24/45	119	Lt/jg. Aubrey Althans	Jake
03/25/45	117	Lt. Arthur Elder	Jake
03/31/45	117	Lt/jg. Edward Jensen	Tabby
03/31/45	117	Lt/jg. Edward Jensen	Tabby
04/01/45	119	Lt/jg. Walter Vogelsang	Val
04/08/45	117	Lt. Robert Garlick	Sonia
04/18/45	117	Lt. Robert Empey	Topsy
04/22/45	104	Lt. George Waldeck	Sally
04/26/45	104	Lt. Raymond Ettinger	Topsy
04/27/45	118	Lt. Phillip Pettes	1/2Val
04/27/45	118	Lt. LeLand McCutcheon	1/2Val
04/28/45	104	Lt. Vance Alder	Betty
05/02/45	109	Lt/jg. George Serbin	Dinah
05/02/45	109	Lt/jg. George Serbin	Jake
05/03/45	111	Lt. Vincent McClintock	Jake
05/05/45	118	Lt. August Lodato	Stella
05/05/45	118	LCDR. Arthur Farwell Jr.	Nick
05/05/45	118	LCDR. Arthur Farwell Jr.	1/2Tess
05/05/45	118	Lt. Norman Keiser	1/2Tess
05/06/45	116	Lt/jg. Frank Garland	K11W
05/07/45	118	LCDR. Athur Farwell Jr.	Val
05/09/45	119	Lt. Frank Matthewson	Val

DATE	SQUADRON	PPC	TYPE
05/09/45	116	LCDR. Allen Waggoner	Mavis
05/11/45	116	Lt. "W" Redwine	Nell
05/12/45	111	LCDR. Albert Ellingson	Topsy
05/13/45	111	Lt. William Bender	1/2Sonia
05/13/45	111	Lt. Wilbur Paris	1/2Sonia
05/13/45	111	LCDR. Richard Field	Pete
05/16/45	118	LCDR. Arthur Farwell Jr.	George
05/16/45	118	Lt. Robert Finley	George
05/16/45	111	Lt. Frank Gibson	Tabby
05/17/45	109	Lt. William Warren	George
05/17/45	109	Lt. William Warren	George
05/17/45	109	Lt. George Fairbanks	1/2George
05/21/45	102	Lt. Otis Andrews	Glider
05/23/45	102	Lt/jg. Stanley Oset	Nick
05/24/45	109	Lt. Donald Chay	Rufe
05/24/45	109	Lt. Floyd Hewitt	Tony
05/24/45	102	Lt/jg. Allen Morgan	Nick
05/30/45	102	LCDR. Louis Pressler	Tabby
05/30/45	106	Lt/jg. Vernon Smith	Jake
05/30/45	106	Lt/jg. Vernon Smith	Oscar
05/31/45	102	Lt/jg. Allen Morgan	Pete
05/31/45	102	Lt/jg. Allen Morgan	Pete
05/31/45	123	Lt. George McDonald	1/2Frank
05/31/45	123	Lt. Robert Monahan	1/2Frank
06/01/45	111	Lt/jg. Romayn Heyler	Oscar
06/03/45	123	Lt. George McDonald	1/2Pete
06/03/45	123	Lt. Robert Monahan	1/2Pete
06/04/45	102	Lt. Elwood Mildahn	1/2Jack
06/04/45	102	Lt/jg. Jack Scott	1/2Jack
06/06/45	123	Lt/jg. Erwin Klein	1/2Tony
06/06/45	123	Lt/jg. Harold Sanderson	1/2Tony
06/08/45	123	LCDR. Samuel Shilling	Rex
06/08/45	123	Lt. Alfred McCuaig	Tojo
06/16/45	108	Lt. Charles Idle	Zeke
06/16/45	108	Lt. Charles Idle	Zeke
06/17/45	102	Lt. Thomas Copeland	1/2Tojo
06/17/45	102	Lt. Robert Barnes	1/2Tojo
06/17/45	102	Lt. Thomas Copeland	Oscar
06/17/45	102	Lt. Robert Barnes	Oscar
06/18/45	117	Lt. Robert Empey	1/3 Oscar
06/18/45	117	Lt/jg. Joseph Hellrung	1/3 Oscar
06/18/45	117	Lt/jg. William Crawford	1/3 Oscar
06/18/45	117	Lt/jg. Joseph Hellrung	Oscar
06/18/45	117	Lt/jg. William Crawford	Oscar
06/19/45	102	Lt. Erwin Copeland	Oscar
06/20/45	108	Lt. Charles Baumgartner	1/2Oscar
06/20/45	108	Lt. William Hazlett	1/2 Oscar
06/26/45	111	Lt. William Bender	Tojo
07/03/45	123	Lt. Alfred McCuaig	Tojo
07/06/45	124	Lt. John Ramsey	Val
07/07/45	124	Lt/jg. Everett Osborn Jr.	Rex
07/07/45	124	Lt/jg. Everett Osborn Jr.	Rex
07/19/45	111	Lt. Burges Smith	Jake
07/22/45	111	Lt. Floyd Misner	Dinah
07/23/45	118	Lt. Robert De Golia	1/2Topsy
07/23/45	118	Lt. George Shortlidge	1/2Topsy
07/23/45	123	Lt/jg. Terence Cassidy	Tojo
07/26/45	123	Lt/jg. Terence Cassidy	Tojo
07/26/45	123	Lt/jg. Richard Treat	Tojo
07/31/45	121	Lt. Albert Magie Jr.	1/2Zeke
07/31/45	121	Lt. Richard Donahue	1/2Zeke
08/03/45	121	LCDR. Raymond Pflum	1/2Pete
08/03/45	121	Lt. Ralph Ettinger	1/2Pete
08/03/45	121	LCDR. Raymond Pflum	1/2Pete
08/03/45	121	Lt. Ralph Ettinger	1/2Pete
08/08/45	117	Lt. Raymond Klassy	Nell
08/11/45	121	Lt. Thomas Allen	Zeke

Appendix E
Listing of Known PB4Y-1 Liberators Assigned to Pacific-based Squadrons February 1943–August 1945

Some squadrons transferred aircraft and thus are noted.

Bureau Numbers 31936 to 32335 B-24Ds			
BuNo	**Squadron(s)**	**Name**	**Remarks**
31939	VB-101		
31941	VB-101		
31946	VB-108/122/123		
31947	VB-101		Lost in Action 3/3/43
31948	VB-101		Lost in Action 3/5/43
31950	VB-101		Lost in Action 3/5/43?
31951	VB-101/VD-5		
31952	VB-101/102		Lost in Action 12/15/43
31953	VB-101/VD-5/VPB-121		
31954	VB-101/115/VPB-120		
31955	VB-102		
31959	VMB-154/VB-108/VPB-123/122		
31960	VB-101		
31970	VB-101		Lost in Action 2/14/43
31972	VB-102/VB-115/VPB-120		
31975	VB-102/106	*Stoop-N-Droop It*	
31976	VD-1/VB-102	*Spirit of 76*	
31980	VD-1		Operational Loss 7/43
31981	VD-1/VB-102		Operational Loss 2/10/44
31982	VD-1	*Satan's Wagon*	
31984	VB-101/VPB-117		
31986	VD-3		Scrapped at Stillwater, Oklahoma
31987	VD-3/VD-5		
31989	VB-102		Operational Loss 4/7/43
31990	VB-102/VPB-109		Scrapped at Stillwater, Oklahoma
31992	VB-102		Lost in Action 7/7/43
31995	VD-1/VB-102	*Hell's Angels*	Operational Loss 2/14/44
31996	VD-1/VB-102		
31997	VD-1		Operational Loss 9/19/43
31998	VPB-VD-1/122/124	*Butch*	
32003	VD-3/VPB-119		
32005	VD-3		Operational Loss 7/7/43
32006	VD-3/VD-5		
32007	VD-3/VB-115/VPB-120		
32008	VD-3		
32009	VB-102/104/108/122	*America's Playground*	
32010	VB-102		
32011	VD-3		
32012	VB-101/102/104	*Jungle Fever*	Operational Loss 11/15/43

BuNo	Squadron(s)	Name	Remarks
32016	VB-102		Operational Loss 2/26/43
32019	VD-3		Lost in Action 1/4/44
32069	VB-102	*The Schooner*	Lost in Action 3/9/43
32073	VB-104/VPB-117	*Pistol Packin' Mama*	Operational Loss 6/6/44
32074	VB-104	*Donald's Duck*	Operational Loss 1/29/44
32077	VB-104	*Vulnerable Virgin*	Lost in Action 1/8/44
32078	VB-106/115/120		
32079	VB-104	*Wata Honey*	Lost in Action 3/7/44
32080	VB-104/115/120	*Unapproachable*	
32081	VB-104/VPB-118	*Whit's Shits*	
32084	VB-106/ VPB-118		
32085	VB-106		Operational Loss 2/10/44
32087	VB-106	*Fatso*	
32091	VB-106	*Mitzi-Bishi*	
32092	VB-106		Operational Loss 12/25/43
32093	VB-106		Operational Loss 12/15/43
32094	VB-106/115/120		
32097	VPB-122		
32098	VB-108/VD-3/122/123	*Sugar*	
32099	VB-108		Lost in Action 12/12/43
32100	VB-108		Operational Loss 3/21/44
32102	VB-106		Operational Loss 10/20/43
32103	VB-108	*Flying Dutchman*	
32104	VD-4		
32105	VB-108/106/VD-4	*Pistol Packin' Mama*	
32106	VB-108/VD-1/VD-4	*Wabbit Twacks*	Scrapped at Stillwater, Oklahoma
32108	VB-109	*Thunder Mug*	Crashed on Landing 06/44
32109	VB-108/VD-1/VD-4	*Little Joe*	
32112	VB-109	*Mission Belle*	
32113	VD-3/VMB-254		
32114	VB-106		
32115	VD-4/VB-115		Operational Loss 5/17/44
32116	VB-108/VPB-124/VD-4	*Nippo Nippin' Kitten*	
32118	VB-109	*No Foolin*	
32119	VD-4	*Overexposed*	
32120	VB-108	*Virgin Sturgeon*	Lost in Action 12/28/43?
32121	VB-109	*Sky Cow* aka *Big Cow*	Operational Loss 7/21/44
32122	VD-4	*Sleepy Time Gal*	
32123	VB-108		Operational Loss 11/18/44
32124	VB-106/108	*Nobody's Baby*	
32125	VB-108/VD-1/VD-4	*Nucky No No Maru*	
32128	VD-4		
32130	VB-109	*The Stork*	Scrapped at Stillwater, Oklahoma
32131	VB-109	*Consolidated's Mistake*	
32132	VPB-121		
32136	VB-109	*Our Baby*	Operational Loss 1/03/44
32137	VB-109	*Helldorado*	
32138	VB-108/109		
32139	VB-109		Lost in Action 1/13/44
32140	VB-109/VPB-122/123	*Pacific Vagabond/Climbaboard*	
32141	VB-109		Operational Loss 1/44
32142	VB-108/VPB-119	*Lady Luck*	
32143	VD-4	*Witchcraft*	
32145	VB-109	*Urge Me*	
32146	VB-101		Operational Loss 2/17/44
32148	VB-109	*Flying Circus*	
32149	VB-109/VD-1/VD-4	*Available Jones*	
32150	VB-115		Lost in Action 6/5/44
32152	VB-106/VPB-109		Scrapped at Stillwater, Oklahoma
32154	VB-106/VPB-109		Scrapped at Stillwater, Oklahoma

BuNo	Squadron(s)	Name	Remarks
32155	VB-108/VPB-119	*Hells's Belle*	
32156	VPB-102/VPB-122		Scrapped at Stillwater, Oklahoma
32157	VD-4/VPB-102/VD-4		
32158	VB-108	*Dinah II*	Scrapped at Stillwater, Oklahoma
32159	VB-115		Operational Loss 5/20/44
32162	VB-115		
32163	VB-101		Operational Loss 1/20/44
32164	VD-4		
32165	VPB-101		
32166	VPB-101		
32168	VB-115		
32169	VB-115	*Loose Livin II*	
32170	VB-115	*Saints and Sinners*	Operational Loss 4/20/44
32171	VB-106		Operational Loss 5/28/44
32172	VB-106		Lost in Action 4/6/44
32174	VD-1		Operational Loss 5/30/44
32175	VB-106	*Mark*	Lost in Action 5/1/44
32176	VB-115		
32177	VB-115		Lost in Action 6/5/4
32178	VB-115		
32182	VB-115	*Snuffy's Mischief Maker*	
32215	VB-115		Operational Loss 5/15/44
32216	VPB-101		
32119	VB-106		Operational Loss 3/22/44
32220	VB-115		
32221	VPB-115/116	*Rita's Rebel*	
32222	VB-115		Lost in Action 4/22/44
32225	VB-115		
32228	VPB-101/VPB-111		
32229	VD-1		
32231	VD-1		
32238	VB-106/115	*Chick's Chick*	
32240	VD-1	*Little Joe*	Operational Loss 4/30/44
32241	VB-109	*Sugar Queen*	
32243	VB-106/115	*Bales Baby*	Operational Loss 10/26/44
32247	VPB-116		
32260	VPB-101		Operational Loss 11/25/44
32263	VB-109		Lost in Action 8/5/44
32264	VD-4		
32265	VPB-101		
32266	VPB-101		Lost in Action 10/20/44
32267	VD-1	*Little Green Apples*	
32269	VPB-104		Lost in Action 10/25/44
32272	VPB-101		
32273	VB-115		
32274	VB-115	*Snuffy's Mischief Maker II*	
32275	VPB-101		
32276	VPB-101	*Comair Wolfpac II*	
32277	VPB-101	*Big Op*	Lost in Action 10/23/44
32278	VB-101		Operational Loss 5/6/44
32279	VPB-101		
32280	VPB-101	*Miller's High Life*	Lost in Action 10/20/44
32283	VB-115	*Snuffy's Mischief Maker*	
32284	VD-4		
32887	VD-1		
32998	VPB-115		
32299	VPB-101		
32300	VB-116		Operational Loss 5/26/44
32301	VPB-115		
32302	VPB-115	*Loose Livin*	?
32304	VPB-115		

BuNo	Squadron(s)	Name	Remarks
32305	VPB-116		
32306	VPB-116	*Bodashus Idjuts*	
32307	VB-116		
32308	VB-116		
32309	VB-116		
32310	VB-116		
32311	VD-1		Scrapped at Stillwater, Oklahoma
32312	VD-1		
32313	VD-1		
32314	VD-1/VPB-122		Scrapped at Stillwater, Oklahoma
32316	VPB-102		
32317	VPB-102		
32318	VPB-102		
32319	VPB-102		Operational Loss 9/9/44
32320	VPB-102		
32321	VPB-102		Converted for Adm. Earnest L. Gunther, Commander Air Force Pacific Fleet, Subordinate Command, Forward Area
32322	VPB-102		Operational Loss 9/8/44
32323	VPB-102	*Easy Maid*	Lost in Action 8/23/44
32324	VPB-102		
32325	VPB-102		Loss 3/3/45
32326	VPB-102		Loss 3/3/45
32327	VPB-116		
32328	VPB-106		Operational Loss 12/19/44
32329	VPB-111		
32330	VPB-111		
32331	VPB-111		
32332	VPB-111		
32333	VPB-102		

Bureau Numbers 38733 to 38979 B-24Js			
38733	VPB-111	*Modest Miss*, may also be *Chief's Filly*	
38734	VPB-102/116	*Dazy May*	
38735	VPB-117	*Pop's Cannon Ball*	
38736	VPB-117	*Uncle Sam*	
38737	VPB-117	*Uncle Tom's Cabin*	
38738	VPB-117	*Queen Bee*	Lost in Action 1/27/45
38739	VPB-117		Operational Loss 8/9/44
38740	VPB-117	*Daring Dame*	
38741	VPB-117	*The Lewd Nude*	Operational Loss 2/17/45
38742	VPB-117	*The Stinger*	
38743	VPB-117/119	*Sweet Marie*	
38744	VPB-117	*Torchy Tess*	
38745	VPB-111/117		
38746	VPB-111/106	*Doc's Delight*	
38747	VPB-111	*Too Hot To Handle*	
38749	VPB-111	*Three Dreams and a Drink*	
38750	VPB-111	*The Snooper*	
38754	VPB-104		Operational Loss
38755	VPB-116	*Peace Feeler*	
38756	VPB-111/VD-5?		
38757	VPB-117		
38758	VPB-117		
38759	VPB-117	*Ready, Willing, and Able*	
38760	VPB-117	*Sweating It Out*	Lost in Action 11/12/44
38761	VPB-117/104	*Neptune's Virgin*	
38762	VD-5		
38764	VD-5		
38766	VPB-102/116	*Lady Lib*	Operational Loss 8/9/44
38767	VPB-102		
38768	VPB-116		

BuNo	Squadron(s)	Name	Remarks
38769	VPB-116		Operational Loss 6/26/44
38773	VPB-117		
38774	VPB-104	*The Frumious Bandersnatch*	
38776	VPB-116		Lost in Action 10/11/44
38777	VPB-116	*Sleepy Time Gal*	
38779	VB-109/116		
38780	VPB-116		
38781	VD-5		
38783	VPB-102	*No Strain II*	
38788	VD-5		
38789	VPB-104		
38791	VPB-102		
38792	VPB-102		Loss 3/10/45
38794	VPB-102		Operational Loss 4/1/45
38795	VPB-104	*Bandersnatch*	
38799	VPB-116		
38800	VPB-116	*Tin Yan Ty Foon*	Loss 3/3/45
38801	VPB-104		
38802	VD-5		Loss 5/22/45
38803	VPB-116		Loss 4/13/45
38804	VPB-102		
38805	VD-5		Loss 5/22/45
38806	VPB-104		
38807	VPB-104		Operational Loss 1/24/45
38808	VD-5		
38809	VPB-104/119		
38812	VD-5		
38813	VPB-104		
38814	VPB-104		
38815	VD-5		Operational Loss 3/6/45
38816	VPB-104		
38817	VD-3		
38818	VD-3		
38819	VPB-116/102		Loss 4/17/45
38820	VPB-116		
38821	VD-3		
38822	VPB-111		
38823	VPB-117		Operational Loss 5/12/44
38827	VD-3		
38828	VPB-102		Loss 3/27/45
38829	VB-115/101		
38830	VD-3		
38831	VD-3		
38832	VD-1		
38833	VPB-117/111	*Chief's Filly*	
38834	VPB-104	*Here She Is Again*	
38835	VPB-104		
38836	VPB-111		
38840	VPB-101		Operational Loss 1/15/45
38843	VPB-102	*Lil Effie*, aka *Boss Burton's Nightmare*	Operational Loss 5/23/45
38844	VPB-116		Loss 4/11/45
38845	VPB-116	*Willie's Wild Cats II*	Loss 4/14/45
38846	VPB-117		
38847	VPB-101/117		
38848	VPB-101		
38849	VPB-104		Operational Loss 12/30/44
38852	VPB-101/104/117		
38853	VPB-116/117/121	*Low Blow*	
38854	VPB-116		Loss 5/18/45
38855	VPB-116		Loss 7/28/45
38856	VPB-101/104		

BuNo	Squadron(s)	Name	Remarks
38857	VPB-102		Loss 5/9/45
38858	VPB-116		Loss 7/28/45
38859	VPB-104		
38860	VPB-116		Loss
38861	VPB-117		
38862	VPB-116		
38863	VPB-117		Operational Loss 5/14/45
38836	VPB-111	*Little Snatch*	
38866	VPB-111	*Cherie and Toni*	
38867	VPB-102		Loss 3/23/45
38868	VPB-116		Loss 7/28/45
38869	VPB-104		Operational Loss 5/13/45
38870	VPB-104		Operational Loss 5/13/45
38871	VPB-102		Loss 4/23/45
38872	VPB-101		
38873	VPB-116		Operational Loss 4/2/45
38874	VPB-104		
38875	VPB-104		
38876	VPB-104		Lost in Action 1/11/45
38880	VPB-102		
38882	VPB-111/117		Operational Loss 7/4/45
38883	VPB-117		
38889	VPB-104		
38890	VPB-104		
38891	VPB-101/117		Operational Loss 2/23/45
38892	VPB-111	*Lady Luck*	
38893	VPB-123		Operational Loss 4/6/45
38894	VD-1		
38895	VPB-111	*Mucalone*	
38896	VPB-117	*Lucky Puss*	Operational Loss 4/18/45
38897	VPB-111		
38898	VPB-101/117		
38899	VD-3/VD-1		
38900	VPB-111		Operational Loss 1/10/45
38901	VPB-111	*Slidin Home*	
38904	VD-3		
38905	VPB-102		Loss 6/10/45
38906	VPB-111	*Reputation Cloudy*	
38908	VD-3		
38909	VPB-117		Lost in Action 7/1/45
38913	VPB-111	*Rugged Beloved*	
38914	VPB-116		Operational Loss 1/12/45
38915	VPB-116		Loss 7/28/45
38916	VPB-102		
38917	VPB-104/111		
38918	VPB-102		Loss 7/2/45
38920	VPB-102	*Impatient Virgin*	
38922	VPB-116		Loss 7/28/45
38923	VPB-116	*Easy Maid*	
38924	VPB-104		
38925	VPB-117		
38926	VPB-101/104		
38927	VPB-104		Operational Loss 12/12/44
38932	VPB-102		Operational Loss 5/9/45
38933	VPB-104		Operational Loss 3/45
38934	VPB-117		Operational Loss 6/22/45
38935	VPB-102		Operational Loss 7/10/45
38939	VPB-102		
38940	VPB-111		
38942	VPB-111		
38943	VPB-102		

BuNo	Squadron(s)	Name	Remarks
38944	VPB-116		
38945	VPB-111		Operational Loss on 7/5/45
38946	VPB-117		
38951	VPB-111		
38953	VPB-116		
38954	VD-5		
38955	VD-1/VPB-108		
38956	VD-4		
38957	VPB-111		
38958	VD-4		
38959	VPB-102	*Cuntry Cuzin*	
38960	VPB-116	*Worrybird*	
38961	VPB-117		
38962	VPB-102		
38963	VPB-117		
38964	VPB-102		
38965	VPB-102		Loss 7/30/45
38970	VPB-117		Scrapped at Stillwater, Oklahoma
38971	VPB-111/119		
38972	VPB-104		Operational Loss 1/17/45
38973	VPB-104		
38974	VPB-101/104		
38975	VPB-102		
38976	VPB-111		Operational Loss 6/20/45
38977	VPB-116/VD-5		
38978	VPB-117		
38979	VPB-111/104		

Bureau Numbers 46725 to 46737 B-24Ls			
46725	VPB-104		Operational Loss 7/9/45
46726	VPB-111		
46728	VD-1		
46729	VPB-104		
46730	VPB-104		Operational Loss 8/1/45
46731	VPB-102		
43746	VPB-104		
46737	VD-4		

Bureau Numbers 63915 to 63991 B-24Ds			
63813:	VPB-104		Operational Loss 1/2/45

Bureau Numbers 65287 to 65396 B-24L and M			
65298	VD-5		
65299	VD-1	*Rovin' Redhead*	
65320	VD-5		
65327	VD-5		
65328	VD-5		
65338	VD-5		
65339	VD-5		
65341	VD-5		
65385	Possibly VD-1	*Brown Baggers Retreat*	

Bureau Numbers 90462 to 90483 B-24Ms			
90471	VPB-102		Operational Loss 8/10/45
90478	VPB-116		Loss 5/18/45
90479	VPB-116		
90482	VPB-104		Loss 6/29/45
90482	VPB-116/VPB-200	*Call House Madam*	
90483	VPB-102	*The Lady*	

Appendix F
PB4Y-2 Privateers Assigned to Pacific Combat Squadrons
1944–1945 Delivered Before 1 August 1945

BuNo	Unit(s)	Name	Remarks
59357	VPB-106/109/115/120/122/124		
59358	VPB-101/108/115/120/123		
59359	VPB-101/108/115/122/123		
59360	PB-101/108/115/123 Els Nocho		
59361	VPB-108/118/122/123		
59362	VPB-101/108/115/118/122/123		
59363	VPB-101/108/115/118/122/123		
59364	VPB-121/124		
59365	VPB-106/115/116/119/120/124		
59366	VPB-106/109/115/116/120/122		
59367	VPB-109/119/124		
59368	VPB-119		
59369	VPB-119/121/124		
59370	VPB-106		
59371	VPB-109/119		
59372	VPB-108/109/115/119/120/122/124		
59373	VPB-115/120/121/124		
59374	VPB-115/117/120/121/124		
59375	VPB-109/121		
59376	VPB-121/124		
59377	VPB-118		Crashed while taxing at NAS Kaneohe, Hawaii on 12/25/44
59378	VPB-118		Combat loss 5/6/45 surveyed
59379	VPB-106/118	Flying Tail	
59380	VPB-118 Summer Storm		
59381	VPB-118		Crashed while taking off from Midway on 12/17/44
59382	VPB-106/118	A-Tease	VPB-123 La Cherrie?
59383	VPB-118	Navy's Torchy Tess	
59384	VPB-106		Nude woman straddling tiger head
59385	VPB-106		
59386	VPB-106		Struck coral boulder on runway on 2/16/45 Operational Loss 2/16/45
59387	VPB-118		
59388	VPB-118	Soaring Fin	Combat Loss 5/6/45
59389	VPB-106		
59390	VPB-106	Umbriago	
59391	VPB-106		
59392	VPB-118	Miss Behavin	Wrecked 5/25/45
59393	VPB-106		
59394	VPB-106		Ditched in Gulf of California on 10/24/44
59395	VPB-106		
59396	VPB-106	Blue Diamond	Operational Loss 5/24/45
59397	VPB-106	Lucky Levin	

BuNo	Unit(s)	Name	Remarks
59398	VPB-106	*Baldy Tortilla Flat*	
59400	VPB-106	*Super Chief*	
59401	VPB-118		Ditched two miles from base on 4/13/45
59402	VPB-118	*Modest O Miss*	Crashed while landing at Iwo Jima, loss 3/6/45
59403	VPB-104/119		
59404	VPB-118	*Pirate Princess*	Combat Loss 7/29/45
59405	VPB-118	*Miss Natch* (previously named *Mark's Farts II*)	Burned on ground at Tinian on 6/2/45
59406	VPB-121	*Naval Body Angel in D'Skies*	
59409	VPB-121	*Come N' Get It*	
59410	VPB-118	*Miss Lottatail*	Loss 8/06/45
59411	VPB-119		
59412	VPB-106		Lost in Action 6/14/45
59413	VPB-119	*Holt's Patches*	
59414	VPB-119		Lost in Action 4/11/45
59415	VPB-119		
59416	VPB-119		
59417	VPB-119		
59418	VPB-119		
59419	VPB-104/119	*Elizabeth Ann*	
59420	VPB-104/119		
59422	VPB-119		Lost in Action 5/19/45
59423	VPB-104/119		
59424	VPB-121	*Mr. Kip*	
59426	VPB-119		Lost in Action 3/22/45
59427	VPB-119		Lost in Action 6/17/45
59428	VPB-104/119		
59429	VPB-121/119		Collided with a PB4Y-1 of VPB-104 on runway at Clark Field, Philippines on 3/8/45
59430	VPB-118	*Twitchy Bitch*	
59431	VPB-121 Little Patrica		
59432	VPB-106/118	*Tarfu*	
59433	VPB-106		Lost in Action 7/1/45
59436	VPB-121		Operational Loss
59438	VPB-123	*Lady of Leisure*	Crashed at Okinawa on 6/19/45
59439	VPB-108/111		
59440	VPB-108 The Outlaw		
59441	VPB-108	*Accentuate the Positive*	Wrecked 8/13/45
59442	VPB-108		Ditched while on patrol on 4/8/45
59443	VPB-108		
59444	VPB-108/109?		Combat loss *Shanghai Lil*
59445	VPB-108		Combat loss 6/5/45
59446	VPB-108	*Lady Luck II*	6/11/45
59447	VPB-108/121	*Dangerous Dan*	
59448	VPB-108/118	*Modest O' Miss II*	Lost 7/27/45 may have belonged to VPB-108
59449	VPB-108/118	*Vulnerable Virgin*	Combat damage surveyed 5/6/45
59450	VPB-121	*Abroad for Action*	
59451	VPB-118		
59452	VPB-119	*Bales Baby*	Lost in Action 4/1/45
59453	VPB-106/111/117		
59454	VPB-106		
59455	VPB-106		
59456	VPB-111/119		
59457	VPB-119		
59458	VPB-118		Combat damage surveyed 7/22/45
59459	VPB-108/111	*Lady Luck III*	
59460	VPB-108	*Els-Notcho*	
59461	VPB-106/118		
59462	VPB-116/121		
59463	VPB-104/124		
59464	VPB-104		

BuNo	Unit(s)	Name	Remarks
59467	VPB-119		Crashed while landing at Nichols Field, Philippines Operational Loss 3/23/45
59468	VPB-119		
59469	VPB-104/106?		
59470	VPB-108/118		
59471	VPB-104/119		
59474	VPB-121		Lost in Action 3/06/45
59475	VPB-121	*Louisiana Lil*	
59476	VPB-123	*Pirate Princess*	
59477	VPB-121		Dicthed off Kaneohe, Hawaii. Operational Loss on 1/11/45
59478	VPB-121	*Buccaneer Bunny*	
59479	VPB-121	*After Hours*	Loss 5/28/45
59480	VPB-108	*Hippin Kitten II*	
59481	VPB-121		
59482	VPB-104/108/118/119	*Miss You*	
59483	VPB-108	*Anchors Aweigh*	
59484	VPB-121	*Lotta Tayle*	
59485	VPB-108		
59486	VPB-108/118		
59487	VPB-123	*Vagrant Verago*	
59488	VPB-109		
59489	VPB-108/121	*La Cherie*	
59490	VPB-108	*Sailor's Dream*	
59491	VPB-121	*Tail Chaser/Indian Made*	
59492	VPB-121/119?	*Pirate Princess*	
59494	VPB-117		
59495	VPB-121		Lost in Action 8/11/45
59496	VPB-108		
59497	VPB-106		Lost in Action 3/9/45
59498	VPB-108	*Super Snooper*	
59499	VPB-118	*Beer Virgin IV*	
59500	VPB-123	*Jackass Jenny*	Surveyed Battle Damage 6/9/45
59501	VPB-109	*Punkie*	
59502	VPB-109	*Green Cherries*	
59503	VPB-122/123	*Whistlin Outhouse*	
59504	VPB-124/123	*Pastime*	
59505	VPB-123	*Red Wing*	
59506	VPB-123	*Little Skipper*	
59508	VPB-123		
59509	VPB-123	*Jacqueline*	
59510	VPB-124/123	*Jackson's Jail*	
59511	VPB-123		
59512	VPB-109		
59513	VPB-109/124		Crashed due to fuel exhaustion 6/6/45
59514	VPB-109	*Blind Bomber*	
59515	VPB-109	*Hogan's Goat*	
59516	VPB-109/124		
59517	VPB-124		
59518	VPB-109		
59519	VPB-124	*Gear Locked and Down*	Lost 7/21/45
59520	VPB-123	*No Body Else's Butt*	
59521	VPB-109	*Bachelor's Delight*	Lost 8/05/45
59522	VPB-109	*Miss Lotta Tail*	
59523	VPB-109		
59524	VPB-123	*Balls of Fire*	
59525	VPB-106/123	*Our Baby*	
59526	VPB-109		Destroyed in bombing 5/19/45
59527	VPB-109		
59528	VPB-109	*Lambaster*	
59529	VPB-109		Loss 5/24/45
59530	VPB-109		Surveyed 6/6/45

BuNo	Unit(s)	Name	Remarks
59531	VPB-123/124		
59532	VPB-124		Combat Loss 6/26/45
59533	VPB-109/123	*Sleepy Time Gal*	Surveyed 5/24/45
59534	VPB-124		Combat Loss 7/2/45
59535	VPB-124		Combat Loss 6/27/45
59536	VPB-123/124		
59537	VPB-124		
59538	VPB-124		Combat damage surveyed 7/7/45
59540	VPB-123/124	*No Strain*	
59541	VPB-109		
59542	VPB-109/104		
59543	VPB-119		Battle damage surveyed on 3/29/45
59545	VPB-123/124	*Little Joe*	
59546	VPB-119		Operational Loss 6/24/45
59547	VPB-106		
59548	VPB-123	*Typhoon*	Surveyed
59549	VPB-124		Crashed at Tinian on 6/17/45
59550	VPB-118		Operational Loss 7/23/45
59551	VPB-104		
59552	VPB-108		
59553	VPB-119		Lost in Action 6/24/45
59554	VPB-106		
59555	VPB-106/111/120		
59556	VPB-118		Combat Loss 8/8/45
59557	VPB-124		Combat Lost 6/26/45
59558	VPB-119		Burned on ground at Clark Field on Loss 3/22/45
59559	VPB-119		Lost in Action 5/1/45
59561	VPB-106/111		
59562	VPB-108/116		
59563	VPB-106		Lost in Action 6/01/45
59564	VPB-121	*Ol' Blunderbuss*	
59565	VPB-119		
59566	VPB-121	*The Mad Frenchman*	
59567	VPB-102/118		
59568	VPB-119		
59569	VPB-106/111		
59571	VPB-106		
59572	VPB-119		
59573	VPB-111		
59574	VPB-104		
59575	VPB-111		
59578	VPB-119/120		
59579	VPB-101/115/122		
58581	VPB-109		
58582	VPB-116	*Miss Sea-ducer*	
58583	VPB-116		
58584	VPB-119		
58585	VPB-116/118/120		
58588	VPB-102		
58589	VPB-111/120		
59590	VPB-104/119		
59591	VPB-117/120		
59592	VPB-116/118		
59594	VPB-119		
59595	VPB-117		
59596	VPB-120		
59597	VPB-117		
59599	VPB-102		
59600	VPB-118/124		
59601	VPB-120/121		
59602	VPB-121		

BuNo	Unit(s)	Name	Remarks
59604	VPB-102/120		
59605	VPB-124		
59606	VPB-106/119/120		
59607	VPB-104		
59608	VPB-102/120		
59609	VPB-106		
59611	VPB-102		
59612	VPB-102/120		
59613	VPB-109		
59614	VPB-106/119/120		
59615	VPB-117/118/120/124		
59616	VPB-117/119		
59617	VPB-116/121	*Miss Milovin*	
59619	VPB-117		
59620	VPB-106/119/120		
59621	VPB-117		
59622	VPB-121		
59626	VPB-106		
59629	VPB-124		
59631	VPB-124		
59636	VPB-116		
59637	VPB-124		
59638	VPB-121		
59639	VPB-111		
59641	VPB-122		
59643	VPB-122		
59644	VPB-122		
59645	VPB-122	*The Black Shee*	
59646	VPB-122		
59647	VPB-122		
59656	VPB-119		
59658	VPB-118/124		
59660	VPB-109		
59663	VPB-119		
59666	VPB-102/108		
59668	VPB-108		
59669	VPB-102	*Zoot Suit*	
59671	VPB-102/106		
59673	VPB-108		
59675	VPB-119		
59676	VPB-116		
59677	VPB-119		
59678	VPB-122		
59679	VPB-108		
59682	VPB-116	*Water Spy*	Crashed while landing at West Field, Tinian, on 09/28/45
59684	VPB-109		
59689	VPB-116		
59698	VPB-115		
59700	VPB-124		
59701	VPB-120		
59704	VPB-120		
59710	VPB-120		
59713	VPB-115		
59716	VPB-120		
59718	VPB-115		
59728	VPB-111/117		
59732	VPB-123		
59741	VPB-120	*Bouncing Betty*	
59745	VPB-120		
59747	VPB-124		Missing in action 7/24/45
59749	VPB-108		

BuNo	Unit(s)	Name	Remarks
59750	VPB-104/119		
59751	VPB-106/111/119		
59752	VPB-101/115/122		
59753	VPB-106/111/119		
59754	VPB-116		
59755	VPB-122/116	*Peace Feeler*	
59756	VPB-108/123/124		
59757	VPB-124		
59758	VPB-117		
59759	VPB-108/116/118/124		
59760	VPB-116	*Cover Girl*	
59761	VPB-106/116		
59762	VPB-117	*Granite State Express*	
59763	VPB-106/108/111		
59764	VPB-108/124		
59765	VPB-108		
59766	VPB-108		
59767	VPB-117		
59768	VPB-102/106		
59769	VPB-116		
59770	VPB-116		
59771	VPB-108/118/124		
59772	VPB-118		
59773	VPB-102		
59774	VPB-116/122		
59775	VPB-122		
59776	VPB-108		
59777	VPB-122		
59778	VPB-122		
59779	VPB-122		
59780	VPB-122		
59781	VPB-122		
59782	VPB-106/119		
59783	VPB-122		
59786	VPB-111	*Lili*	
59788	VPB-122	*Black Mac II*	
59789	VPB-102		
59791	VPB-124		
59792	VPB-124		
59793	VPB-108/123		
59796	VPB-108/118/124		
59798	VPB-108/123/124		
59801	VPB-108/123/124		
59803	VPB-108/123/124		
59804	VPB-108/123/124		
59806	VPB-108/123/124		
59807	VPB-120		
59809	VPB-120		
59813	VPB-120		
59816	VPB-120		
59818	VPB-108/123/124		
59819	VPB-120		
59821	VPB-120		
59822	VPB-104		
59823	VPB-120		
59827	VPB-120		
59838	VPB-120		
59844	VPB-108/123/124		
59846	VPB-122		
59850	VPB-124		
59852	VPB-124		

Bibliography

Government Documents

Aircraft Seventh Fleet, Summary of Operations. Secret Bulletin No. 11, 18 July 1945.

Air Force Combat Units of World War II. Washington, DC. US Government Printing Office, 1961.

Case No. 32. *Trial of Lieutenant General Harukei Isayama and Seven Others, 1st-25th July, 1946*. United States Military Commission, Shanghai.

Naval Aviation Combat Statistics: World War II. Air Branch, Office of Naval Intelligence, Office of the Chief of Naval Operations. Navy Department. OPNAV-P-23V No. A129. 17 June 1946. After Action Reports and War Diaries from various squadrons available through the National Archives and Records Administration at College Park, Maryland, and Aircraft Accident Reports and Aircraft History Cards available through the Naval Historical Center.

U.S. Naval Aviation in the Pacific. Office of the Chief of Naval Operations. US Navy, 1947.

Published Works

Birdsall, Steve. *Log of the Liberators*. Garden City, New York. Doubleday & Company, 1973

Boyd, Karl and Akihiko Yoshida. *The Japanese Submarine Force and World War II*. Annapolis, MD: Naval Institute Press, 1995.

Carey, Alan C. *Consolidated PB4Y-2 Privateer: The Operational History of the US Navy's World War II Patrol/Bomber Aircraft*. Atglen, PA: Schiffer Publishing, Ltd., 2005.

Carey, Alan C. *The Reluctant Raiders: The Story of United States Navy Bombing Squadron VB/VPB-109 in World War II*. Atglen, PA: Schiffer Publishing, Ltd., 1999.

Cleary, John P. Article on Charles Reddon, *Elmira Star Gazette*. 9 January 2006.

Hata, Ikuhiko and Yasuho Izawa. Translated by Don Cyril Gorham. *Japanese Naval Aces and Fighter Units in World War II*. Annapolis, Maryland: Naval Institute Press, 1989.

Heimann, Judith M. *The Airmen and the Headhunters*. Harcourt, Inc., 2007.

Ito, Masanori. *The End of the Imperial Japanese Navy*. New York: Mackadden-Bartell, 1962.

Morison, Samuel E. *History of United States Navy Operations in World War II*. Leyte, Vol. XII.

Morison. *The Liberation of the Philippines*, Vol. XIII.

Morison. *Victory in the Pacific 1945*, Vol. XIV.

Pettit, James T. *The History of Navy Bombing Squadron 118: "The Old Crows."* 1992.

Sanford, Kenneth F. *Crew Six*. Port Ludlow, WA: Sanford Publishing Group, 1996.

Stevens, Paul F. *Low Level Liberators*. El Cajon, CA: Whitmar Electronic Press, 1997.

Wolpert, Robert L. *The Story of One Eleven*. Emerson, NJ: Emerson Quality Press, Inc., 1990.

Woolf, Joseph. *Pacific Privateers*, 1976.

Unpublished Works

Navy Patrol Bombing Squadron 117 Association. The Blue Raiders: VPB-117, United States Navy, 1944-1945. Alexandria, Virginia: Navy Bombing Squadron Association, 1984.

Thoman, Louise C., Editor. U.S. Navy Squadrons VP-14/VB-102/VPB-102: A Chronicle-1938 to 1994, 1998.

Notes

Chapter 1

1. U.S. Naval Operations in World War II. Leyte, Vol. XII, 20–21.
2. Morison, 25.
3. The story of *Miller's High Life* from the accounts of Martin and Read.
4. Paul Stevens, letter to the author.
5. Paul F. Stevens. Low Level Liberators, 81–82.
6. From the account of Joe Wasneski.

Chapter 2

1. From an unpublished history of The Blue Raiders: VPB-117.
2. Stevens, 94.
3. Ibid.
4. Ibid, 126.
5. Ibid, 127.
6. Morison, 42.
7. VPB-117 Squadron History.
8. United States Military Commission, Shanghai. Case No. 32. *Trial of Lieutenant General Harukei Isayama and Seven Others, 1st-25th July, 1946.*

Chapter 3

1. Information squadron after action reports and data compiled by James C. Sawruk.

Chapter 4

1. VPB-117 Squadron History.
2. Letter to Peter P. Bresciano from Farville K. "Bud" Mills.
3. Letter from "Bud" Mills Topsy kill to Peter P. Bresciano.
4. Excerpts of the trial were found in the VPB-117 squadron book. The original document originates from the Office of the Judge Advocate General.

Chapter 5

1. A majority of this story comes from Secret Bulletin No. 11, Aircraft Seventh Fleet, Summary of Operations, dated 18 July 1945.
2. For a comprehensive work about the Army airmen and their stories please read Judith M. Heimann's, *The Airmen and the Headhunters: A True Story of Lost Soldiers, A Heroic Tribesmen and the Unlikeliest Rescue of World War II.*
3. Heimann, 176. 4. Ibid, 174-175.
4. Secret Bulletin.
5. VPB-117 Squadron History.
6. From Thomas Hepting, nephew of Robert Hepting.

Chapter 6

1. Paul Stevens.
2. VPB-104 History Records.
3. Ibid.

Chapter 7

1. Letter to Peter P. Bresciano from Farville K. "Bud" Mills.
2. Robert L. Wolpert. *The Story of One Eleven*, 67–68.
3. Bresciano from Mills.
4. Sawruk.
5. Wolpert, 87.
6. Ibid.

Chapter 8

1. Peter P. Bresciano from Farville K. "Bud" Mills.
2. Louise C. Thoman, Editor. U.S. Navy Squadrons VP-14/VB-102/VPB-102.
3. Sawruk. Japanese pilots engaged and battle damage to aircraft in this attack were CPO Ushio Nishimura damaged with one

hit, Lt. Shigehiro Nakama damaged with five hits, CPO Toshiro Yanagisawa, and CPO Ushio Nishimura damaged with one hit.

4. VPB-117. Lt. (jg) Harold J. Boss wrote the original story under the title *Blue Monsters*. Boss was killed during the squadron's deployment.

Chapter 9

1. James T. Pettit, The History of Navy Bombing Squadron 118: "The Old Crows.

2. Letter to the author from Billy Buckley.

3. VB/VPB-102 History.

4. John P. Cleary. Article on Charles Reddon, *Elmira Star Gazette.* 9 January 2006.

5. Lt.Cdr. Pressler, Lt. Barnes, and Lt. Holohan commanded VPB-102 aircraft. Information compiled from the VB/VPB-102 History and squadron after action reports.

6. Taped interview provided to the author from Hal Olsen. Original interview conducted by Florida State University Institute on World War II & the Human Experience, 30 June 1999.

7. Karen Nilsson Brandt, Los Alamos Monitor, Sunday, August 13, 1995.

Chapter 10

1. Carey, *Reluctant Raiders.*

2. VB/VPB-102 History.

3. Taped interview of Allen Morgan by his son Joseph Morgan

4. Carey, *Raiders.*

5. VPB-102.

Chapter 11

1. Information on VPB-118 activities from squadron history and after action reports.

Chapter 12

1. The Old Crows.

2. From an oral recording of Val M. Higgins to the author.

3. Sawruk. The Japanese pilots involved in the battle were: Ens. Mitsuo Ishizuka, CPO Shigeru Aoyagi, CPO Tomio Yamamoto, PO1 Yasuo Matsumoto, CPO Toshio Tanaka, CPO Hideo Nakao (ordered to return and did not engage), CPO Hisamitsu Watanabe, PO2 Ei Hoshino, CPO Sanpei Shiono, CPO Shiro Hirotome, CPO Junichi Miyake, and PO2 Masayuki Tashiro.

4. Ships sunk that day may have been the 834-ton tanker *Takasago Maru* Number 2; the 1,004-ton cargo ship Taiun Maru Number 9, and the 834-ton tanker Takasago Maru Number 15.

5. Carey, *The Reluctant Raiders.*

6. Information on the Japanese vessel struck by the missile from Minoru Kamada.

Chapter 13

1. Kenneth F Sanford, Crew Six. Port Ludlow, WA, Sanford Publishing Group, 1996, 112.

2. Sanford pp. 122–38.

3. Sanford, 143.

4. The flight included Lt. Leland McCutcheon, William N. Lloyd, Henry J. Thompson, and N. M. Keiser.

Chapter 14

1. Reflections by Ted Rowcliffe.

2. Ted Rowcliffe.

3. Letter from Donald H. Van Steenwyk to Francis C. Wellman April 2, 2004. Copy sent to author by Van Steenwyk.

4. Carey, *PB4Y-2 Privateer Operations*, p. 79.

5. Interview with F. T. Pierce.

6. This is information obtained by Jim Sawruk. However, there is some question about these Privateers being Ramsey and Miller, as the squadron believes they were flying their sector on the Northwest coast of Korea, not the southern tip near Saishu-To Island.

7. Conversation with the author.

8. Interview with the author.

9. Sanford.

10. Conversation with Ted Rowcliffe by the author.

11. A conversation with the author.

12. Ted Rowcliffe.

Chapter 15

1. Lt. Hewitt was patrol commander of the second VPB-109 Privateer. Patrol plane commanders for VPB-118 were Lt.Cdr. Rinehart and Lt. G. H. Shortlidge. For VPB-123, Lt. Sam R. Pepe and Lt. (jg) Richard Treat commanded the planes.

2. Sawruk.

Index